To Dad

lots of love

Ron, Julie, Hele

Chrystal. Tips and Alistair

Christmas 1994 x x x x x x

THE BURIED PAST
IN FAMILY HISTORY

The Haynes family group, about 1900. Grandfather and
Grandmother Haynes (seated) Ernie, Nellie and Harry
showing off his Boer War uniform.

THE
BURIED PAST
IN
FAMILY HISTORY

G. Letitia Haynes

The Book Guild Ltd
Sussex, England

The Book Guild
25 High Street,
Lewes, Sussex.

First published 1993
© G. Letitia Haynes 1993
Set in Baskerville

Typesetting by Kudos Graphics
Slinfold, Horsham, West Sussex
Printed in Great Britain by
Antony Rowe Ltd.,
Chippenham, Wiltshire.

A catalogue record for this book is
available from the British Library

ISBN 0 86332 743 5

CONTENTS

List of Illustrations   6
Introduction   7

Part 1:   **Ambitious Striving**
Chapter 1   *Family Origins*   13
Chapter 2   *Background to Grandfather Haynes's Business
               Its Inspiration to Ernie*   18
Chapter 3   *Great Grandmother Haynes's Family – Their
               Marriages and In-laws*   30
Chapter 4   *Grandfather Haynes's Home*   39
Chapter 5   *The Children's Education and Play*   48
Chapter 6   *A Prosperous Family With a Social Conscience*   58
Chapter 7   *Young Harry's Recollections*   70
Chapter 8   *Friendships, Holidays and Recreation*   86
Chapter 9   *Gathering Shadows*   94
Chapter 10   *Life's Path Takes New Directions*   103

Part 2:   **In Parish Bounds**
Chapter 11   *Gertie's Family and Place of Origin*   115
Chapter 12   *Victorian Values*   128
Chapter 13   *Roots in the Past*   137
Chapter 14   *Life in Bartley*   148
Chapter 15   *Jane Partridge's Marriage*   159
Chapter 16   *Life in the Cottages*   166
Chapter 17   *The Witherford Family*   175
Chapter 18   *School and School Days*   185
Chapter 19   *In the Streets*   194
Chapter 20   *Social Life*   202

Chapter 21   *The Daily Food*   208
Chapter 22   *Clothes and Things for the Home*   218
Chapter 23   *In Times of Trouble*   228
Chapter 24   *The Girls Grow Up*   235
Chapter 25   *The War Years*   245

LIST OF ILLUSTRATIONS

The Haynes Family, c. 1900   Frontispiece

Old Mint Ropery   33

Staffordshire Knot Trademark   37

The Beehive Stores   61

Nailers Cottages at Northfield   123

Great Grandmother Partridge   151

Gertie aged 18   238

INTRODUCTION

There is nothing predictable in life except the certainty of change.

Throughout our history, except in the times of national upheaval that seem to have occurred every two or three centuries, the patterns of life for common people, although constantly changing, have changed so slowly that conditions in one generation have merged almost imperceptibly into the next.

Our last great upheaval was in the middle of the eighteenth century with the simultaneous, interrelated changes of enclosure of common land and the Industrial Revolution. The changes that took place were so profound, they inspired the interest and compassion of many thinkers, philosophers, politicians, philanthropists, writers and others. But the minutiae of the domestic conditions which were destroyed are almost completely lost, and few traces remain, either in the countryside or in folk memory.

Right through civilisation there have been few records of the everyday life of common people, their food, home, clothes, family life, division of their day, their troubles, their thoughts of their own world around them. Almost all we know of them is through the artifacts they may have left behind, their architecture, and what is recorded incidently in current literature and art by the erudite and cultured of their time. Through these sources we believe we know a great deal about our ancestors, but nevertheless most of it is conjecture and deduction.

Now in the twentieth century, another upheaval is in the process of taking place, the changes being so profound, universal, and proceeding with such mind-confusing acceleration that those born into it see the pattern of their young days compared with those of their parents', and certainly of their grandparents', as belonging to another world, locked securely back behind the iron door of Time. In every tiny detail, life has altered; no longer exists the fire burning in the hearth, all the family sitting round the table for their meals, mother always there, busy in the home with household tasks; people whistling or singing to themselves as they worked; dogs running freely, fighting each other, or romping and scampering with children at play; fowls in pens in the back garden or scratching round the farmyard; fields with sheep, cattle and pigs. All such basic, elemental things, constant through all past changes, for the most part exist now only in memory.

Not only have home life and the social pattern changed, but so also, with far deeper effect, have the habits and ideals of thought, which, from the beginning of our culture, through countless generations, have emanated from Church, State and schools, and were directed with single-minded emphasis on Christian virtues, universally believed and respected, even by those who fell short in their practice. A society has evolved where free education is universal, accepted as a matter of course, and rarely valued as it once was, as a precious privilege, to be embraced to the full with effort and perseverance, and where the knowledge introduced into schools to children is now as different as the methods by which it is taught and the behaviour and response expected from the pupils.

Many people feel instinctively that if the everyday life in Victorian, Edwardian and early twentieth century England is not quickly recorded while there are still some left who remember firsthand at least its circumstances and particulars, its spirit and nuances will be lost just as completely as earlier ways of life have been lost to history. The following pages attempt to relive a bygone way of life and thought, and awaken memories of people in and around two branches of one simple, working-class family, and the environment and background in which their lives took place.

This family is exceptional in that so much information about the early life and personalities has survived, through the stories of Ernie, one of its third generation, and his wife Gertie, and recorded by their daughter. Although they represented families that were different in many respects, their two records complement each other, giving descriptions of late Victorian and early twentieth century everyday life in typical industrial suburbs, fast emerging from their rural past. Throughout their lives the two loved to relate their parallel experiences in conversation by the fireside. They were both acutely observant of all that went on around them and were enchanting raconteurs.

The record of Ernie's family is mainly a framework on which he hung hundreds of stories about everything and everybody, all told with sparkling eyes and enthusiasm, brimming over with fun and humour. He enjoyed his early life immensely, and to the end loved to tell the old stories on which his brother and sister also loved to reminisce when they visited him. It was impossible not to help enjoying them because he enjoyed them so much himself, running his fingers through his hair till it stood on end as the tales unfolded. It is a pity they were not recorded while they, and the spirit in which they were told, were still vivid in mind as well as in memory.

In recording these family stories it has become impossible not to become aware of their significance as social documents of the nineteenth and early twentieth centuries, as so many social aspects are mirrored in them: workers from Ireland, emigration to the colonies, for adventure, to better the way of life, to escape from the consequences of youthful indiscretions, and the varying degrees of success; philosophical adjustment of marital and domestic morality to the realities of life, which families took in their stride, working out their difficulties without help or interference from the Church or State.

It revealed in the young generation the existence of a sense of responsibility that struggled to maintain the old and needy, and kept them from the dreaded institution of the workhouse.

There was an eagerness to grasp the new opportunities of education, if too late for themselves, certainly for their children, and to direct their ambitions higher than would scarcely have been deemed possible in earlier generations.

9

There were seeds of compassion for those less fortunate than themselves, which flowered into the Welfare State, which, in its turn, so some people thought, overbloomed with excesses of inappropriate assistance, undermining resourcefulness in the individual, even threatening society itself.

Above all, there was a new sense of dignity and self-confidence, that public service and the manipulation of public policy were open to them too, and not solely the prerogative of ruling aristocracy and wealthy families.

In distant future, if civilisation survives so long, maybe the descendants of these families, and others like them with a sense of history, will treasure such memories as being typical of the roots from which they, and a great many twentieth century professional people have sprung, and of which they can have no cause to feel ashamed. Rather, they can have cause for pride that many among their ancestors, struggling with troubles such as long since have disappeared, could show such courage, resourcefulness, patience, uncomplaining fortitude, such generosity. Their descendants may well hope that, if life in the Welfare State should one day evolve beyond the festoons of social safety nets ready to catch young and old alike, sick and healthy, provident and inprovident, deserving and undeserving, indigenous and alien, when assorted difficulties threaten, they too will prove to have inherited deep within themselves seeds of the same qualities, to germinate and flourish in time of need.

Part 1

AMBITIOUS STRIVING

1

Family Origins

Herewith the history of the Haynes family from the nineteenth century, through five generations.

It is the story of how one dynamic family exploited the conditions created by the Industrial Revolution to heave itself upwards, with nothing whatever to stimulate its ambition except its own skills, initiative and tireless energy.

Victorian England had many such families, and it is in them that a great many twentieth century professional men and women have their roots.

Great-grandfather Richard Haynes came from the district around Bromyard, Bringsty Common and Whitbourne in the County of Hereford, a borderland between England and Wales. He was a gardener at Brockhampton Court, the seat of Lord Lutley. It is recorded in family tradition that one of his forebears, Nathaniel by name, was sufficiently implicated in a political plot, to get himself hung at Worcester Gaol for treason. The exact nature of his offence has been lost in the passage of time, but it was most likely connected with events during, or immediately after the Napoleonic Wars, when social unrest found expression greatly disturbing to the government of the day. Who knows? Perhaps it was from him that certain of the family's descendants in the latter part of the nineteenth century, and later again in the first part of the twentieth, inherited their instinct for social reform, which in one case found expression in philanthropic and political activity, in another in Socialist agitation, which in an earlier age would have undoubtedly brought down upon him a fate similar to that of the unfortunate Nathaniel.

Richard's wife, Emma, was a descendant from the Lloyd

family of Bringsty Common.

The name Lloyd is of Welsh origin, as are a number of both personal and place names in that borderland district. Bringsty Common was a wild, remote, rural area, covered with bracken, wild thyme and harebells, traversed by sheep tracks as smooth as lawns, and scattered with stone or black and white, half-timbered, wattle and daub cottages hidden in the hollows. These cottages were set in little orchards of apple, pear, cherry, and above all damson and plum trees. Of course the area has changed a lot, and is now unrecognisable as the wild lonely place it still was, even between the two great twentieth century wars. Nevertheless, in spite of its changes, very much for the worst, it is still National Trust property, preserved as a place of outstanding natural beauty.

Emma's father, John Lloyd, as a young man had left Bringsty at the end of the eighteenth century to live in Rugely in Staffordshire, where he ran a livery stable and trained racehorses. One of his clients was the notorious Dr Palmer, known later as 'Palmer the Poisoner' on account of his nefarious activities, for which he was in due course executed. The two horses John Lloyd trained for Dr Palmer were called 'Strychnine' and 'Gold Finder', and these horse names were used at the trial to influence the jury to find that gentleman guilty, which, according to family inside knowledge, they believed he undoubtedly was. At his execution, as the drop fell, he cried out, 'Now for the Great Secret,' and thus became recorded for posterity.

When Emma was old enough to work, she was sent back to her relations at Bringsty, who found a 'place' for her at Brockhampton Court, there being practically no employment possible to country girls except to go out to 'service'. She was a handsome, intelligent girl who conducted herself well, and in the course of time became personal maid to Lady Lutley, a position of which she could be justly proud, and eventually married Richard Haynes, a gardener at the same house. On her marriage, Lady Lutley gave her, among other things, a small white porcelain bowl with a picture of Brockhampton Court and its deer park painted on it in black, as a souvenir of her life in service. This was treasured in the family, and passed in time to her youngest daughter,

14

Mary Ellen, and is still in the possession of the Haynes family at the end of the twentieth century.

As often happened in service to maids coming from humble homes, close association with the intimate life and culture of the 'gentry' resulted in some of it rubbing off on them. This was the case with the young Emma. In her later years, in spite of her explosive Celtic temperament, her son's children always stood in awe of her as a 'lady'. They kept their distance and took no liberties, as they certainly did with their maternal grandmother.

In their early married life, the young Emma and Richard moved to the parish of St John's on the outskirts of Worcester where Richard established his own market garden. Most of the early history of this family came down from their eldest grandson, Harry, and from their younger daughter Ellen, who did not die till 1934. She talked freely about her early life, but only vague memories now remain after such a passage of time, and although family stories are always interesting to the younger generation and listened to eagerly, nobody thought to question further. It is a pity her stories were not recorded at the time.

In Emma's early married days, the family was successful. Ellen loved to tell how she remembered her parents quarrelling when her father one night took out several silk dresses (given to his wife as lady's maid to Lady Lutley, as the custom then was) to cover over his young plants as protection from the frost.

Apart from the above incident, little is remembered of what was told about Great-grandfather Haynes, and in any case he faded out of the story at an early stage, as he abandoned his wife and family to elope with another woman and was never heard of again.

Be that as it may, while the children were young, the family undoubtedly fell on very hard times. Their second son, Harry Walter, who is the Grandfather Haynes of this family history, and his brothers too, although highly intelligent, were almost illiterate, being able to read very little and to write still less, although in later years Harry at least was very sensitive on the matter and used to pretend that he could. Their youngest sister Ellen did not suffer from this disadvantage. She too was very intelligent, and her three brothers saw to it that she had the advantages that had been denied them in their childhood.

At this period there were many schools for the poor, from the cottage 'dame schools' to the Church or Chapel schools. It was a matter of luck whether or not there was one in the village in which one lived, and even then many families were too poor to pay the penny or twopence per week demanded from each pupil. Sometimes the girls went to school till they were old enough to go into service, while the boys did not go at all, being useful to help on the land or in a family cottage industry, or they left at the age of eight or nine to find employment, scaring birds from fields or orchards, or finding work in a local factory. Sometimes too, the teacher accepted produce or service in lieu of payment, or took different members of a family on different days of the week for one fee.

Early poverty and distress is confirmed in the Haynes family by the fact that all the boys when young were apprenticed to White and Pike Ropery, near Worcester. At this time ropers were amongst the poorest and least respected members of the community, and employment on a rope walk was considered a thing of last resort. The main reason for this was the uncertain nature of the work, which had to be carried out in the open; when the weather was bad, sometimes for months at a time in the winter, the ropers had to be laid off, their masters giving them a 'sub' to carry them over the bad patch, and this had to be worked out later when the weather improved.

Ambitious for her young family, Emma brought them from Worcester to the rapidly developing town of Birmingham, where they lived in Great Colmore Street, a rundown area that had once been fashionable. They did we.., and some time after, in 1866, decided to found their own rope business. Each of the brothers bought a piece of land where he could do his own spinning, but they combined together for other aspects of the business, including travelling and selling. They took the 'Staffordshire Knot' as their trade mark, a knot, so it was said, that could hang three prisoners at once. The original wooden block still exists. The venture prospered well, and would have prospered even better if the brothers could have got on better and trusted one another

16

instead of quarrelling.

'The trouble was,' said their sister Ellen, 'there was one big bone, and they all wanted to pick it.'

Harry, the second son, found ideal premises about two miles outside Birmingham, at Soho in the suburb of Handsworth, where he procured a large field known locally as 'the daisy field'. Through it flowed a sizeable stream, the Hockley Brook, which was a tributary of the River Tame, and this supplied the water necessary for rope manufacture. The field was flanked on one side by a row of pleasant shady trees. The site had considerable historic interest, as it was within the boundaries of Handsworth that inventions took place or were exploited, that gave impetus to the Industrial Revolution, and changed the face of the world. Above all, the very kernel of this was on the site of Haynes's rope walk, just where Matthew Boulton's factory and mint had formerly stood, and on account of this the new business was named 'Old Mint Ropery'.

Grandfather Haynes's second son, Ernie, who was himself of an inventive turn of mind and fascinated by anything mechanical, was inspired by the family association with this birthplace of the Industrial Revolution, and always considered himself as a kindred soul to some of these eager inventors who in the early days found their way there.

2

Background to Grandfather Haynes's Business
Its Inspiration to Ernie

Up to the middle of the eighteenth century, Handsworth
was a pretty Staffordshire village between the Black
Country and Birmingham. It stood in the middle of
Handsworth Heath, a wild remote spot covered with
heather, gorse and fern. Although the old Roman road from
Chester ran near, there were no proper roads over the
heath, only rough tracks.

The forerunner of local development was the building of
a turnpike road over the heath in 1727, and in 1752 the first
coach from Chester to the developing town of Birmingham
included it in its itinerary. Soon the road was being used to
carry coal in panniers on the backs of donkeys from the
mines in the Black Country to the new industries in
Birmingham. Later in the century it became known as one
of the chief routes along which itinerant Irish labourers
came for fitful and seasonal work in agriculture or the
digging of the new canals. Later still, Irish immigrants came
this way when they flooded over from Dublin in the time of
the potato famine in the eighteen-forties.

At that time the sole distinction of the area lay in the
reputation a number of its inhabitants had won for themselves on account of their skill in coin forgery, not so much
for the coins of the realm as for tradesmens' tokens, which
employers had struck and with which they used to pay their
workpeople, as, for some reason, national coinage was in
short supply at the end of the eighteenth century. The
ringleader and most noted of the forgers was one William
Booth, who inhabited a lonely farmhouse deep in the Heath
where he kept his presses, dies and the materials he needed.
His accomplices were at times caught and hanged on

Handsworth Heath, where their bodies, after first being tarred to preserve them better, were left on the gallows to creak and rattle in the wind till they rotted away, as a warning to others likely to succumb to similar temptations. The sight of the corpses does not seem to have been a great deterrent, as the rewards were so great, and in a time of real poverty and great hunger there were always those ready to take a chance in a business so lucrative and hard to catch.

The practice continued till the end of the century and beyond, when Booth's house was raided and he himself caught red-handed, destroying forged banknotes and other incriminating evidence, but not before much of it, and also the dies from which he worked, had been salted away in various places around, to come to light from time to time for the next forty years and more.

Booth himself was executed at Stafford Gaol. Not only his life but even his death was memorable, there being so much difficulty in hanging him. At the first attempt the rope slipped. His unconscious body was resuscitated and a second attempt made. This time the 'drop' refused to work. Everything went smoothly and according to plan the third time round.

By this time Matthew Boulton had established his mint using the newly-invented steel presses, the coins from which, for the first time in history, were perfectly symmetrical and could not be counterfeited, and hence the local malpractice came to a natural conclusion.

It was the coming in 1764 of Matthew Boulton, the son of a prosperous button manufacturer in Birmingham, that before long gave the area international fame. He had recently made a wealthy marriage, and intended to use his newly acquired riches to start a factory of his own on revolutionary lines. His interest fastened on Soho, (named after the hunters' cry to their dogs, 'So' (see) 'Ho' (after him), which was traversed by the Hockley Brook. It was then a sandy rabbit warren in the middle of the Heath, at a time when rabbits, far from being considered wild creatures and vermin, belonged only to the gentry and were carefully kept in specially secured warrens, preserved by keepers called warreners. The only solitary dwelling on this common was the warrener's hut, on the site of which Matthew

19

Boulton built Soho House, an elegant mansion of great distinction.

The first industrial building Boulton erected was a metal rolling mill, using the Hockley Brook for the necessary water power. Then nearby he built a factory, a very large one costing what at that time was considered an astronomical sum of £20,000. Here were made what were known in the trade as 'steel toys', small metal objects such as buckles, door handles, lamps, chains, snuff boxes, watchcases, candelabra and the like. The nearby area in the Black Country had always, since the Civil War, had the reputation of making small metal objects, but it had been done as a home industry, a forge and smithy being attached to almost every farm and cottage.

Boulton's new manufactury became a showplace. It became the first factory in the world to use modern mass-production methods. He assembled under one roof a number of skilled workmen who, with the aid of machinery, produced articles of greater precision more cheaply than had ever been done before by individual craftsmen. Each product circulated round the works from one specialist to another till it was completed. This division of labour, where each worker kept to one particular occupation, necessitated new organisation and control, and so arose the employment of a trusted foreman in the roll of a small master of each workshop. In ten years Boulton had built up a labour force of a thousand men, women and children, among whom were skilled artists, designers and craftsmen from abroad. In all this he was helped by his friends John Lloyd (founder of the bank of that name) and John Wedgewood the potter, who collaborated with him for many beautiful articles, and copied his methods in his own pottery works in Etruria. The organisation of the factory came to be considered as the starting point of the Industrial Revolution, and served as a model for many others.

Boulton's products were exquisite, and quickly achieved a reputation for excellence. Through his shrewd and superbly skilful marketing in London, his goods were sent all over the world, and every Royal Household in Europe was numbered among his customers

At first the products of the factory had to be sent either to

Chester or to London to be assayed. These were long journeys and the goods often got damaged, so application was made for the founding of a new Assay Office in Birmingham for the convenience of the Boulton factory, and such was its reputation that the request was granted, and the new Assay Office was built in 1773, with an anchor chosen as its sign.

To visit his famous workshops and admire its mechanical and artistic productions came sightseers from all quarters of the civilised world, including the most illustrious names in literature, art, science and philosophy, as well as soldiers, statesmen, even royalty, including Catherine the Great of Russia herself, and many others. His newly erected mansion of Soho House, with its pleasure gardens, lake, lawns and beautiful avenues, was always filled with such visitors. The area was described at the time:

'Soho, where Genius and the Arts Provide, Europe's wonder and Britannia's pride.'

The work that went on in Boulton's factory was the focus of intense outside interest, and there were always spies hovering around, not only from other parts of Britain, but also from abroad, particularly Germany, all trying to probe the secrets of what was going on there. A favourite spot for them to haunt was the Wagon and Horses public house, where the men from the factory used to gather for a drink in the evening. The strangers used to chat with them and bribe them with drinks to talk about their work, and describe the machinery and what they were doing. This was not always easy. Few of the men could read or write, but they did the best they could by making in chalk on the floor quarries rough drawings of the parts of the machinery with which they worked, and much valuable knowledge was gained by this method.

Boulton tried to frustrate the spies by engaging a tough old seafaring man named Blower to patrol round the factory night and day with a musket, and in Ernie's time there were still folks around who told tales of people they had known in their young days who on occasion had been threatened by him. According to local memory, Blower had lived in a wooden hut surrounded by fowls that at night roosted in the rafters, and with no company other that these and the two goats he kept, he was always referred to as Robinson Crusoe.

Boulton himself could scarcely have complained too severely when some of his secrets became known, as he too had agents practicing like espionage and deception round places where work interesting to him was being done. It was by such methods that he discovered and exploited the secrets of Sheffield Plate shortly after it was invented.

The manufactury became so successful, it became the Mecca for many other inventors, all eager to join the venture, but Boulton was very selective as to whom he accepted. Foremost among the many applicants was James Watt, who came in 1773, and it was in Boulton's factory that the first steam engine was perfected.

A clumsy steam engine had already been invented for pumping water out of mines, but it was not used extensively as it needed so much fuel. Watt invented improvements so that it took only a quarter of the fuel hitherto needed, and extended its scope for other purposes. By this time Boulton's factory had outgrown the water capacity of the Hockley Brook, and Watt's perfected steam engine was adapted to supply power for the machinery without the need of water, and a patent was taken out for its manufacture. From then on, the reputation of the Soho factory increased still further. Even more visitors arrived, and the factory's new steam engine was widely sold.

When asked why so many famous people visited him, Boulton replied with a laugh, 'Do I not sell what all the world desires? Power.'

Verses of the time extolled the virtues of the steam engine:

'Engine of Watt, unrivalled is thy sway.
Compared with thee, what is the tyrant's power?
His might destroys, while thine creates and saves.
Thy triumphs live and grow like fruit and flower,
But his are writ in blood and read on graves.'

Another famous arrival, who walked down from Scotland, was William Murdoch, who came in 1777. He was a poor

Scottish boy whose father had known and worked with James Watt in years gone by. This boy had shown early an instinct for mechanical invention, and his father sent him to the Boulton and Watt factory in Soho to get a job and learn about the new steam engines being made there. The quiet, shy young man dressed himself up for the interview with Mr Boulton. The occasion needed a top hat, and as he could not afford to buy one, he 'turned' one himself out of wood on a lathe with which he was very skilful. The interview did not go well, and he was dismissed. As the embarrassed, disappointed young man turned to go, his hat dropped to the floor with a clatter. The noise aroused the attention of Mr Boulton who asked to examine it, and heard the story of how it had been made by oval turning, a process which his factory had unsuccessfully been trying to achieve for a long time. He changed his mind about the applicant and gave him a job.

Murdoch was a willing and skilful pupil. His gifts lay as a practical engineer and craftsman, and it was not long before Watt, a draughtsman with theoretical engineering ability, was consulting him on the practical application of his drawings and designs. After a few years he was sent to Cornwall as area manager to give instruction on the installation of the new steam pumping engines used in the mines down there. In his leisure time he turned his hand to many inventions of one kind and another, including amusing gadgetry and the lighting of his home with natural gas, pockets of which were found near the mines, and with which he terrified the locals, who thought it was the work of the Devil. Even more frightening was the model he made from his own idea of a steam engine locomotive. It was a small affair, but proved a success. Early one morning he got out on the road to test it. When he lighted the fire and the steam was generated, the engine started to move so fast he could not keep up with it. The parson from the church, taking an early morning walk, saw the curious contraption making a bee-line for him and, scared almost to death, immediately turned right about, and fled over the fields to find shelter at a farm, where he told the woman there that he had seen the Devil himself, and advised her to bolt the door and hide in the house.

A few days later Watt came to see Murdoch, and was told by the parson of his terrible experience. Murdoch was severely reprimanded, and told to pay attention to his work and not play about with useless toys. Soon after he was recalled to Soho where his employers kept an eye on him, but they allowed him to continue his experiments.

In 1802, national celebrations were called for to celebrate the Peace of Amiens in the Napoleonic War. Murdoch organized the celebrations at the Soho factory by installing gas burners all round the building. This was the first public exhibition in England of coal gas lighting; the lamps were naked and 26,000 were used, but no accident occurred. In *Aris's Gazette* for 1802, the novel illuminations are thus described:

> 'On top of the roof was a great star, while above
> the central figure was a transparency, showing a
> female figure giving thanks for the return of Peace.'

Neither Boulton nor Watt ever tried to push the invention, although Murdoch and his assistants continued experimenting. Before Murdoch died in 1839, a gas meter and gas oven had been invented in the Soho factory.

Not only in England but also in Germany, experiments in gas lighting were taking place, and indeed in 1803 a German named Winsor had been invited to London to arrange a gas lighting display in the Strand, and another took place in 1805 to mark George III's birthday. Far greater publicity was given to these displays than the earlier one at Soho.

Among other inventors who established themselves at Soho was Francis Egington, who invented the japanning process and the revival of the medieval art of glass staining using enamel colours. John Houghton, one of the famous eighteenth century clock makers, also found his way there. Various printing processes were invented here, including the processing of photographic plates known as 'sun pictures', although the inventor never discovered how to 'fix' them. Oil paintings were reproduced mechanically. A copying machine was also invented, so accurate it alarmed the government, which thought it might be used to counterfeit bank notes. No doubt they had not yet forgotten the earlier reputation of the area.

It was in 1786 that Boulton opened a mint on the opposite side of the road to the factory, and installed the new steel presses for making both coins of the realm and tradesmen's tokens, and entrusted it to Kirchler, the celebrated medallist of that time. Here for the first time, British coins were struck in copper instead of the traditional bronze, and were designed to make a connection between coinage, weight and length:

> The two pence piece weighed two ounces, and fifteen placed end to end measured two feet.
>
> The one pence piece weighed one ounce, seventeen of which placed end to end measured two feet.
>
> The half pence piece weighed half an ounce, ten of which placed end to end measured one foot.
>
> There were further coins of a farthing, half a farthing and a quarter of a farthing, of corresponding weight and measurements.

Often these coins were used as weights by the shopkeepers, and even at the end of the nineteenth century there were many old people who could remember when butter, sugar and the like were weighed by placing the appropriate number of Boulton coins in the scale.

The mint continued here till 1851, when it was dismantled and the machinery and presses removed to Birmingham, where a new mint had been built. This was the site Grandfather Haynes bought for his ropery, and his son Ernie loved to tell how, as a small boy, he used to spend hours with an old knife digging out these big, heavy Boulton pennies, at that time considered worthless junk, but later much sought after as collectors' pieces.

The inventors and famous men associated with the manufactory, including John Bright and Dr Priestley (of oxygen fame), were mostly members of the National Scientific Royal Society. They met every month for discussion and conviviality at the house of one of them. They called their club 'The Lunar Society', as their meetings were always timed for the full moon, so that they could walk or ride back home over the heath in greater safety from muddy potholes or from footpads. After a time the society lost one of its most famous members: Dr Priestley was known to be sympathetic to the French Revolution at a time when England was at war with France, and in July 1791, while he was out at dinner celebrating the taking of the Bastille, his house was sacked, and he thought it prudent to beat a hasty retreat from Handsworth, and never came back.

Of course this highly successful venture attracted a great influx of population, at first from the rural districts of England, just at that time being tragically affected by the increasing number of Enclosure Acts, whereby land, common to the use of local inhabitants for various agricultural purposes from time immemorial, was being appropriated to their own use by those knowledgeable enough to manipulate the law, and against whom the simple, uneducated, dispossessed peasant was quite powerless. With their traditional living taken away from them, these unhappy folk had to leave their homes and seek work in the new factories springing up all over the place, including that of Matthew Boulton in Soho. In succeeding generations these were augmented by Irish immigrants, who, for one reason or another, flooded down from the Chester turnpike, which connected with the Irish crossing from Dublin.

It was not long before a great number of workmen's cottages mushroomed up, but nevertheless for a great many years the area remained pleasant and desirable, not only for the labourers but also for the factory owners themselves, seeking a pleasant and convenient home out in the country, not too far away from their businesses in Birmingham or the Black Country.

An entry in 1819 in Pye's *Description of Modern Birmingham* calls Handsworth:

> '. . . the elegant village of Handsworth where the common lands of the parish, being enclosed by acts of parliament in 1793 . . . there are at least 150 respectable houses erected upon ground which formerly was entirely waste (heath land)

and plots of the same ground have been sold for £200 to £1,000 per acre,' (an incredibly high price at that time for land).

James Watt built here for himself a house which he named 'Heathfield'. He fitted up the garret as a workshop where he could plan out his drawings and equipment undisturbed. It was a cosy little room and here he shut himself up, sometimes for weeks, cooking any small repast he needed on a frying pan he kept there, getting a servant to push food to him through a hatch, especially grapes of which he was particularly fond, although sometimes he was so absorbed in his work they remained uneaten for days.

In 1819, James Watt died in his garret and the house was bought by one of the Tangye family, who, like a number of other manufacturers, had gravitated to the area with his engineering business. The new owners sealed up the room in the garret, leaving everything there, including the frying pan with its last fat, and the tools Watt had used just where his hand had last placed them. For the next fifty years it remained unopened and unattended except by his ghost, which, according to local belief, paid a visit there every year on the anniversary of his death. Eventually it was opened as a museum and the dust of ages cleared away, but everything else was left undisturbed as it had been in the great man's time, even to the last bunch of withered grapes.

And so it was in Ernie's time. He visited it time and time again, Watt's solitary way of life exercising for him an immeasurable fascination, and indeed, from childhood to old age, while not being quite so committed in his dedication to solitude, he was never happier than when he had locked himself in his room or shed, alone with his own experiments and 'inventions'. All these local associates, with the Industrial Revolution, both humble and renowned, were to him living personalities of character and individuality; he knew them and their lives as well as he knew members of his own family. Although he never had anything but a poor opinion of Boulton, whom he thought an unscrupulous villain, picking and exploiting other peoples brains to his own advantages, his hero worship for Watt and Murdoch never waned. It never seemed to occur to him that maybe the great inventors who worked at the factory might not have got so far if they had not been backed by Boulton's wealth and interest.

According to local records, some of the new inhabitants were far from desirable. In the early days of the nineteenth century, a wild, coarse bunch of lock filers established themselves here, and they really stirred the place up, bull-baiting, badger-baiting and cock-fighting being amongst their milder and more pardonable iniquities. So great were their vices, the places where they lived became known as 'Nineveh' and 'Bacchus', words perpetuated in local street names to this day.

Of course the new Methodist Revivalists wrung their hands at such depravity, and soon arrived in fighting force, clad in the armour of the Lord to pursue the art of conversion. They started by holding meetings in the open, which led them on to congregations in some of the little cottages. Later they rented a little workshop over a wash house, and finally built a little chapel which they called 'Nineveh Chapel', next door to an inn called 'The Beehive', which years later became Grandfather Haynes's home, his mother-in-law fitfully patronising the adjacent chapel from time to time.

The evangelists worked very hard and very skilfully to draw people away from the sources of many of their vices, the principal ones being Handsworth Wake and other similar although lesser occasions during the year, when there were booths and entertainments all along Soho, and the public houses, particularly the 'Wagon and Horses', became centres for the popular bull- and badger-baiting and cock-fighting, and there was an ox roast in the streets.

On these occasions the 'Ranters', as the Methodists were called, organized their own tea party as a counter-attraction, all the inhabitants of Handsworth being supplied beforehand with tracts and being given a free and open invitation. They had a considerable measure of success. Other chapels opened, and in the course of time the area settled down to an acceptable level of sin.

Matthew Boulton died in 1809, at the age of eighty-one. He had a lavish funeral costing two thousand pounds at which six hundred of his workers attended, each of whom was given a hat band, gloves and a silver medal. Later there were entertainments and a sumptuous dinner; no doubt all Soho, including his own family, were satisfied he had had 'a good send off'.

The manufactory continued to thrive and prosper until Murdoch's death in 1839, after which its complexity became unwieldy. There was a dispersal of skills, and finally it was demolished in 1862, although fragments remained and were preserved as a museum by Avery's Weighing Machine Company, one of a number of firms that established themselves there.

In spite of the population explosion in the eighteenth and nineteenth centuries, numbers were, by modern viewpoint, not overwhelming. In the census of 1871, twenty-two thousand were recorded, in that of 1901 fifty-one thousand, but this pales into insignificance against modern comparison.

Grandfather Haynes and all his children were fascinated by the local history of the place in which they lived and with which they felt so closely associated. To the end of their lives, Ernie told the stories of Matthew Boulton, James Watt, Murdoch and the rest, to his own family and friends as they sat by the fireside, till they knew them as well as he did. It must be remembered that these renowned men had lived on into the nineteenth century, and had not been dead a great many years in Grandfather Haynes's time. There were many people in Handsworth who had known them, and whose parents and certainly grandparents had worked for them from their earliest development. They too were proud of their own connection with these world-famous personalities and their achievements.

Grandfather Haynes and his family were not so far removed from even the beginning of the Industrial Revolution as we today are from Victorian times. Now, at the end of the twentieth century, densely-populated Handsworth has achieved a national reputation very different in character from that which first focused the eyes of the world.

3

Great Grandmother Haynes's Family.
Their Marriages and In-laws.

Great-grandmother Haynes's family was a strange assortment. Harriet, the eldest daughter, worked in the jewellery
quarter of Birmingham after her mother brought the family
from Worcester. She married, when young, a pleasant,
estimable young man named Joe Harvey, who was a roper
like her brothers, and also a lightweight boxer of some
repute, and they had several children. Later she abandoned
them all to elope with a married man, a public house keeper
who had come down from Barrow-in-Furness. Her younger
sister Ellen followed her to London where they had gone, to
plead with her to return, but she would not come back and,
as far as is known, no member of her family ever saw her
again.

Poor Joe was broken-hearted. He took to drink in a big
way, and refused to go to church ever again. Ellen and her
brother Harry wrestled with him for his soul, and after
weeks of supplication eventually won and persuaded him to
accompany them to church to be reconciled with the
Almighty. It was a great day when Joe, escorted by Harry
and Ellen, attended his first service again. At first he bore
up well, but unfortunately he had fortified himself for the
occasion, not wisely but too well, and to the eternal
disgrace of the family, during the singing of the Psalms
suddenly stood out in the aisle, and with arms raised aloft,
above the noise of the service, roared out to God to pour
down curses on the erring Harriet.

After this, the Haynes family disowned him completely;
they had done their best. Joe never went to church again,
till he was carried there in a box from which he could not
escape many years later.

Richard (Dick), the eldest of Great-grandmother's sons, was the 'gentleman' of the family. He was a master roper like his two brothers, and did the distant travelling for the firm, getting orders, making deliveries and the like right through Staffordshire and the Potteries in the North, south down to Worcester, Bromyard and Hereford, while his two brothers worked the Midlands and the Black Country. He was often away from home for weeks at a time. He was remarkable to his friends and acquaintances for always wearing a top hat and playing a concertina as he drove along the country lanes, and he turned the heads and hearts of a number of girls on his travels. Indeed, in the early nineteen-twenties, his nephew Ernie's family, when holidaying at Bromyard, well remembered an old lady in a shop there talking about the Haynes family, and saying how once she thought Dick wanted to marry her.

With his brother Harry he had a rope walk in Handsworth, and also a retail shop in Hill Street in the centre of Birmingham, and was helped by his sister Ellen, who knew the rope trade just as well as her brothers did.

Dick did not marry until late in life, his bride being a solicitor's widow with two boys, Percy and Aquilla, who were at boarding school near Bromyard. She was the only real 'lady' by birth and education in the family, and had considerable wealth and property. Dick managed to get through all this in no time at all; soon they were comparatively poor, and the marriage was not a happy one. In any case the union got off to a bad start, as soon after the wedding a barmaid in Stafford brought a paternity suit against him. He denied his guilt and refused to pay maintenance, choosing instead to go to prison. This was only the beginning of a succession of infidelities. His unfortunate, unhappy wife put up with him for a number of years, but eventually had a legal separation from him, divorce in Victorian times being rare and considered a great disgrace for everyone concerned, guilty and innocent alike.

Although very lavish in expenditure on himself, Dick was very mean with everyone else, which made him very unpopular with Grandfather Haynes's family, who saw little of him except on Sunday mornings after church, when he used to come and help himself to the whiskey, of which he

31

was extraordinarily fond and drank far too much. Although he was a pillar of the local church, his brothers despised him as an arch-hypocrite and a snob of snobs.

Charlie, the youngest brother, was very fat, good-natured and rough. Although a rogue and a tippler and the black sheep of the family, according to his nephews, in many ways he had a fine character, and was amongst the 'whitest', kindest and most lovable of men they ever knew, always ready to share his last shilling with anyone harder up than himself. He had never been known to wear a belt or braces, but to the day he died he always kept up his trousers with a piece of rope tied round his waist and the legs tied up under the knees with string. He was a very large man with an enormous appetite - herrings he bought by the barrel and kippers by the box. At every meal, as additional accompaniment to whatever was provided, he demanded that his wife should cook a large saucepan of potatoes for himself alone.

He was a shocking drinker, a real boozer, and although he only drank fourpenny ale, he drank prodigious quantities of it. He often went out on business for the firm, and his nephew Ernie loved to go with him. He was instructed that if his uncle stopped at a public house, he was to turn the horse's head round immediately and come straight back home. Charlie used to bribe his nephew's silence with a penny for every public house stop, so Ernie was always happy to accompany him.

Charlie's wife, Chrissy, was fat and good-natured too, and they had a number of children, one of whom had a leg that did not grow. Over many months, so the story went, for hours at a stretch his mother used to sit him on the table with a weight attached to his leg, till eventually it started to grow again. The children did not have constant or regular contact with their Uncle Harry's family, although one daughter was much liked by her Aunt Ellen, whom she constantly visited right through life.

All the brothers liked and understood horses, no doubt much of their interest and skill being inherited from their grandfather, who had run the livery stables in Rugeley when they were young, and also from their mother, who had been brought up with the animals. Charlie was especially skilful; as a horse dealer he had a considerable reputation, much

Old Mint Ropery (by permission of Archive Dept Birmingham Central Library) Grandfather Haynes on 'Bunch' accompanied by dog 'Joe'.

knowledge and more trickery. Before he sold any horse he would open its mouth and push down its throat a great lump of fat bacon, which, for the time being, quite disguised any difficulty it might have with breathing. He once bought very cheaply a horse that kicked badly. He operated on it and inserted a steel knitting needle under its tail, so that it was painful for it to press down its tail to kick. He sold the animal soon after and it worked well for about three years till the needle worked out, when the horse returned to its former iniquitous habit. On another occasion he inserted a tube in the throat of a horse belonging to a cabby, and although it improved its wind, it roared and snorted beyond description on ascending a hill, and became known all over Birmingham.

In defiance of the law, he was willing to cure anyone's horse of 'frog' by standing its feet in strong soda water, regardless of its suffering. But not all of his methods were so cruel. He cured several horses of kicking by fastening to their backs long strings with tin cans attached, leaving the animals tied up to be frightened by their own noise.

As a roper, Charlie was the most skilful of the three brothers, and had his own rope walk in another part of Birmingham. In summertime he was down on the walk at three in the morning with his men, working till midday, when he stopped for a snack, perhaps of a large, meaty hambone, washed down with huge quantities of ale. After a short rest, they would go on working as long as it was light.

Charlie had a sub-contract with Wright's, the firm entrusted wiith the spinning of the first Atlantic cable, which had to be spun on the Thames Embankment, as this was considered the most convenient place with a long enough stretch of suitable flat land for the job. A few of the firm's most trusted sub-contractors were invited to help spin the cable, and the Haynes family were always proud of the fact that Charlie was one of those chosen. He took a team of his men from Small Heath railway station to London for this purpose, each man being given £2 as a 'sub' before starting. On arrival, they immediately disappeared, and did not reappear till all the money was gone.

In Grandfather Haynes's family, Charlie was definitely the favourite uncle, although he certainly did not deserve this distinction through any gentleness in his treatment of his nephews. His contact with them was rough and ready, to say the least. One family story tells how, coming one day to visit his brother, he tied his horse outside the back gate. On leaving later in the dusk, having imbibed freely of liquid refreshment, he could not get his horse to move in spite of beating, curses and threats. Eventually he noticed that one back leg and one front one were tied together. At that moment his brother's eldest son, also named Harry, came out of the gate, and putting two and two together, Charlie immediately set about the lad instead of the horse, to the immense delight of the young brother Ernie, who was

34

watching from an upstairs window, and who was the perpetrator of the trick.

Great-grandmother Haynes's daughter Ellen lived with her mother till the old lady died. She had, through the church, formed a friendship with a lady older than herself named Miss Shooter, a kindly, gentle, cultured woman, very different from the forceful, domineering Ellen. She was the adopted daughter of Mr Gooch, a wealthy landowner, and had travelled with him in India and the Far East. She was at that time living with her guardian in Edgbaston, one of the fashionable parts of Birmingham, in a lovely house filled with oriental carpets, silks and many art treasures. After her mother died, Ellen joined them in this house as 'lady's companion' to Miss Shooter.

Although Ellen never married, she had had, so she said, no less than five proposals of marriage, one from a wealthy silk merchant, another from Mr Gooch himself, and three others, details of which were lost over the years. Among this collection, she sued one of them for 'breach of promise', and the matter was taken to court, where she was awarded one thousand five hundred pounds damages, a considerable sum of money in those days. Ellen certainly had 'something' about her that gave an air of distinction even in her most penurious years. Her manners were beyond reproach, and her personality full of self-confidence and assurance without being 'forward' in any way. She was completely natural, entirely without pretence of any kind, but penetrating in her observations and cynical judgement of people and situations, particularly in regard to her own relations.

When Mr Gooch died, for some reason (could it have had anything to do with Ellen and her 'breach of promise'?), Miss Shooter was left with only a very small part of his fortune, and it was necessary for her and her companion to find a way of earning a living. Ellen's favourite brother, Harry, who nevertheless always described his sister as 'funny un', set up the two women in a retail rope and twine business in Pershore Street in the heart of Birmingham. Ellen's own knowledge of the trade, her business intelligence and her family connections were a great help, and the shop prospered. Ellen was in her element, but Miss Shooter was never happy there.

In due course Miss Shooter died, leaving all she had to

Ellen, who lived there alone in the shop, carrying on the business till she died in 1934, in the course of which time she had wasted all her money in a lengthy lawsuit with her next door neighbour, who, so she said, had poisoned her dog.

Soon after coming to Birmingham, Harry, the second son, fell in love with and wanted to marry an Irish girl named Hannah Russell, who worked at a local bedstead factory painting decorations. There was considerable opposition from his mother and sister Ellen, who did not like the girl, considering the family not good enough and the match unsuitable because she was nine years his senior. Her father had disappeared shortly before in very dubious circumstances, and the Haynes family found themselves getting involved in the police enquiries. The story goes that Harry used to lie on the sofa in the evening pretending to be asleep, and muttering to himself, 'Oh Hannah, Hannah, I do love you,' over and over again.

The mother's reluctance for her son to become connected with Hannah's family was quite understandable. The girl's father, Harry Russell, was no credit to any family. He was a rascally Irishman who had fled to England from Dublin when his own country got too hot for him, but nothing could keep him out of trouble for long. He became a committee member of the Fenian movement, and with four others was involved in the attempted rescue in Manchester of members of the society who were being transported along the street in a prison van. In the incident, a policeman was killed and the five rescuers apprehended. At the trial that ensued, Harry Russell was lucky and reprieved; one other was transported and the other three were hanged, public opinion being that Harry Russell was just as bad and should have been with them. As the noble-hearted three waited for the executioner to release the drop, they sang at the top of their voices, 'God save Ireland', in consequence of which they were ever afterwards known in sympathetic circles as the 'Manchester Martyrs'.

From Manchester Harry Russell went to Chester where he married a Chester girl by whom he had a large family. He became Clerk of the Course at Chester Races, and he remained in that position for some time. Then one day he disappeared, and a large sum of money disappeared at the same time, it being suspected they had gone together. Nobody

Woodblock Trademark of Old Mint Ropery. 'The Staffordshire Knot'. A gallows knot that could hang three felons at the same time.

ever again heard of him or the money, and his wife, Carrie, brought her children to Birmingham.

This was by no means the only skeleton to which the Russell family could lay claim. It had a great many others too numerous to mention. Carrie's eldest son, Timothy, was kidnapped when young by bargees, and kept by them for a long time travelling the canals of England. Eventually he escaped and got a job as a telegraph messenger in the postal service, and by ability and industry rose to a good position. He married and had an incredibly large family, two of whom, each in his own way, became famous.

The eldest son, James, became known as 'Jim the Penman', on account of his skill in perfecting the art of forging other people's signatures on cheques.

A second son, Thomas, like his father, joined the postal service as a telegraph messenger. He got to the top and became Sir Thomas Russell, OBE.

Another son, William, also did well in the Postal Service, but did not distinguish himself as his illlustrious brothers had done.

In spite of Hannah's unfortunate relations, Harry eventually married her, and worshipped her for the rest of his life.

Great-grandmother Haynes certainly had a handful to cope with in her wilful, tempestuous brood. Her photographs and family recollections indicate her as a very determined woman, and heaven knows how she must have needed to be, as a deserted wife left with such a handful. All her children were skilful, highly intelligent and industrious. The business her sons started was greatly successful, and would have been even more so if they could have agreed together and worked in harmony instead of quarrelling so much. Harry and Ellen had a justly deserved reputation for scrupulous honesty, but not so the others. Their business affiliations were constantly interrupted by innumerable petty court cases against each other, in which the younger generation were often bribed as accomplices in iniquity. Harry's son, Ernie, in later years used to tell how he was approached by his Uncle Dick to burn down one of his Aunt Ellen's sheds and intercept her letters. His father found out just in time, or presumably he might have succumbed to the temptation. And this was only one of many such stories.

Their mother however does not seem to have been daunted by her children, helped no doubt by her hot, impulsive, Celtic, Welsh blood. Even in later years, when she became very lame and could only walk with a stick, she kept them where she wanted and stood no nonsense. It is told that one day one of her grown-up sons, sitting down to a dinner she had cooked for him, complained the meat was tough. Instantly, without a word she picked up her stick, and cracked him on the head with it – hard!

All the same, her family always spoke of her with deep affection, and treated her with the greatest respect to the end of her life.

4

Grandfather Haynes's Home

Early in his married life, Harry bought a sizeable house near the rope walk. It had eight bedrooms, attics, a stable yard and considerable stabling. It had once been a public house called The Beehive, and the inn sign was still there. On the opposite side of the road was a piece of waste ground called the Pleck.

The front rooms of the house were fitted up as an ironmonger's shop and general stores and called the 'Beehive Stores'. Here was sold not only ironmongery but hardware of all kinds, crockery, watches and clocks, ready-made working men's clothes, as well as the products of the ropery. Harry's children all their lives remembered with delight the saucy advertisement their father thought up one day, 'Haynes's Trousers Down Again', which at that time was considered breathtakingly daring, but which achieved record sales success.

Hannah helped her husband considerably with the business, as she was quick and intelligent with accounts and correspondence. She managed the shop and employed two girls to help in the house. One of these girls, Bertha Mason, had originally come from the Black Country to help her aunt who had a local fried fish shop, but her aunt had not liked the look of the girl and intended to send her back. Hannah was very sorry for her, and, as she was at the time looking for a new servant, she said she would take her on and give her a trial. Bertha fitted in perfectly and adored the family, particularly her mistress, and she stayed with them till the family broke up many years later.

At least five children were born to Harry and Hannah, two sons, Harry Walter, named after his father, and Ernest

Gordon, named after the national hero General Gordon, who died in the year of the child's birth. There were also three daughters, Nellie, Gertie and Florrie. The latter two died when they were quite small, one of some sort of convulsion, the other of excitement on receiving the gift of a toy on her father's return from one of his business trips. Many years later, Nellie, on the birth of her only child, developed epileptic fits, and one cannot help wondering if the earlier deaths of her sisters might not have been from some form of the disease.

Hannah, in those early years, was a tiny, slight, placid woman, very kind and unpretentious, and greatly beloved by everyone except her mother-in-law and sister-in-law Ellen. One cannot help wondering if she brought to her home any sense of tenderness, a quality in which her husband's family, and indeed her own children, were strangely lacking, in spite of their generosity and many obvious virtues.

Harry, Nellie and Ernie were of very different temperaments, but with a strong, unmistakable family resemblance running through all of them. Perhaps because of early jealousy (who knows?), but from the day they were born to the day they died, they were never compatible with each other, and never ceased to argue and quarrel the minute they met, although right through life they could never sever contact. All this was strongly reminiscent of their father's family relationships among his brothers and sisters. Indeed, many members of the Haynes family in later generations, in spite of, or perhaps because of the strongest and most pronounced resemblances in virtues and vices alike, have often found it hard to harmonize and draw the best out of each other.

With a large house and a strong sense of responsibility that it was his duty to care for the older generation when their time of need came, Harry invited his wife's mother to live with them, and also his own mother and unmarried sister. These three did not get on at all well together, and were very jealous of each other. On one occasion, so it is told, Harry brought home as presents for the two elderly ladies, pieces of silk to be made up into dresses. His own mother, seeing that hers was the same and not better than that for her hated rival, immediately stuffed hers up the chimney.

Great-grandmother Haynes, acting very genteel and on her dignity, seemed to bring out the worst in Great-grandmother Russell (affectionately called 'Gaggy' by her grandchildren), and the three in-laws quarrelled violently, ending one day in a pitched battle, when Gaggy, with difficulty, was intercepted striking out with a poker. Harry decided this could not go on, so he bought a house nearby for his own mother and sister, and kept his wife's mother in his own home.

Gaggy was definitely the favourite grandmother and spoilt the children dreadfully, particularly Ernie, the youngest, even taking a glass of milk every day to him in the school playground when he was small. When they were little, the two boys slept in her room. Her sight was poor, and young Harry loved to tease her by hiding his little brother under the bed and then putting a bundle of clothes in Gaggy's bed to make believe he had crept in to her, and then laughing to hear her drooling over and caressing it before she discovered her mistake.

Gaggy always had a bag of biscuits each week delivered with the grocery, and these she took upstairs and locked away in a tin box. Every morning, when Bertha brought them a cup of tea in bed, she produced the box of biscuits. When it came to Ernie's turn to choose one, he used to tease by constantly changing his mind till she looked away, when he would grab several and run off. Later, when she died, he was asked if there was anything of hers he would like; he chose this box, believing it would in some magical way always contain biscuits. He was very disappointed when he found this was not so, but nevertheless this same box survived right through his life and to the generation after.

Young Harry exploited shamefully his grandmother's poor eyesight, asking her, for instance, to boil a crock egg for him out of the coop, and complaining it was too hard, or drawing bones, knives, spoons and other objects on the kitchen floor tiles, and persuading her to try and pick them up.

All the children loved to go to town with Gaggy on the

41

tram. She kept her money in a bag tied up with a long piece of tape, and this she put safely in the top of her stocking. The whole tram watched with interest while she lifted up her skirts to get at it, holding the tape in her mouth the while. On one occasion she found difficulty in getting at it, and it was with huge delight the children heard the conductor say, 'Hey Missus, p'raps yo'll gie me the fare when yo've finished scratching yerself.'

When they got to town she always took them to the Market Hall, underneath which in the cellars was a working man's cafe known as 'Nelson's Cabin'. Here a good dinner was served every day for fourpence halfpenny, and the place was always packed. It was owned by a stout, flamboyant, large-hearted woman named Mrs Mountford, who had made a fortune out of it. She no longer worked seriously on the premises, but each day, about one o'clock, she arrived in her carriage drawn by two lively-stepping horses, all dressed up in a cartwheel hat with enormous ostrich feathers and decked out with the largest and most ostentatious rings and assorted jewellery, and would alight and enter her eating house, where a huge, steaming joint of meat was waiting for her. This she carved with a flourish in front of her customers. When she had finished, a flunkey, dressed equally ostentatiously, arrived with a tray of thick slices of bread. Taking a big, long-handled fork, she would dip them in the gravy in the meat dish, to give to a queue of dirty, ragged little urchins who assembled there. Gaggy always timed the visit to coincide with this spectacle, which the children wouldn't have missed for worlds.

Occasionally Gaggy used to go away from home for a few days on a mysterious visit, the purpose of which was never discussed and about which the children's questions remained unanswered, although it was presumed to have something to do with her lost husband. Nobody ever saw him, and his whereabouts were never revealed.

Gaggy did not go to church with the rest of the family, but patronized the chapel next door. Not that she ever went to a service, but every Sunday she sent along a penny for the collection, and later, when the chapel treat took place, she always received an invitation and was given a prize.

Harry and his wife were regular and conscientious

churchgoers, but when their two boys were small they were left at home in the kitchen on Sunday nights for Bertha to give them their supper of bread and milk while their parents were at the evening service. In these cosy evenings in the kitchen, young Harry used to dress up as a parson and, when the others got back, insisted they took their places on chairs he had set out for them, while he stood up and gave them a sermon. His parents were very proud of him as he was really good at it, so good, in fact, they thought he had a vocation for the church, and encouraged him for all they were worth. They did their best for baby Ernie too. After Harry's sermon, the big, illustrated family Bible used to come out, and the little Ernie was told the stories and shown the pictures, which he would kiss or thump as he considered appropriate.

As Harry got older, he was taken to church with his parents and sister, where they all sat in a family pew shared by his Aunt Ellen and her mother as long as the old lady was able to get there. Young Ernie was left at home for some time yet, it being considered he was not old enough to sit through the service and be well-behaved during the long sermons of those days.

Harry and Ernie both grew to be dreadful teases, particularly Harry. A poor old woman named Mrs Reeve used to do some washing for the family. She could never prevent the buttons from coming off in the mangle, and 'to teach her a lesson', Harry one day got a large tin plate, bored two holes in it, and sewed it on his shirt before sending it to the wash. This same old soul used to hang about the kitchen before going home, and always finished by asking if they had got a bit of dripping she could have. Young Harry one day, thinking himself very clever, made up a little song about the shirt buttons and the dripping, and recorded it on a blank gramophone record which he played to her the next time she came, with smug satisfaction at the poor woman's discomfiture.

Many such tales were told about young Harry, episodes which were equally enjoyed by his brother and sister, even though they had not initiated them. These stories are quite typical of one side of the Haynes nature – of being indifferent, sometimes, though not always, unconscious of the hurtfulness of their words and deeds towards other people, particularly if any wit could be associated. They could be completely lacking in tact and sensitivity, and the self-control and courtesy that goes with these qualities. Instead of the parents being amused at their son's smartness, they should have given him a good reprimand, or a thrashing as would have been more customary at that period, and the fact that they did not seems to indicate that they too possessed this family flaw, in spite of their strong and obvious virtues of kindness and liberality in so many ways.

All three children were alike in this way to a greater or lesser extent; even Nellie, married later to the gentlest, kindest husband, who came from a family outstanding in thoughtfulness not only to strangers but above all in their own family circle, never grew out of it. To the end of their lives they were all capable of doing and saying things that were breath-taking in their insensitivity.

(Knowing how strongly the Haynes characteristics could be inherited, perhaps it would not do any of their descendants any harm to 'look themselves over' now and again. No doubt each would be convinced he or she had been lucky and had escaped; hopefully their friends and relations would be equally convinced.)

Both grandmothers died when the children were still quite young. Their Haynes grandmother had become very lame with the years, at first walking with a stick, which later, with increasing infirmity, was replaced by a bath chair, bought for her by her son Harry. When she died, this chair was kept in the home and lent out in local need. His two sons would watch till their father had gone out, when they would take it to the top of nearby St Michael's Hill and ride down it in turns. They gave it so much use that eventually a wheel came off one day when Ernie, commandeered by his father for the job, was pushing a fat old chap in it up to the hospital. And that was that!

One can only wonder what the old lady, so conscious of decorum, would have thought of her own funeral. The meal, always provided on these occasions for the mourners, was a hilarious affair when her son Charlie, always full of fun and merriment, kept the company in such stitches of laughter, they were reluctant to break up the party and go home.

Only Ellen was shocked beyond measure and haughty with disapproval; she had already been put out that day to learn from the will that her mother had left her much admired and coveted gold watch to her eldest grandson Harry instead of to her. However, she obtained it before long by offering to take it to be cleaned, and never remembered to give it back to him.

One of the family's most attractive qualities was their love of animals, particularly horses, with which they were familiar all their lives. Harry owned a number of horses and stables on his premises, and these he not only used for his own business, but hired them out to his neighbours. One of Ernie's earliest recollections was of playing in the stables between the horses' hooves, his mother's fears that he would get trampled, and his father's reassurance he would come to no harm and insisting she should leave him alone. Young Harry became particularly clever at handling the horses, and many tales are told.

Of all the horses they had, one was held in particular affection, and they never tired of talking about him to the end of their lives and laughing about his tricks.

The horse's name was Bunch. He was a strong, rough, sturdy animal with a reddish coat and the distinction of possessing a very stiff mane which stood straight up from his neck. He had an ugly look in his eye, and would bite with or without provocation. The family believed he was a Russian horse, and he had so many tricks they felt sure he must once have been in a circus. If he felt like rearing at any time on the journey, he reared on the spot without warning. Likewise, if he felt like kicking the back of the cart, he stopped in his tracks and went ahead with kicks. For these practices the whip was called for, but he had another habit which at first was far more puzzling; if he felt tired or perverse, he simply stopped dead still wherever he was and lay down, and no amount of beating, swearing or tugging would induce him to budge. Only young Harry found a solution; if he were tickled gently on his back with a cane, he would instantly get up and set off as if nothing had happened. So a cane in the back of the cart became routine equipment.

The boys loved to tell how, one cold, foggy, November

45

night, they were returning home very late through Hockley Heath. At a lonely, deserted stretch of the journey, Bunch decided he wanted a drink of water from a quarry pond below the level of the roadway. They could not control the animal and down he went, slipping on the muddy bank into the deep water, cart and all, the boys jumping to safety only just in time. They went to find help but there was none, so they had to return, expecting to find the horse dead. Not one bit of it. He had managed to drag himself out as well as the cart, and so they continued home. They said they thought at first he must have drunk the pond dry, and would not have put it beyond him.

Eventually Bunch was sold to a local milkman. For the most part he was a good worker but sometimes he got bored with the routine, when he made for his old home at a gallop, rattling the churns behind him. The milkman, on missing the horse in his rounds, learned to go to the Haynes's stable yard to collect him.

Some of the family dogs were also remembered with delight. There was Joe, the deaf bull terrier who never barked. There was Vic, a vicous little mongrel terrier whom nobody dared touch, except Hannah. The animal often went out in the cart, and on one occasion, when Harry was travelling in the Black Country, the dog strayed away and could not be found. He had to return home without him, and it was with much trepidation he faced his wife, who was devoted to her pet.

Two weeks later, when the family were having their supper in the kitchen, on opening the back door there was poor little Vic, dirty, starved, and feet covered in blisters. He went straight to Hannah, who took him on her lap where he went instantly to sleep. Oh, what a fuss they made of him. He was honoured by having his picture taken and made into a trade calendar for that year, entitled 'The Wanderer's Return'.

Another affectionately remembered pet was a contemporary of Vic, a handsome golden retriever called Lion. The animals were great friends and, so the family asserted, used to help each other out in a variety of iniquities, which included stealing meat from a nearby butcher's shop, and ingenuity in frustrating the butcher's attempts at giving

46

chase. Vic, so they said, spent a lot of time lying in wait in a back entry to pounce on and fight any unsuspecting dogs going by, fetching Lion to help him out with any too big to tackle on his own.

On one occasion Harry had had the retriever clipped close, leaving only his 'mane' and tuft at the end of his tail. Ernie passed it among schoolmates that his father had bought a lion, and the little urchins, wide-eyed with awe, believed him, and spread it around to each other, 'Haynes's have got a really lion now.'

The next step, of course, was to tame the lion. Ernie was quite equal to the occasion, and the next time his father was out of the way, he fastened the dog up in a big crate in the yard, which had held a consignment of crockery from the Potteries. Then he invited his pals in, and set them up on a high wall to watch. Everything went well. The animal was tormented with brooms, poked with mops and sticks, terrified with lighted newspaper till he was frantic, and would have devoured his captor if he could have got him. Then the audience on the top of the wall began to melt away as if by magic, although the show was by no means over. Ernie's dad was spotted coming back.

It was the lion tamer's turn now to feel panic. He knew his father would have thrashed him within an inch of his life if he had seen the animal in that state imprisoned in the crate, but he was terrified of letting him out. He had to work fast; he fastened a long piece of cord to the catch on the crate, and removed himself to the top of the wall before pulling it. He got back in the kitchen just in time to be sitting by the fire reading a book as his father returned for his tea. It was several hours before the tormented animal had settled down and could be approached.

5

The Children's Education and Play

The business prospered exceedingly, and Harry tried to give his own children the advantages of education he and his brothers and sisters had missed. His two elder children, young Harry and Nellie, were sent to a local private school, Harry going on later to King Edward VI Grammar School, which had then, and still has today, the reputation of being one of the best schools in the country. Every year scholarships were awarded for places, and the examination was open to boys from all over the country. Harry won one of their scholarships, and in his year came fourth in the examination.

At that time State Schools for Higher Education had not yet been founded and the few boys who won scholarships to the old Grammar Schools were very conscious of the honour and proud of their school, and Harry was no exception. The history and tradition of his school burnt itself into his consciousness and all through his life he was always ready to talk about it and extol its merits.

Harry was proud to tell how the first foundation of his school was on 28th October, 1382, in the reign of Richard II, and a licence was granted to four wealthy and philanthropic men of Birmingham ' . . . to found a chauntry (chapel) to the honour of God and the Blessed Mary, His mother, to be endowed with lands, tenements and rents in Bermyngehame and Edgbaston to the value of twenty marks per annum, to maintain two chaplains for celebrating divine service in the church of Saint Martin' (Birmingham's Parish Church). These chantry schools were widespread in the Middle Ages, and in them a considerable number of boys of promising ability were educated for the

48

priesthood.

The Birmingham Chantry, and the religious Guild of the Holy Cross of which it was part, was broken up, and its funds confiscated by the Protestant Commissioners of Edward VI in 1547. Members of the Guild petitioned that some of these funds should be restored as an educational endowment, and the petition was granted. Many old chantry schools in many parts of the country made similar petitions and were similarly treated.

In 1552 a Free School was ordered to be erected by the Commissioners of Edward VI '. . . to bring uppe the youth boathe in the same town nigh thereabouts for instruction of children and younge men in Grammar for ever to endure one Schole Master and one Usher' (undermaster). The king entrusted to 'twenty honest and discreet inhabitants the business of establishing and administering the school'. The governors of these newly founded schools were given the choice of having their endowments either in land or money. The Birmingham governors wisely chose land, which increased in value. Schools who chose money, which decreased in value over the years, found themselves in difficulties, and eventually many ceased to exist.

The old fourteenth century building was abandoned, and the newly-founded school housed in the Old Guildhall in New Street, Birmingham. Here it functioned smoothly till 1604, when two of the governors were charged with embezzlement of the school funds, making over school possessions by secret conveyance to their own friends and relations, destroying evidence of their iniquities by removing ancient deeds and leases of the Guild of the Holy Cross, kept at that time in a 'three-man' triple locked chest in Saint Martin's Church together with the cash of the School funds.

There were countercharges of misapplication of the charity which, incredibly, had increased by twenty times, the governors giving only the original amount to the school and keeping the increase for themselves. So much for the 'twenty honest and discreet inhabitants'.

In 1734 the old Guildhall building was demolished, and the school rehoused in New Street in a new building nearby. It was this school that Harry attended. Here it remained till

49

well on in the twentieth century, when it was removed to a more spacious site in Edgbaston.

Harry's education at King Edward's Grammar School was interrupted for a while by the boy's sickness, it being feared he had consumption, so thin and emaciated had he become. On doctor's advice he was sent to 'run wild' on Bringsty Common, where his father's mother had a cousin, Polly Lloyd, married to a local sheep farmer named Emanuel Roper (known in the family as Uncle Manny), and here he stayed with them, learning to shoot, shear sheep, trap rabbits, and other rural activities which were full of interest and delight.

Later still, Harry's schooldays were punctuated by an accident which could have finished them altogther. This was concerned with his impulse to make fireworks after a demonstration lesson at school. He and his pals, including one of his Russell cousins, were having great fun on the rope walk one afternoon putting charges in tin cans and blowing them up from a distance. All went well till one failed to blow up; Harry approached to investigate, and the delayed action went off just as he got there, blowing the boy's eye on to his cheek. With great presence of mind his father took out his handkerchief, bound the eye back into place, and then hurried to the nearby hospital. Contrary to all expectation, the sight of the eye was saved. This incident made a great impression locally, and was talked about till well after the Second World War by old inhabitants of Handsworth who were still alive then.

After the 1870 Education Act, when school attendance became free and compulsory, the existing church and nonconformist national schools became too small for the new influx of children, and were soon augmented by government-sponsored 'Board Schools'. One of the first of these schools in Birmingham was built near the Beehive Stores. The little Ernie watched it being built and, so the story goes, went each day for weeks, dressed for school, with a slate and slate pencil in a bag, to ask the workmen if the school was ready yet. He was promised that his name would be the first on the admission register when the school was opened, and so indeed it was, Ernie at the time being three and a half years of age. He started school in a little

50

velvet suit with a needlework collar out of regard for his tender years, but before long this was exchanged for more manly attire of a sailor suit, matching hat, and a lanyard with a whistle attached. Many years later in old age, Ernie used to go down occasionally to the school, where the staff made a lot of fuss of him, and got him to talk about old Handsworth, to the mutual delight of Ernie himself and his enthralled audience.

Ernie had many vivid memories of the school, even from his earliest infant days. He remembered the maypole fitted into a socket in the school hall, and the children regularly dancing round it as one of their 'drill' lessons, and also the entertainment they gave to their parents at various social occasions. Miss Pringle, the Headmistress, was full of encouraging ideas for her small pupils. One of them centred round a model cow placed in a large glass case known as 'The Museum'. The cow would moo when its head was turned, and a scholar who had done something very well or had tried very hard was allowed, as a great honour and privilege, to turn the head and hear its plaintive moo. This cow Ernie remembered as a highlight of those early years.

At Christmas time, as a gift from Miss Pringle, there was always a big tree loaded with little presents for all who went to the school party, to qualify for which the little pupils had to attend school regularly all the year. At the end of every week, on Friday afternoon, every scholar who had put in a full week's attendance was given a red card with his or her name on it, to be saved and brought to school a week before Christmas, those who had the required number of cards being eligible for admittance to the party. Miss Pringle was very strict in this matter, said Ernie, and no favouritism was shown. Also every Christmas time a play and entertainment was given for the parents. When Ernie was old enough to take part, he was cast as Jack in *The House that Jack Built*. As he stood in the centre of the stage, the words went completely out of his mind; all he could think of was to point to the back of the room and say, 'That's my daddy over there,' which of course brought the house down.

In due course the children were promoted to the 'Big School' next door, where most of them remained until the

51

leaving age of thirteen, a few of them leaving at the age of eleven if they were bright enough to pass the 'Labour Exam', and family circumstances were such that contributions from them were needed to help support the home. Here in the 'Big School' the boys and girls were separated into different classes, but Mr Hackwood was Head of the whole school.

The 'Big School' also produced an entertainment every year. Ernie, who was very musical, took part in two of them, the first of which was called *The White Garland*, and the second one, *Cinderella*, in which he was one of the Ugly Sisters. He never forgot the names of the other members of the cast, which included Daphne Quance as Prince Charming and Principal Boy, Clara Pank as Cinderella and Arthur Pank as the other Ugly Sister. These were most ambitious affairs in the form of cantatas. The performers were organized and trained by Harry Davies, who was a Welshman and very musical, and the teacher of the top class, Standard Six as it was called. All the cast were chosen from the top classes of the school.

Much money was spent on these productions, professional costumes being hired from theatrical agents, as also was scenery, footlights and props, even the scene shifters being professional. The stage was raised by desks and platforms erected at the lower end of the hall. They drew very good audiences, and were performed on two nights, Thursday and Friday, the tickets for which, sold by the children, were snapped up like hot cakes. They made good profits which were used to finance a school outing in the summer, and a teachers' 'soirée' about Christmastime. Those were hectic times, said Ernie, and were talked about by children and parents for many days.

Not only for these outstanding occasions, but in every other way did Ernie enjoy his school days. He liked and respected his teachers and, so he asserted, did most of the pupils, always considering them as their friends, particularly Mr Davies, who, although very strict, was recognized by parents and children alike as well as other members of the staff as being a most conscientious and excellent gentleman, and always very fair in all things. The children did not see much of the Headmaster, who held himself aloof, running his school from the background, and delegating authority to the members of his staff, but he was greatly liked and trusted.

Ernie was grateful, so he said, for the fair share he received as an ordinary, mischievous boy, of the corporal punishment meted out in those days. He remembered with sparkling eyes and huge delight circumstances that led up to these whackings. One story revolved round an old lady by the name of Mrs Winkles, who kept a little shop a few yards from the school. She was a very amiable old lady, said Ernie, and the children looked upon her as a kind of fairy godmother, keeping the tuck shop of the locality. She made all kinds of boiled sugar sweets, but her speciality was lemondrops, which were always in great demand. This sweetmeat had a very strong flavour, but unfortunately it had an even stronger smell, which greatly annoyed the teachers, who warned the children they must not be brought to school. Of course, he continued, they often smuggled them in, and there was a kind of 'hunt the thimble' game with the teacher trying to sniff out the culprit. Even if the teacher managed to locate the smell, they usually got away with it by a big gulp at the last minute. If luck was against one of them, and after severe cross-examination he was declared to be guilty, the sentence was the cane, the sweets put in the waste paper basket, to be thrown away by the caretaker when he made his nightly cleaning rounds, and staying in after school to write out a hundred lines: 'I must not bring lemondrops to school'. But the culprit was not always found, and the class, chuckled Ernie, had a very merry afternoon, which most of them thought was worth the risk of punishment.

The fun went on for a long time, till eventually Mrs Winkles refused to supply lemondrops till after school. This may have been a coincidence, but Ernie doubted it. He was very partial to lemondrops, and sometimes got caught with them in school, when he suffered the appropriate penalty, although he never mentioned it at home, knowing he would have received further punishment from his father, as was then the accepted practice of the time.

Even greater fun for the boys was the afternoon they spent in the Manual Centre connected with the school, where they learned to do woodwork and various kinds of metalwork. The Centre was some distance from the school and reached by a walk along the canal, at one point of which a neighbouring factory discharged into it warm water which contained some substance causing a kind of lather. This spot was known locally as 'the soap hole'. On their way back from the 'Manual', the boys loved to strip and swim and sport around in the warm water. Sometimes the police tried to catch them by confiscating their clothes, but the boys got the better of them by swimming with their clothes over to the other bank where there was no towpath, and laughed at them from the water. There were stern warnings from their parents, and their disobedience was always discovered by the smell of the canal they brought back with them. Ernie's father regularly punished him for this offence, but its appeal was irresistible.

There was a lot of fun to be had out of the school too, particularly on the 'Black Patch', a piece of waste ground opposite the school, recognized as the local playground for all the children. Here the girls played at skipping, hopscotch, Tinker's ground and all the other well-known singing and traditional games, while the boys spun tops, flew kites, played marbles, Hi Ackee (hide and seek), Bedlam (a noisy chasing game), Duck (tip cat), and Birds in the Bush. Boys and girls always played separately, and the games came round regularly in their season. Most popular with the boys was 'Kick the Can' (a primitive form of football). Ernie's brother Harry was particularly good at this, and was always chosen as leader. When picking his side he always picked Hetty Garrett among them, in spite of opposition from the team to 'playing with a wench'. Hetty, who worked on his father's rope walk, was a madcap and a better footballer than any of the boys.

A very old lady who lived alone in a cottage adjacent to the Black Patch was often teased by naughty boys on dark winter nights. They tied a button to a long piece of strong black cotton, which they fastened with a pin to the wood of the window frame and then retreated with the end of the thread into bushes a little distance away. When everything was quiet, they gently pulled the thread so that the button tapped on the pane, and continued to do this until she came out to see who was there. Seeing the place deserted, she went back inside again, and so they kept her going in and out till they themselves were tired of the sport.

Old Mrs James also lived near the school, and made ginger

beer, which the children called 'pop', and this she sold at a halfpenny and a farthing a bottle. She was an enterprising old lady and used to get the children to gather the dandelions, nettles and other plants she needed from the numerous fields in the neighbourhood, particularly from Haynes's rope walk. They were always rewarded with a large glass of the delicious brew and smacked their lips over it, considering themselves amply repaid.

Mrs James had two sons who, when the cycle boom started, repaired bikes. The bicycles in those days were the penny-farthings, with a very large wheel at the front and a very small one at the back. The riders were very high up and had a good view of the countryside, although they had to be very skilful in getting on and off and managing them generally. These bicycles were dying out in Ernie's day, although there were still quite a number about. Later in the nineties, they were replaced by the so-called 'safety cycle'. These had solid tyres, so it can be imagined how one felt after riding a few miles, and the name 'boneshakers' bestowed on them was a very appropriate title.

The business started by Mrs James's sons flourished, and they transferred it to another part of Birmingham. By hard work and enterprise they extended it into a large and well-known company. They often came to see their old mother and tried to persuade her to leave the district, but she never did. She lived to a ripe old age in her little cottage, still making her bottles of pop, although she was no longer poor and it was not necessary for her to do so.

Regularly during the year, bands of gipsies used to camp on the Black Patch, when the children were warned to keep away because of their reputation for child-stealing, although, as far as Ernie knew, no child had ever been missed during any time of their stay. It was always the same families who came, selling their pegs and baskets and artificial flowers from door to door, so they became well-known, and their brightly-painted vans, campfires and cooking pots, babies slung in shawls on their mothers' backs, tethered horses and dogs, fowls imprisoned in coops, were the focus of aroused interest as well as apprehension. During the last decade of the century, the head, or king of the gipsy families was a very old man well into his nineties, by the name of Esau Smith. He died on the

Black Patch, and his burial service took place in Handsworth Old Church. His funeral was an occasion of great interest, many other gipsy families coming from all over the country for the occasion. According to gipsy custom, as soon as he had died a few of his clothes were placed in the coffin, and a mirror and a number of valuable ornaments broken. At midnight following the funeral, his caravan, containing all his possessions with the exception of the few clothes which had been placed in the coffin, was ignited with shavings soaked in paraffin and burned completely to ashes.

Esau was succeeded as head by another member of his family, Sentima Smith, who also lived to be very old, almost a hundred years of age before she died. She too had a similar funeral service on the Black Patch. After her death the authorities, in spite of considerable resistance, evicted the gipsies, who henceforth had to camp elsewhere.

Not only the Black Patch but also the streets around were always full of interest. There were often street orators at the corner, or musicians of one sort or another, playing in a band or singly with a fiddle or concertina. The hurdy-gurdy came regularly with a monkey on top and a pair of lovebirds in a cage, and for a small coin picked out little written love messages from a basket. To all this music the children joined in and danced quite spontaneously.

Sometimes the travelling players visited for a few days. Their plays were always very gruesome and advertised as 'seven murders for sixpence', and their theatre was called 'The Blood Tub'. Here the audience was entertained to *Carl the Clockmaker*, and *Maria Marten, or Murder in the Red Barn*, or *The Face at the Window*, or *Why Girls Leave Home*, and other dramatic renderings equally titillating.

Barnum and Bailey's circus came sometimes, with elephant rides, hungry tigers and performing lions, as well as the handless man, or the fattest or thinnest or tallest or smallest man or woman on earth, as they advertised.

May Day was a red-letter day for Handsworth. All the horses and carts were decorated with bells, coloured braids and artificial flowers and horse brasses polished to gleaming splendour. They then processed round the streets and onto the Black Patch, where some of the prosperous tradespeople, including the Haynes family, used to award prizes for the best.

In Harry and Ernie's young days, there was still plenty of

evidence left of Handsworth's rural past. In the neighbourhood were several tollhouses and tollgates left standing,
one of which was still working up to the end of the century.
There were also pounds where stray animals were locked up.
These lockups were usually built close to a church, and a
black-smith's forge was always near. The smith had a key
and was responsible for the animals, and had to feed and
water them till they were claimed. At the end of the nineteenth century, the police fee when they were claimed was
five shillings, and the smith made a charge for their maintenance. Sometimes the animals were pounded for a long
time without any protection from the weather, and obviously
got in a bad condition. There were several of these places
round Handsworth, one being next to Handsworth Old
Church, and the smith's forge opposite. Grandfather Haynes
once had a horse that was lost for a considerable time before
being discovered right the other side of Birmingham in the
pound next to Northfield Church, and nobody could imagine
how it had come to stray so far.

6

A Prosperous Family with a Social Conscience

The latter half of the nineteenth century was a time when a number of philanthopists, the Cadbury, Fry and Lever families conspicuous among many others, tried to relieve the sufferings of the poor. Harry Haynes had these selfsame instincts, and did much the same kind of things in a smaller way.

Before long, Old Mint Ropery employed some fifty workpeople, many of them very poor, under a foreman named Charlie Bull. Harry bought a row of little houses which he rented to some of these workers. There was great competition to live in them, as the family was so kind-hearted the tenants were never pressed for rent, and soon felt they had no obligation to pay. These workers had to start very early in the morning, and as a number of them were too poor to buy an alarm clock, they clubbed together a copper or two every week to pay an old woman as a 'knocker-up'. Young Ernie well remembered hearing her go by in the early hours, singing hymns to herself for company. Of like fraternity was 'Arry, the 'babby minder', who came round on Mondays, and for a copper took the tiny ones off their mothers' hands while she got on with the washing. He used to take the whole collection of them into a brewhouse somewhere, and entertain them with rattles and whistles till their mothers were ready to have them back.

If any of the Haynes's workers were sick or in trouble, each day when meat was served for the family dinner, extra plates were set out for the unfortunates before the family had theirs, and Bertha was despatched to deliver them. On one occasion it was reported that a workman had stolen a fowl from off the rope walk; Harry replied he must have been hungry to have taken it, and immediately sent Bertha to buy a joint of meat to go with it.

At Christmastime Harry always gave to each of his employees a joint of beef and one of his own fowl, of which he had a considerable number running on the rope walk, and also a Christmas pudding made by Bertha. The recipe for this pudding, and also the corresponding Christmas cake, were carefully preserved and used in the family for the next century and more.

According to the custom of the day, when the rope walk was first established, a number of children as young as six to eight years of age were employed for various menial tasks. Hannah, who fully supported her husband in his kindness and generosity, was so sorry for these little urchins she made a big pot of hot stew every day, and gathering them in her kitchen, gave them a bowlful each with a great hunk of bread. One of these children, little Willie, whose job was to turn a big wheel for the men, diligently set about the task of teaching himself to read and write, and progressed in self-education from strength to strength, till in later years he became a Member of Parliament, retaining his seat for many years well into his eighties, and became known in his time as 'Father of the House'. Right to his death in the Second World War, Will preserved intermittent contact with the family that had once been so kind to him. He died a wealthy man, leaving £48,000, a great sum of money at that time.

Ernie, the only one who went to the Board School, had quite different school pals from the other two. His family said he always found out the dirtiest and scruffiest little ragamuffins who did not have a jacket between them, and used to bring them to play in 'his yard'. Among them was a poor little waif, an imbecile boy nicknamed Happy, who was employed on the rope walk. He often came to join in the games, one of the favourites of which was 'hurdy-gurdies', when the children pranced round, pretending to be fair horses. Happy enjoyed this best of all, and always insisted on being in the middle, pretending to turn the handle of the organ, and as musical accompaniment chanting 'airdy-gairdy, airdy-gairdy' in his strong Brum-magem speech. Nellie and young Harry often came to watch, and sometimes to join in. On one occasion young Harry arrived with a paper of shrimps, which he ate while watching, putting the heads and tails on one side. On finishing them he called Happy over, and asking him if he wanted any shrimps, gave him the heads and tails. 'One, Two, Three, Gone', the boy ate the lot, to the delight of the spectators.

Mockery of this simple lad almost went too far one day. In the yard was a well young Harry said needed cleaning out, and told Happy to jump in and do it. His faith and trust were such, he started immediately to get down the well, and was pulled up only just in time. Such was Harry's sense of humour, although neither his brother nor his sister found in it anything amiss.

An outstanding example of the overflowing generosity and compassion of Harry and Hannah was in their kindness to the Hooley children. Mr Hooley, at that time in South Africa (which he later was forced to flee for keeping a gaming den), had been an illegitimate son of one of the Kynocks, a wealthy arms manufacturing family in Soho. His wife had left him, and gone off on her own to America, leaving three small children, Wally, Hetty and Jim, with their disreputable, drunken old grandmother, Mrs Cropper, whose husband had long since left her, and an aunt, Mrs McNabb, also deserted by her husband, whose life and habits were no better. She was financed by royalties due to her husband when he had patented a percussion cap for guns at Kynock's. They gave her the money till she died, even after her 'old man' ran away and left her.

The Kynocks provided for the children, and every Saturday morning the little Hooleys had to fetch a gold sovereign (a great deal of money in those days) from the factory, and the Haynes children, with whom they were friendly, often went with them. Money and gifts were never short from the Kynocks, and the Haynes children, themselves by no means deprived, were wide-eyed sometimes at the lavishness bestowed on the Hooley children, who often spent the money on childish frivolities even before they got home.

One day Old Gell Cropper, as she was known, had a drunken quarrel with her daughter, who pushed her down-

The Beehive stores (formerly The Beehive Inn)
Left to right: Harry, Ernie, Mrs Reeve (servant), Grandma
Haynes, Nellie, Polly (servant), Bertha (servant), Charlie
Bull (foreman of rope walk).

stairs and killed her.

Nobody wanted those unhappy children. Harry and
Hannah took them in and looked after them as their own,
waiting for one of their parents to return and claim them,
but they never did. They kept them for more than three
years before settling them in a very good orphanage, the
Blue Coat School, where they received an excellent education. The three kept contact with the Haynes children to the
end of their lives, and Jim, the youngest, was in later years
best man at Ernie's wedding.

The family business went from strength to strength. The
policy of 'small profits, quick returns' paid off. Harry, so the
story goes, on returning from his business trips, would go

straight to his wife and ask her to hold her apron out, when he would pour into it all the gold sovereigns he had taken on his travels. Not only did he set up his sister, Ellen, and her friend Miss Shooter in business in the town, but took over extensive premises in Edgbasten Street in the very centre of Birmingham, which he used as a warehouse, with a shop in front for selling, wholesale and retail, all kinds of rope and twine, pig and cattle nets, jute bags, hessian, sacks of various kinds, and the innumerable products of his ropery. When she was older, his daughter Nellie was put in charge of it, and she proved to be an efficient manager.

Among the many contracts he obtained at the time were some for supplying the various rope and twine products needed in the interior of ships, even some of the big ocean liners then being built. These contracts were of considerable value at a time when most of the crew and deck hands slept in hammocks, and nets were used at sea to hold all sorts of articles not associated on land with net containers.

Winson Green prison was very near. Ernie never forgot how frightened he used to be as a little boy when he heard the prison bell toll as a sign that a prisoner had been hanged, and how he would cover his eyes and run to his mother and hide his head in her lap. The hangman was seen about locally, and although he went along to the public house like all the other men, everyone avoided him. When he came into the various shops, as he sometimes did, he was courteously served, but no effort was made to chat with him or get into conversation, and he was surreptitiously pointed out to strangers passing down the road.

Harry had a contract with the prison, and supplied all kinds of products they needed, including jute and hessian for the mail bags the prisoners made, and also the rope used for the hangings. Every such rope had to be specially ordered and individually spun. Many of these ropes were later preserved in Madame Tussaud's wax-work museum in the 'Chamber of Horrors', and it would be interesting to know which of them started life on Haynes's rope walk.

The Prison Governor became a close friend of Harry Haynes, and there were exchange visits between the two families. As he got older, Ernie, like his brother and sister, used to sit round the fire and listen enthralled to the tales

62

his father's friend told of prison life. He heard how the prisoners working in the workshops were paid twopence a day, with which, at the end of the month, they could buy cigarettes and tobacco, or any other little luxuries they might want. They were allowed to smoke only once a week, and they might have one cup of tea after dinner on Sunday; the rest of the week only cocoa was given. A penny per month was charged for the tea on Sundays, and another penny was put aside for celebrations at Christmas, when the prisoners themselves made and carried out all the arrangements. One Christmas, said the Governor, they had asked for turkey, but this was not allowed, so they contented themselves with fried ham, eggs and sausages and fried bread.

Occasionally the cell doors were unlocked and the prisoners could sit out in the passage, although they could not speak to each other except for once a week, when they could have a quarter of an hour's conversation. At the weekend they were locked in their cell with a Bible and a book on health, and did not come out again till Monday morning, except for a short service at Chapel, when each man sat in a special box with a little window through which he could see the chaplain. None of his fellow prisoners were visible to him, and a warder overlooked them all.

The Governor brought along a cat-o'-nine-tails for the boys to see. The cords were very thin, with a knot every three inches. A new 'cat' was provided afresh for each prisoner on each occasion it was required, and it was sent to him, so he said, in a specially sealed package direct from the Home Office. The birch was given to delinquent boys for lesser offences. Ernie remembered only one boy in Handsworth having it in his time, and that was for throwing bricks under a passing train.

The Governor told them how any man who was to be hanged was always well doped the night before, and that the hangman always tried the 'drop' previously with a sandbag the same weight as the prisoner, because if the rope was too long the prisoner did not die, and if it was too short it took his head off. The bodies were usually buried under the prison walls, the spot marked with the man's initials and the date.

63

Harry Haynes had more than once been over the prison with his friend, and told his family of what he had seen there; the condemned cell; the treadmill, composed of a hollow wooden cylinder on an iron frame, with steps about seven or eight inches apart, and a handrail for the prisoners to hold as they monotonously and laboriously trod on each step, so making the wheel turn; the crank, a similar appliance consisting of a revolving circular disk. All male prisoners over sixteen years of age and sentenced to hard labour, so he was informed, had to do at least three months on the treadmill or crank. When they were released, they could be recognized by the heavy, measured tread they had acquired by their punishment.

Ernie and his brother were often sent to the prison to deliver goods from the shop or rope walk. The prisoners always unloaded the cart, and sometimes the boys left tobacco among the packages for them to find.

Harry Haynes had a great sense of public service. He became a Church Warden, Superintendent of the Sunday School and Young Men's Bible Society, and other organizations of like nature, where he organized treats and all sorts of local activities. He became one of the managers of the new Board School, and showed considerable patronage towards it, lending his rope walk for their treats, donating the little presents for the Christmas tree, supplying boots from his shop for the desperately poor and needy children. Nor were the teachers forgotten. On Shrove Tuesday, Bertha was sent in with a dish of pancakes for them, eggs at Eastertime, and mince pies and cakes at Christmas, as well as showing on innumerable other occasions little kindly acts of thoughtful generosity. No doubt some of this rubbed off on Ernie, who was treated with deference, at least from his fellow pupils. The Haynes family were very big frogs in a little pool, and thoroughly enjoyed the experience.

Hannah, as well as her husband, played her part in the social life of Handsworth. She was elected Secretary of the newly-founded Mothers' Union, and in 1896 was presented with an inscribed silver teapot by the appreciative members. Her daughter, Nellie, later inherited this, and treasured it till her husband died and she went to live with her daughter's family. They had no regard for it whatsoever, so one day she handed it over to Ernie, together with framed portraits of her parents.

These portraits were very attractive. Harry had had the portrait of his wife done after the birth of their eldest son, as an expression of his affection, and liked it so much that he had one of himself done soon after to match and make the pair. The portraits and the teapot are now with some of their great-grandchildren.

Politics was another of Harry's enthusiastic interests. He was elected a comitee member of the local Conservative Association, and spent much time and money on their behalf. When election time came along, he and his family, even Ernie, the youngest, were busy for days beforehand with canvassing and other aspects of the occasion. At that time political propaganda could only be dispersed through the newspapers or at public meetings, which were held both indoors and in the open. Most people did not take a regular newspaper, so that public meetings had great significance and were always well attended. Harry had an instinctive talent for public speaking, and whenever there was a crowd on an outing, on the beach or the like, he would, according to his sister Ellen, get up and address it on some religious, political, or other theme relevant to the circumstance and occasion, causing the family, so she said, sometimes to feel very ashamed of him. So at election time he was in his element, and meetings at which he spoke were always packed out. As appreciation for the work he did, the Conservative party presented him with an illuminated address of which he was very proud, and he had it framed, together with a similar one from the church, in appreciation of his work with the Young Men's Bible Class, both of which are preserved and valued by his grandchildren more than a century later. He was asked on several occasions by the Conservative party to put up as the local parliamentary candidate, as they felt sure no opponent would stand a chance against a man so beloved and popular among those with whom he lived. Surprisingly, he always refused, perhaps because of his lack of literacy, of which in his later years he was very sensitive, and which it would have been impossible to conceal.

Election day, as Ernie and his brother Harry remembered

it, was a great occasion, when feeling ran very high. Slogans were painted or chalked up on every conveniently situated wall, and as the time drew nearer, comments, approving or scurrilous, were chalked alongside, according to individual fancy and opinion. Everybody, from the youngest to the oldest, got very excited, and prepared to enjoy themselves to the full. As the school was a polling station, the children had a holiday, and throughout the day they gathered together in spontaneous, sprawling, untidy gangs according to the political allegiance of their fathers, many of them sporting favours or ribbons of their chosen party, and waving little flags, some of the less inhibited mothers also joining in with equal enthusiasm, even though, as yet, the women did not have the vote.

And so they paraded round the streets and on the Black Patch, banging dustbin lids, bowls, buckets, rattles and the like, and bawling political slogans at the tops of their voices:

'Vote, Vote, Vote for Joey CHAMberlain' over and over again, and 'Lloyd George for EVER' from the Liberal opposition.

The Tories, strong supporters of the Boer War then being waged in far away South Africa, were lusty in their rendering of 'Goodbye Dolly Grey', and even more lusty with:

'We don't want to fight, but by Jingo if we do,
We've got the men, we've got the ships
And we've got the money too'

The Liberals were no match in patriotism, but they made up for this by equally loud and vociferous support, with music hall choruses of the day, scuffles breaking out from time to time as rival gangs crossed each other's path. Public houses sold record quantities of beer on election night, and many of the voters staggered unsteadily and loudly home at a very late hour.

The Liberals at that time seldom made much showing in elections, mostly owing to their condemnation of the Boer War, which attracted almost universal patriotic fervour,

66

and in which so many lads were fighting. Ernie and his father went one day to the Town Hall in Birmingham to hear Lloyd George speak, intent on doing their bit in heckling and interrupting, but they were forestalled; they found such great , milling, angry crowds outside, bursting to get at Lloyd George who was inside the building, and thirsting for his blood, that they could not get near the place. Mounted police kept the crowds back, while others went inside and managed to get Lloyd George out through a back door disguised in a police uniform. Then two returned home, staunchier Tories than ever.

Politics at all times inspired strong, even acrimonious feelings, and many people were ready to keep apart from their neighbours, even actively to dislike them, on no other grounds than that they held another political opinion. This was equally true in religion; members of the Church of England always considered themselves on a distinctly higher level than the Noncomformists, who, while indulgently acknowledged as fellow Protestants, were, for the most part, patronisingly tolerated as belonging to a lower social strata, and their pastors were often disparingly referred to as 'Ranty Parsons'. But all this was sweetness and light compared with their feelings towards Roman Catholics, whom they regarded as idolators and hypocrites, who could commit the most heinous sins over and over again, provided they went to confession and receited prayers the priest gave them as penance. Tracts and stories were written, or told with bated breath, of nuns imprisoned, even walled up in convents, where unimaginable events took place. Undoubtedly the Roman Catholic priest exercised a far greater influence over his flock than did any of the Protestant dignitaries, and this was considered very sinister, as also the conducting of the mysterious service in Latin, a language even most of their own congregation did not understand.

Much the same could be said of their attitude towards the Jews, except that the focus of their mistrust was not alleged worship of Mary and statues and idols and the influence of the priests, but their refusal to eat pork or any product from pig, a circumstance much less comprehensible. There was a belief too that they were mean and hard and exacting

67

in money dealings, no doubt an inherited distrust reaching back to the Middle Ages, when Jews were most distrusted and feared on account of their monopoly in the business of moneylending. So it was understandable that both Roman Catholics and Jews tended to live in close communities apart from their neighbours. Fortunately there was a widely accepted etiquette that it was inexcusable bad manners to enquire from anyone what his politics or religious beliefs might be, and this, no doubt, helped to make social contact smoother than it might otherwise have been.

Harry always prided himself on his own toleration. He allowed the chapel near his home to hold its Sunday School treat on his rope walk, and gave them generous donations on many occasions in both cash and kind. He employed for some years a Roman Catholic servant girl in the house. Polly was sometimes visited by the priest, of whom she was greatly afraid, and would runaway and hide if she spotted him in time. Her fear was believed to have its origin in an uneasy conscience over her irregular and fitful appearance at Mass on Sundays. Harry also had frequent business dealings with Jews, whose shrewdness and scrupulous honesty greatly impressed him.

Harry and Hannah tried their best to set a good example to their children and direct theit steps in the way of practical Christianity. And they suceeded. All their lives, not one of the three deviated from the acceptance of Christian values they had learned in their home. They trained their own children in the same way and passed these values on to them, whatever they came to think of the doctrine and the story on which Christianity was founded.

Neither Nellie or Ernie ever suffered intellectual problems or doubt. All her life, Nellie accepted her childhood faith just as it had been presented to her, and undoubtedly found it great help and comfort. She married into a family which accepted it in just the same way. Ernie never had a deep interest in religion. He accepted it without much thought in his early days, graduated from Sunday School to singing in the choir, to Young Men's Bible Class, enjoying each in turn. As he got older, he never consciously thought about relgion, either to accept or reject it; he simply ceased to think about it at all.

With Harry it was quite different. He was the only one of the three who had an inherent interest in religion, although in later years his ponderings led him to agnosticism and a rejection of Christianity.

7

Young Harry's Recollections
(The Making of an Agnostic)

All Saints Church in the Nineties

'There' said my Aunt Ellen, hastening with short, quick-steps, her eyes, as they always were when she walked, upon the ground, 'that's the second bell.'

The carillon had ceased in the square, Victorian Gothic tower which overlooked the churchyard. There was a minute or two of silence which the blackbirds filled with hymns of their own. Then the bell began again on a single, more insistent note; it was five minutes to eleven. From all directions along the streets the faithful were converging upon the church, summoned somewhat more urgently now by the monotone of the bell that tolled above the trees.

In the high, arched, over-decorated interior, the congregation were settling into their pews. Through the green baize west door we entered – my aunt, my mother, Nellie and I – and settled into ours. Our pew was marked by visiting cards, my grandmother's, my mother's and my father's – in metal holders at the end of the narrow shelf which held prayer and hymn books. My father's name was included, I suppose, out of courtesy, for, being a Church Warden, he seldom made use of his seat in this pew. Those cards proclaimed our indisputable right to that much space in God's house. After all, we had paid for it. The house was God's but the pew was ours; and if, as sometimes happened, we arrived to find our pew occupied, there was some indignant whispering and shuffling and hostile staring. Sometimes even, my father, or another frock-coated Church Warden, had to come forward and make sibilant apologies and explanations. Then, the battle won and the intruders routed, we could settle down to the comfortable, rather drowsy business of worship.

There was a ritual about this. My aunt entered the pew first, making in the aisle a genuflection to the alter as she did so. I stood behind her, hat in hand, wondering shyly whether I ought not perhaps to make some similar obeisance, but feeling too self-conscious to do so. I edged into the pew and sat down between my aunt and my mother. Nellie sat on the other side of my mother at the end of the pew. On alternate Sundays we exchanged positions, and quarrelled all the way to the church about whose turn it was to sit in the middle. After some manoeuvring with umbrellas, hassocks and hymnbooks, we all four knelt on our hassocks and covered our faces with our hands. Every member of the congregation did this as a preliminary; it was the correct procedure, part of the way to behave in church. Knowing how to behave in church was one of the signs of being well-bred, I had been told, and so I did the same as everyone else, although I am afraid that nothing much happened during those few minutes. I looked between my fingers at the elaborate grain of the deal shelf in front of me and at the pattern on the coat of the lady in front. She, I was often shocked to notice, was not kneeling at all, but only pretending to kneel. Her behind was still resting on the edge of the pew. I noticed with disapproval that quite a lot of grown-up people did this, and came to the conclusion that they were not very well-bred and hadn't been told about it when young.

After a few moments in the kneeling position, we sat back in our pew and waited. The interior of the church was dim and vaguely Gothic. It was suffused by a red, blue and golden light which shone through melancholy bearded figures in perpetual benediction, and gazed down upon us in irremediable sorrow. There was so much ironwork everywhere in the form of screens and rails and hanging constellations of lights; iron curled into leaves, and efflor-esced into stiff flowers with gilded centres, fleurs-de-lys and roses. There was much gleaming brass; a brass eagle bore the Book upon its wings, a cross of brass by the parson's chair took the light of the hanging constellations, a cross of brass gleamed high above the altar behind a brass rail.

Above, where I sat, trefoiled pillars of polished granite shot up into the gloomy roof and there spread branches which joined and crossed with little stone roses at their intercessions, so high above my head that if I looked at them, my mother touched me gently on the knee with her gloved hand. I was not behaving.

Architecturally perhaps, the church was bad, over-elaborate and sham. But to me it was exceedingly beautiful, familiar, dear and holy. It was all that it should be, it was Church – with a capital C. I knew by name all the sorrowful, gentle figures in the windows and the stone, carved heads on the pillars supporting the roof, and every Sunday felt devout and humble before these pale and distant effigies.

The faithful, who sat delicately coughing and fidgeting around me, were also part of that Sunday performance known as Church, and with Church marking Sunday as a day apart, went clean clothes, my Eton suit and mortar-board cap, roast beef and rhubarb tart and a fire in the parlour. For Church, my Aunt Ellen always wore a hat with feathers on it, furs, and things that swung and glittered. She emanated a pleasant Sunday smell of eau-de-Cologne, camphor and leather, as did my mother. So did all the other ladies, though few of them had hats with feathers on them; and I was clean and proudly uncomfortable in the Eton suit and white collar. All the other male members of the congregation, both young and old, looked proudly, self consciously clean, pressed and uncomfortable. It was part of Sunday.

There was a subdued expectancy in these minutes of waiting, though what was expected, apart from the entry of the choir and the two clergymen, it would have been difficult to say. Certainly no-one was anticipating any alarming or inconvenient manifestations of divine power. If any had taken place, there would have been general consternation and disapproval. It would have made us late for dinner. Through the shuffling of feet, the muffled whisperings and smothered coughing, the organ, invisible but vibrant, maintained a continuous melodious hum – a sound indissolubly associated in one's mind with Church.

Presently the bell, tolling faintly above the branches of the stone forest, stopped. There was a moment's silence, then the organ boomed from its many pipes that looked like

72

rows of gigantic inverted pencils. Everyone stood up, and I became suddenly conscious of backs in front of me, tassels of fur and buns of hair and hats. From a wide door in the chancel, a procession of black and white robed figures emerged, little ones in front and larger ones behind. Their hair was brushed and their collars were clean; their eyes, behind spectacles more often than not, had a devout and downcast look. I was aware of boots below their black skirts, for somehow one half expected them to move on wheels. The procession divided at the chancel steps, opening out right and left into the choir stalls below the rows of inverted pencils. It disclosed, in so doing, the Vicar and his Curate in their surplices and stoles.

The Vicar was a large man with a long beard; he was very fond of gardening and cricket. His frail, tired little wife sat in the front pew beneath the pulpit with her offspring, over which her hands fluttered throughout the service, hushing, admonishing, fussing. Now the Vicar took up his position in his stall, where gleamed the cross of brass. He clasped his hands in front of him and turned his large, bewhiskered face, remarkably like that of a biblical prophet in our illustrated Family Bible, towards the congregation.

'When' he intoned in his mellifluous voice, 'the wicked man turneth away from his wickedness that he hath committed and doeth that which is lawful and right, he shall save his soul alive.'

Ah! When! '. . .' The familiar proceedings had begun.

It was always the same. All my life it has been the same, whether it was in the dim, many-coloured interior of that church many years ago, or in the red-brick chapel at school, or in a garrison church, or on board a troop ship with ranks of soldiers clean and shining for Sunday services. Always these same prayers in their lovely language, so right, so appropriate, so pleasant in the sight of God, but yet so often galloped through or swallowed or mispronounced so as to become an offence to the ear. The same oriental, savage old psalms, with chants much too difficult for the congregation and words that could only be fitted in by means of surprising rushes at the verses, several words strung together, and disgorged at one breath. The hymns too, in which the congregation joined with a gusto sometimes unsuited to the sentiment, or manfully strove with the unexpected intricacies of melody and phrasing; and the same sermons. Always among this there has returned to me that smell of eau-de-Cologne, camphor and leather. In my imagination, my hand has stolen into my mother's muff, for thus I used to sit during the lessons and during the Vicar's sermons. I see again those aspiring trees of polished granite, the lianes and tendrils of ironwork and constellations of lights, the sorrowful figures in red and blue robes with their fingers raised in perpetual benediction. It is like a calm, broad, untroubled river, flowing through life; something that was, is and ever shall be.

And yet it has always been Church with a capital C; it has never seemed to have any real relation to life. That has always been part of its beauty and its charm. It never seemed to have anything to do with me; I was just there, watching it and breathing its comforting, easeful atmosphere. It brought me, and still brings me, a strange peace like gentle hands upon the forehead. So remote, indeed, did it seem from life as it is actually lived at any time except between eleven and twelve-thirty on Sunday mornings, that I could contemplate without astonishment, the Misses Jeff and Butterworth, comfortable and well-fed, in their shapeless hats, bending their eyes devoutly upon 'My wounds stink and are corrupt through my foolishness. I am brought into so great trouble and misery, so that I go mourning all day long.' Equally, as a matter of course at school, I joined with two hundred odd other innocents to repeat in that cataract of words inseparable from the psalms, 'Behold, I was shapen in wickedness, and in sin hath my mother conceived me', without astonishment, because quite obviously such words could not possibly relate to me or the Misses Jeff or Butterworth. And while I, young as I was, suspected that the sweet young ladies who lisped so prettily that they had 'done those things they ought not to have done', would box my ears if they heard me repeating their self-accusations outside; I took it as being just part of Church. There was that same remoteness too about the sermons. Those which the Vicar preached in his ornate pulpit differed little from those of the Headmaster in the chapel at school, or indeed from any that I have listened to a thousand times since. There was always the same strange feeling that they were inapplicable. It seemed to communicate itself to the whole congregation, for hardly anyone was really listening, and the sigh of relief when the preacher turned to the East and ascribed, as was most justly due, all might, majesty, dominion, power, was almost audible. It was as if the well-meaning and kindly gentleman, six feet above correction, was striving to make himself understood in a language which his hearers had forgotten. Indeed, perhaps he was. But one reason for this, I think, was possibly the strange trick clergymen have of complicating simple passages from the scriptures. There seems, in fact, to be a lowest common denominator of sermons, the simple text, which has to be juggled with, as one juggles with vulgar fractions, until it comes to mean something quite different from what it seems to mean, and much more obscure.

This lack of human contact in the pulpit, the savagely poetic but improbable words of the psalms, the incongruous religiosity of most of the hymns, as well as the distortion of most of the prayers, so that they sounded like a too-familiar and oft-repeated recitation without any real significance, all combined to make Church a thing quite apart from life, something detached as if railed off, as it were, by that very ironwork and gleaming brass which I admired so much. It was a pleasant Sunday anodyne, distinct from the life which I resumed with my Sunday dinner; and this effect was heightened by what seemed to be an undue emphasis on a wickedness of which I was not at all conscious, and a contrition I never felt.

It never occured to me that Church could be different from this. I knew in a vague sort of way there were other kinds of Church in which another kind of order prevailed; for instance, there was High Church, and there was Low. Sometimes I heard people say they found the service of such and such a Church too high or too low, but I never quite knew what they meant, and my father used this as an excuse for never going to High Church at all. 'Too high for me,' he used to say; 'don't like High Church services, never go to 'em.' As a matter of course, the church we went to was Church of England. I knew there was a Roman Catholic Church because history was full of the dreadful things the

'Catholics' had done, though they never seemed to do them nowadays. The Catholics I met seemed to be ordinary people like my own family and not in the least given to burning and massacring, and yet there seemed to be a slightly sinister significance about the word 'Catholic'. I had heard it said in a mysterious whisper of some new arrivals in the district, 'I believe they are RCs.' This was followed by the reply, 'Oh I see,' with pursed lips and a comprehending look. A distant relation of ours had performed a manoeuvre known as 'Going over to Rome', which was considered in the family as a rather discreditable proceeding, and was always spoken of in subdued tones. Then again, as it were, at the other end of the scale, there was something called 'Chapel', to which peculiar people belonged. This was a free and easy and undecorative form of church. We lived next door to Chapel, and what we called the 'Chapel Yard' was our private playground. Occasionally we peeped in out of curiosity, and once a year we watched the Chapel girls, all in white with pink and blue sashes, entering their unpretentious temple for anniversary services. Nobody whom one knew was Chapel.

I find it difficult to recall what sort of impression I gained from my religious teaching and what seeds of belief, if any, were sown in those days in my shallow and unfruitful soil of brain. At school I must have gathered very little, for my only memory is one of mild boredom. It was Divinity, which was just another lesson, 'Divvers', like French or Maths or Stinks – and a particularly irritating one because it broke into Sunday afternoon. Curiously enough, I was rather good at 'Divvers', and almost ran the risk of being labelled 'Pi', which was liable to fall on anyone who, as I did, became expert at the journeys of St Paul and could enumerate the kings of Israel and Judah in chronological order. And much good that accomplishment has done me.

Such religious teaching as I did absorb, came to me sporadically at home. It came, as it should, at my mother's knee, though the plant that finally flowered from these seeds was a strange one. On Sunday evenings, by the fireside, my mother read to Nellie and me, sitting on either side of her, from two little books called *Precept upon Precept* and *Line upon Line*. They told the stories of the Old and New

Testament; it was, I suppose, a little essay in self-deception, for although it was obviously most sincerely and devoutly written, yet, in the stories which it told with such an air of piety and reverence, the chief characters cheated and betrayed one another, lied, stole and even murdered. And the Deity who ruled their destinies, as petty and vengeful as His subjects, wreaked frightful vengeance upon them as well for small transgressions, such as offering up a sacrifice whose smoke did not ascend straight into Heaven, as for more grave ones such as murdering one's brother. There is something old and almost primaeval about our reverence for their stories, like the reverence and awe of the Greeks for their frail and human gods.

I loved these old fables and found them deeply satisfying. I listened enraptured, letting them sink into my blood so that they became part of me, as they have all that profess and call themselves Christians; but they gave me a somewhat contorted conception of the Almighty. He was presented to me, as to thousands of other Christian children, as an omnipotent and vindictive old gentleman who, mercifully, has long ago ceased to function. He seemed now to have lost that power of sudden, disconcerting intervention in the affairs of his subject mortals, for which, I thought, we must all be truly thankful. For all the evidence of His power, it seemed, had to be dug up out of the remote and fabulous past. All His interests and activities apparently centred round a small corner of the Levant, where a poor, nomadic people, remarkable chiefly for their longevity and their habit of relying entirely upon their Deity to fight their battles for them by means of miracles, inhabited tents in the desert and were as false and unstable as primitive human beings may be expected to be. At the end of each story in *Line upon Line*, there was appended a series of naive questions somewhat as follows:

Q. If I gave you some wood, some nails and a hammer, could you make a box?
A. Yes, I think I could.
Q. But without the wood, the nails and the hammer, could you still make a box?
A. No, I certainly could not.

77

A. Quite right, you could not, but God could make
a box out of nothing.

To which the reply, not in the book certainly, but not far
from my mind was, 'Well, perhaps He could, but He never
does.'

And so religion all seemed to be something fabulous and
concerned with things that happened very, very long ago,
and although I loved these stories, they remained fairy
stories to me, slightly enhanced by a faint gleam of truth.
Nor did I ever really believe in that omnipotent, vengeful
God, or imagine that He ever intervened in human affairs,
the evidence seemed too much to the contrary.

The other little book, *Precept upon Precept*, told the New
Testament stories in the same simple language, but for
some reason it failed to capture the imagination to the same
extent as *Line upon Line*. The central figure remained
nebulous.

Yet I prayed frequently when young, and often when
alone tried to materialize that sad and gentle spirit, as I
tried later to conjure back the loved spirit of Grandmother
after her death. Sometimes I thought I had succeeded,
although I could never be quite sure.

One day, in my second term at Grammar School, the
Headmaster sent for me; a prefect called me across the
quadrangle, 'Hi, you. The Head wants you in his study at
the double.'

Astonished, and remembering previous interviews in
studies, I went with misgivings. The Old Man was sitting
behind his desk, which was, as usual, littered with papers;
shelves of books and high cabinets of drawers surrounded
him on all sides, the room smelt of leather, and, for some
reason, decaying apples. Through the windows I could see
the garden sinking into its winter sleep; no more roses now,
only dead leaves lying in heaps or falling singly with a dry
rustle. I entered timidly, wondering what crime I was about
to answer for, but the Head beamed kindly through his
thick glasses.

'Well, my little man, still happy?'

'Oh yes, Sir. Quite, Sir. Thank you, Sir.'

So this was to be another of those cross-examinations.

78

'How old are you?'

'Fourteen, Sir.'

'Have you been confirmed?'

'No, Sir.'

'Do you want to be?'

I had no idea. It had never occurred to me that one ever actually wanted to be confirmed – one just was confirmed. It was one of life's milestones, an inevitable thing that just happened in the course of time, like being born, baptized and married, like coming of age, like dying. And it was 'the thing'. Everybody did it. But that one should decide for oneself whether it should happen or not was a new idea. I hesitated.

'You know what it means, of course,' continued the Headmaster. Did I? I knew that when I was baptized, my godfathers had vowed and promised three things in my name. The time must arrive when I must take those vows upon myself. These two gentlemen, so I understood, had undertaken to be responsible for all my misdoings until I was confirmed, when I should be responsible for them myself. I cannot say I thought this burden lay very heavily on the shoulders of either of them. It now appeared I must relieve them of it and assume that burden myself.

'Oh yes, Sir. I know what it means,' I said.

'And do you wish to be confirmed?'

'Oh yes, Sir.'

'Good. Confirmation classes are beginning in about a fortnight,' said the Headmaster. 'I will write and tell your parents that you wish to join. I am glad you have taken this decision.'

At that time I was unaware that my father had requested the Reverend E.F.M. McCarthy to speak to me on the matter, as I had shown signs of rebelling, and I felt relieved that the interview had concerned a matter so harmless and of so little moment compared with most interviews I had had in Headmasters' studies. I came away feeling I had made a wise decision which the Head received with favour, for some reason comprehensible only to headmasters.

But the same day, my chum, Fred Taylor, was also summoned into the study and asked the same question. The result in his case, however, was startling and the interview a somewhat unhappy one.

'No, Sir.' was Fred's reply.

The Headmaster appeared dumbfounded, and there was a moment's embarrassing silence. Such a reply to this particular question was evidently something outside his experience.

'Do you mean to tell me,' he said at length, 'that you do not wish to become a communicant member of the Church?'

'No, Sir.'

'Do you know what you are saying?'

'Yes, Sir.'

'What are your reasons?'

'I wish to become a Roman Catholic,' said Fred. The Headmaster was horrified. Papism – for him it was the road to Hell. Was he nurturing a viper in his bosom? He rose from his desk and strode up and down the room, his hands behind his back.

'This is very serious,' he said, 'very serious. It needs deep thought. You should think this over very carefully, you must search your heart thoroughly. I will give you another week for reflection. At the end of that time, I hope – I will not say I expect – I hope you will have come to a different decision. Meanwhile I think I had better write to your parents. They know about this, of course?'

'I don't know, Sir.'

'You don't know. Haven't you said anything to them about this?'

'No, Sir.'

'Dear me, dear me – what do you think they would say if they knew?'

'I don't think they would say anything.'

'Oh, come, come. Do you mean to infer they would have no objection?'

'No, I don't think so, Sir.'

'I see. Most extraordinary! Well, I think it is my duty to write to them. As you know, we do not look with favour upon the Roman persuasion here. I shall write to your parents; meanwhile I shall give you another week to consider what I can only describe as a most unfortunate decision.'

80

If Fred had confessed to a dreadful disease, the Headmaster could not have been more horrified. In fact, in the Head's eyes he had confessed to one, for he was suffering from the insidious disease of heresy.

But there was no need for Fred to think it over, that week was a waste of time. He had arrived at this conclusion which shocked the Headmaster by a process much more sure and compelling in such a connection than any amount of thought, through his instincts and emotions. For, unlike me, Fred was instinctively deeply religious in an intense and emotional way. He had a personal God and believed the Bible literally; for him the miracles were fact, beyond argument. Not beyond reason, as Chesterton has said, but beyond raciocination, He believed that his God did intervene actively in the affairs of mankind, and believing that, there was nothing unreasonable to him in supposing that God could erupt into the profound and flexible verities of science, even to the extent of making the sun stand still or of bringing about a virgin birth. His was a mystic and unshakeable faith, and I am bound to say that he, as are all others like him, was strengthened and made happy by it. In later life, no doubt, he found a rock to lean upon which agnostics such as myself sadly lack, and even, indeed, cry out for. Like many emotional spirits, he was drawn towards the Roman Catholic Church by its very mysticism, by its colour, its magic and its glamour, and by the triumphs in art and music which the human spirit has achieved in its name.

A burning desire to make converts possessed Fred. He itched to proselytize, and since I was his new-found friend, his greatest wish at this time was to convert me. He found it hard going, I am afraid. He talked to me earnestly about it and pressed upon me little leather-bound books, his 'pi' books as the other boys called them. I had never before met anyone who felt at all strongly on the subject, which I somehow conceived as being reserved for clergymen, one just took it all for granted. I was a shallow little boy and grossly lazy intellectually, as I still am. I hated having to think about things, but as Fred talked about the glamour and mystery of his church and the perpetual wonder of the Mass, I was forced to reflect in a dim sort of way about what

81

he was saying. I found I did not want to imagine 'Church' as anything other than I already knew it, something holy and remote from life but very, very familiar, something filled with a peace that was mine alone. So the scent of eau-de-Cologne and camphor and leather, long loved and recognized, like the smell of earth and fields far out at sea, came back to me with a strength of which I had never thought them capable. The sorrowful figures with hands upraised, the homely sweet words I already knew leapt into my mind as they do now, from some recess where they have lodged deep without my knowing. 'Grant us the kindly fruits of the earth, so that in due time we may enjoy them.' 'The Author of Peace and the Lover of Comfort, whose service is perfect freedom.' 'Let your light so shine before men.' All these came pouring into my mind in a torrent; I found that Church – with a capital C – had become part of me. It was in my blood. So I never read those little books, and though I daresay this was largely due to laziness, it was not entirely so. It was the tall pillars branching above my head and those gentle figures with their perpetual benediction.

The curate held his confirmation classes in one of the Sunday School classrooms. He held them without Fred but with me. Fred's father had written, to the disgust of the Head, that his son might please himself, and Fred, in the Head's eyes, was consigned to Eternal Damnation.

'In other words,' Fred explained, 'my old man doesn't care a damn. He hasn't been inside a church himself for twenty years.'

So one evening a week, I and about fifteen others gathered in the classroom and were excused homework. The curate seated himself on a chair in front us on the floor of the room, in order, so we thought, to make us feel more at home, to impart an air of intimacy to the proceedings. At first we rather enjoyed the novelty of these sessions, although they usually began, as any session with a parson was apt to, with an embarrassing few minutes. Also they were a means of escaping homework once a week. This gave us a sense of importance and of being slightly apart from the others. If a class master on the following day asked about our homework, the delighted answer, to which there was no effective reply, was, 'Confirmation Class, Sir.' And if on the following day we were called upon to translate or to recite something we were supposed to have learnt the previous evening, the same effective retort provided a means of escape. Thus we were distinguished from the common herd, who still had to do homework or to get up and construe or recite, while we listened.

'Lucky blighters,' the others whispered. 'Wish I could go to Confirmaggers again myself.'

After the atmosphere had thawed a little, the curate began to talk. He talked for about three-quarters of an hour in the church variation of his voice, a slight additional unction, reserved apparently for religious occasions; he kept his chin sunk upon his black tie, as he always did when he said his prayers. A short prayer ended the proceedings, and we had to turn round and kneel with our elbows upon the seat. Then we were released and went clattering down the stone stairs, glorying in the abandonment of having done no homework – and I very much doubt if any of the fifteen of us gave the matter another thought, except to pipe, 'Confirmation Class, Sir,' in a tone of evil triumph when asked for homework the next day.

But after six or seven of these evenings I began to enjoy them less. A suspicion began to grow that nothing at all was happening to me. These talks, explained the curate, were meant to prepare us for the laying-on of Hands, an outward and visible sign of inward and spiritual grace. And after each class, when I was in bed and the house was silent, I tried to make myself feel prepared for grace. I failed. Nothing seemed to come. I usually fell asleep in the attempt and dreamed I was at Bringsty under the Gospel Oak. I never heard anyone discuss the subject and no-one seemed to take it very seriously. I once tried to open a discussion with a member of the class, but could get no more out of him than he couldn't see why we shouldn't have a real bishop like last year, instead of only a Suffragan, which wasn't the same thing at all. I began to get the idea that neither I nor any of the others had a notion of what the curate was talking about. The light . . . the Word . . . the entry of The Holy Ghost. 'You see that gas jet,' he explained as we gazed at the bubbling gas mantel above our heads, 'you can imagine God like that. The power, the light, the heat, three in one. None can exist without the other.' We were empty vessels into which the Word was about to be poured like a refreshing stream. The Church was the trunk of a tree of which God was the root we the branches. And so on. And soon I began to wonder if the curate believed this either.

I asked my mother, 'Need I be confirmed? I don't think I want to after all.'

Apart from my doubts and the feeling of emptiness, there was another and more earthly consideration, which was turning me against the approaching event. It was being presented to me as a kind of public performance on my part. I had stage fright. It was to be something I was to do in front of an audience, one which I imagined would be about as hostile and critical as any could be, an audience of my own playmates. The Church would be filled with unforgiving eyes. The curate had begun to introduce into his talks a great deal about procedure and deportment, until soon they seemed to be more important than anything else connected with the ceremony. Later there were to be rehearsals in the empty church. The occasion began to assume frightening proportions; I conceived a dislike for the whole business and began to complain to my parents as though I were about to undergo a critical surgical operation.

The Headmaster sent for me again about a week before the event. All preparations and arrangements had already been made for it. He was less benign this time; a wave of disapproval seemed to advance towards me across the desk's disarray, and I saw on it a letter with my mother's writing. He did not ask me if I were happy.

'Your mother writes you do not wish to be confirmed after all,' he said.

'Yes, Sir,' I replied, feeling small and guilty.

'I understand you do not yet feel prepared to receive grace.'

'Yes, Sir, I mean no, Sir.'

'I do not of course wish to press, although I think you might have arrived at this decision sooner. It would have saved a very great deal of inconvenience, since Mr Wilson (the Vicar) must now tell the Bishop there will be another candidate less, and he has lost two already through sickness. However, this is a decision you must, of course, make for yourself. I think perhaps it would be better to leave the matter till you are a little older. You may go.' Disapproval followed me out of the room.

My mother had written I did not seem really to understand the confirmation classes. She could scarcely have said anything more unfortunate and, when I learned of it a long time after, I understood the full measure of disapproval I had earned from the Headmaster. I had indeed fallen from grace. He was gravely disappointed in me; he never again stopped me in the quadrangle or placed his hand upon my shoulder or asked if I were happy, and for this I was not altogether sorry. At the end of the term he wrote under the heading 'Comments':

'He is in danger of becoming a dull and uninteresting boy.'

8

Friendships, Holidays and Recreation

Harry and Hannah became friends with the local upper-working class, teachers, craftsmen and prosperous trades-people like themselves. They had no aspirations to gentility, but were quite content with and confident in their own station, feeling themselves inferior to no-one because they worked with their hands. They believed they could achieve self-respect and win the respect of those around them without needing to assume a 'genteel' way of life which was not theirs by birth. Not all their close descendants shared these sentiments, which sometimes became a source of tension and shame in the years ahead.

It was a time when many of the working class whose homes were not degraded by the misery and squalid poverty that drunkenness caused, looked to people who were socially above them, and tried to follow the example they set in speech, social etiquette, dress and the furnishing of their homes. They made an effort to associate with those they so much admired. The easiest and most usual way of doing this was by contact with the clergy who, in late Victorian times, were increasingly being drawn from the middle classes rather than the younger sons of aristocratic families as had formerly been the case, and who would have been quite unapproachable on any terms of equality or familiarity. Most churches had a nucleus of such socially aspiring people, especially women, who were particularly in evidence when a young unmarried curate came along, and no doubt many of the clergy must have enjoyed and felt flattered by the uncritical respect and veneration shown to them. For the most part, these new 'genteel' were greatly ashamed of their lowly background, and would not acknowledge it. They looked down on those who had no aspirations to assume a like gentility and who, in their turn, despised them as 'snobs', pretending to be what they knew in their own hearts they were not.

Usually these 'genteel' aspirations were limited to a veneer of the superficialities of life, but among these people were a few who were sincerely drawn to the deeper qualities of class distinction, to the cultural interests and the way of thought natural to and enjoyed by the privileged. These people were often to be found among some of the most intelligent lowly folk who had worked in and made their way up in 'good service', where some of the interests and ways of life of their employers had rubbed off onto them; they became interested in and enjoyed the art, beauty and culture around them, and responded to it.

The people in Handsworth considered the Haynes's wealthy, and indeed they were in a moderate way; they lived well in their own family, enjoyed the prosperity their own industry and efforts had created, and shared it with their workpeople and those around less fortunate than themselves, but they were not ashamed of their humble origin, nor did they try to conceal it, and greatly despised those who did. They were all born without the almost universal sense of automatic veneration for those of social superiority or wealth or position, and were cynical beyond measure towards those who considered themselves superior on account of their possessions, lifestyle or associates. Social revolt and arrogance were in their blood; they could not bear even the thought of condescension or control, and although they were the staunchest of Conservatives, egalitarian instincts could not have been more pronounced in any Socialist than they were in them. Harry, particularly, looked on humanity, rich and poor, but especially the poor, as fellow men and worthy of respect, and made every effort to impress these principles on his children. 'I'll make you say 'Sir' to a rag-man,' was one of their father's sayings his children never forgot.

All the Haynes family were highly intelligent, but not one of them had strong cultural leanings towards art, music, flowers or nature. Hannah and Harry provided music lessons for their children as was the custom of the time, but Ernie was the only one who showed any outstanding

aptitude. Young Harry became greatly interested in literature, as did his brother and sister to a lesser degree, and
some of their children too in later years. Although not
greatly sensitive to art or nature, they were all keenly alive
to all that went on in the world around them, and enjoyed
to the full the experiences of the moment.

Every Sunday afternoon, Harry would take his wife out
alone in the trap without the children, and every year they
went together, again without the children, to Blackpool. It
seems very strange that this generous couple should go
every year for a seaside holiday without their children.
Could it perhaps have had any connection with their
enigmatic Russell grandfather, who disappeared in Chester, a town not very far from Blackpool? Who knows?

Often they and their family went together for a holiday to
Bringsty, where they stayed either with 'Aunt' Polly and
'Uncle' Manny in their beautiful little black and white half-
timbered cottage on the common, or with 'Uncle' Tom,
Manny's brother, who lived in the next village of Whitbourne where he was a miller. Manny's cottage was not
really suitable for visitors, as it had had very little alteration
over the centuries, and the upper storey was not divided
into bedrooms, but was one large room without a ceiling,
stretching high up to the thatch-covered rafters, and
divided for sleeping by curtain partitions as appropriate for
current family needs. There was no water near the house;
this had to be fetched from a spring some distance away
through the meadow.

These domestic inconveniences did not trouble the boys,
who much preferred to stay with 'Uncle' Manny, where
there was more to do, looking after the sheep, taking
produce to market, accompanying the postman doing his
rounds on his horse, which he allowed them to ride, cutting
bracken or shooting rabbits or birds in the cherry orchard.
Sometimes they helped to sweep the wide open chimney by
dragging a bush down it, although this last operation was
always concluded by their being forced to drink a cup of
milk in which a large tablespoon of soot had been stirred,
'to clear them out'.

Manny did not own the cottage but was a tenant of Lord
Lutley, to whom he and other tenants used to take their

rent on Quarter days, dressed up in their best suits to do honour to the feast always provided on the occasion. Ernie and his brother were staying at Bringsty when Lord Lutley's eldest son came of age, and they were allowed to go to the party held for all the tenants in honour of the occasion. All the trees along the park drive and round the lake were lit up by thousands of candles in paper lanterns, and the memory of this occasion delighted them for a lifetime.

The rest of the family usually stayed at Whitbourne, where 'Uncle' Tom's wife, helped by his two daughters, Priscilla and Lavinia, ran a select boarding house and the way of life was more 'genteel', with garden parties at the vicarage, croquet and afternoon tea on the lawn and such-like activities, all of which the boys scorned.

Ernie and young Harry left their mark on Bringsty tradition for several generations. They were staying with Manny one summer, and were sent up to bed at the usual time while the family went off with a local party to a whist drive at Whitbourne. Later, the boys heard the revellers in the distance returning home. It was a beautiful, warm, moonlit night, so they crept out of bed, along the drive to the deserted main road, where they hid in the bracken. As the party approached, they jumped out into the moonlit road, and danced about in their nightshirts under the dark, ancient trees. Not one of the party would proceed further along the road, and some went miles round out of their way. Nor would they later be convinced it was only two small boys in nightshirts they had seen. No, it was the Bringsty ghosts, and the story was told and the spot avoided late at night for many years afterwards.

Manny and his wife had no children, but had adopted a little girl, Maud, who was not very popular with the Haynes children. The boys ignored her as being 'only a girl', and with Nellie there was a great deal of jealousy over the local lads. As she grew up, Maud was apprenticed as a dressmaker and became very skilful, making the rounds of a number of aristocratic houses in the area. She remained single till late in life, when she married an elderly widower and left Bringsty. Manny did not like her much, and when he died he left all he had to his nephew Tom at Whitbourne. Many years later Ernie took his young bride to stay at Manny's for their honeymoon, where she was shocked at the economies practiced there, the family having been brought up to put the cores of the apples they were eating in the cider mill to avoid waste.

Manny, as domineering, cantankerous and difficult as they come, had a keen sense of humour, running to practical jokes not always kind in their nature, but he was dearly beloved by both the boys. Almost to the end of his life, he always wore a traditional Herefordshire smock for workdays made and embroidered by his wife, making sure he had a clean one set out for market day in Bromyard. On Sundays he wore his ancient best suit, made many years before with wool from his own sheep, and carefully stored in an ancient wooden chest.

Manny did not end his life in that little wattle and daub cottage on the common, but in another cottage a mile or two away on the road to Malvern. In the latter part of his life he quarrelled with his landlord, and saying nothing to anybody, not even his wife, he bought a little stone cottage and, with nothing but his own labour, patiently built on a new extension at the front. When it was ready, he gave notice to Lord Lutley and also a piece of his mind on grievances stored up in memory for a lifetime, and then removed to his new home.

The cantankerous old man also quarrelled with the parson at Whitbourne, and left the parish church to attend a new tin chapel recently erected on the common. In the course of time he practically ran it, and gained quite a reputation as a lay preacher. He lived well into his nineties and died about 1924, still working on his own land. A photograph taken only a few days before he died showed him, by no means a decrepit-looking old man, cutting bracken on the common with a scythe. Many years later when Ernie died, he was cremated and his ashes cast in the same cherry orchard where he had, as a boy, and then as a young husband, spent some of the happiest days of his life.

There were happy times not only during holidays but in everyday life too. For those who wanted them, plenty of recreational facilities existed, most of which centred round the churches and chapels. Few young children did not go to the Band of Hope, where they enjoyed immensely the games, lectures, talks, recitations they were encouraged to learn and say, the loud and enthusiastic singing of temperance hyms, and above all the magic lantern shows that took place at frequent intervals. Attendance at Sunday School for both boys and girls was almost universal, many of them in the course of time became Sunday School teachers themselves.

Once a week there was choir practice for suitably gifted boys (girls had not yet been admitted to church choirs), or bell-ringing practice for men and boys with less obvious talent. In due course many of the young people went on to Confirmation Classes and Young Men's Bible Class, all of which were well-attended. There was a local brass band for boys and men whose talents led them in that direction. Nor were the women left out; the Mothers' Union, various Sewing Guilds and Chapel Sisterhoods met every week, where, over a cup of tea, there was time and opportunity for pleasurable gossip and scandal as well as serious intent.

There was no lack of more general activities, which included whist drives and the weekly Penny Readings, where those with budding literary interests could taste the delights of poetry, popular classics, adventure and travel tales in social surroundings, even if they could not read or write, and there were a great many people, right on to the end of the century and well beyond, who had to sign their names with a cross and could not profit by the free public libraries that made a start not long after the introduction of compulsory education in 1870.

Some of these groups gave prizes or awards of one sort or another for attendance, and most of them organized winter schools and summer outings for their members, with such delights as trips on the canal (up the 'cut' on a washed-out coal boat), day trips by train to London or the seaside, or by horse-drawn vehicles to places not so far away, Sutton Park, the Lickey or Clent being popular favourites. Some places nearer home were chosen for the little ones, often Haynes's rope walk, which they were always ready to lend to their neighbours for treats and fetes. All these occasions were enjoyed with overflowing eagerness and enthusiasm.

Cycling clubs sprang up everywhere with the invention of the new, more easily-managed safety cycle, which saw the

91

demise of the old penny-farthing. Every Saturday after-noon, club members set off in a group out to the practically deserted country roads, happily singing as they pedalled along, and stopping at one of the tea shops on route for refreshment of a pot of tea, bread and butter, and even fancy cakes if funds allowed. One or two of the girls wore the new fashionable bloomers, but most of them felt they outraged feminine modesty and were content with long, full, cycling skirts, protected from splashes of mud in wet weather by a shield of attractive coloured cords attached to the mudguards of the back wheels.

The Haynes family, from the oldest to the youngest, took part in all these activities, and the recreation of their daily life revolved round them. The young boy Ernie became very fond of his Sunday School teacher, an estimable young man named Edwin Norton, who had spent some time in America, where his father had emigrated a few years earlier. The family had not found America up to their expectations and returned to England, where they had settled in Handsworth. Old Mr Norton, a whiskery man with a very gruff voice, was a carpenter and for that reason given the nickname of 'Old Shavings', as was the custom of the time, particularly among boys and working men, many of whom throughout their lives were hardly known by their real names.

Old Mr Norton was a very intelligent man, not only an excellent craftsmen in his own trade, but master of many other skills, very ingenious and exceedingly industrious, and Edwin, his eldest son, was following in his father's footsteps. Young Mr Norton, as he was called, delighted his Sunday School pupils by telling them tales of his life in America, and entertaining them with all kinds of tricks and amusing gadgetry. Ernie never missed Sunday School, and always insisted on bringing his teacher back home to tea, where he showed him his own 'inventions' he had been working on, and the pieces of carpentry he loved to do in his spare time. Edwin Norton was leader of the Church Cycling Club, and used his ingenuity to tune all the cycle bells to different pitch, so that the club could play tunes on them as they cycled merrily along the lanes.

Young Harry, according to his relations, was a rebellious

wilful lad, more interested in chasing the girls than in hobbies. He and his sister Nellie were nearest in age, and closer to each other than either of them were with Ernie, and did not bother very much about their little brother, who always felt left behind and overlooked in comparison with them. One example of this was Ernie's soreness at the way his sister used to put it over on her parents that she felt sick and had a headache when she wanted to get out of piano practice or a music lesson, and he quite purred with satisfaction to recount how different he was; in fact, so he said, he practiced the piano so many hours, his mother was worried about him and used to insist on putting brown paper and vinegar on his aching head to ease him. It says much for the conviction his stories inspired in his own family many years later, that for a long time they actually believed him.

Nellie showed signs of becoming an exceedingly pretty, gay, happy girl, very popular with the boys. One story she enjoyed telling against herself was how, as she was beginning to grow up and consider herself a smart young lady, she had a new hat she thought very fetching, and wore it proudly off to town one day. She was puzzled why the lads she passed grinned and muttered 'Bombay' under their breath. Coming to the end of the High Street, she understood; the Bombay Tea Company was giving away identical hats with a pound of tea.

9

Gathering Shadows

The Haynes children, greatly spoiled and indulged in many ways, were nevertheless very early on, long before they left school, expected as a matter of course to take part in the family business. All three of them learned to spin the various kinds of rope and twine, to make hammocks, nets and all other products of the rope walk, as well as helping to serve in the shop. At a surprisingly early age the boys were sent out with horses and carts, quite alone, to make deliveries and collect orders, covering a distance of forty miles over two days, as this was the horse's physical capacity, and putting up overnight. Their wishes in the matter were never consulted, their parents taking it as a matter of course they would continue in the family trade and business, just as had been the practice in most trades from time immemorial.

When Nellie and Ernie left school they were absorbed into the business, and Harry, who was at the Grammar School, was expected to do his share at the weekend. After a while, Nellie was sent to work at the shop and warehouse in the town, and showed so much competence that she was after a time promoted to managing it. All three were provided with everything they needed and given pocket money but no wages, even though they worked hard, sometimes for twelve hours a day or even longer, as was not unusual at the time. No doubt their father believed he was giving them training and experience in a business which would one day belong to them, and so in reality they were working for their own advantage. The boys deeply resented this, and came to consider their parents hard and mean to them, while being lavishly open-handed and generous to everyone else. Ernie was particularly resentful. He believed his father did not love him as he did the other two; among examples he would quote how the oldest children had been given bicycles but he had not, and so he shamed his father by getting pieces of wood and metal and old parts, and building one for himself. It was most successful, and he rode it for a long time.

It was not that the youngsters had no time for their own interests and pleasures; far from it. Harry divided his time between his beloved books and various church clubs, where he gravitated instinctively to the company of the girls. Ernie spent a lot of time shut up alone in his room, working at his 'inventions'. He became very skilled at understanding and repairing watches and clocks, a knowledge gained by taking to pieces and putting together again the various timepieces sold in the family shop. Many years later, as a young husband with little money, he made a weight clock for the hall of his home, cutting the wheels out of coins and the rest out of odd bits of metal. It was greatly admired, and kept excellent time for many years. He seems to have inherited some of this mechanical skill from his father, who was himself quite an ingenious man, who among other things had invented and patented a bird drinking fountain, a design that remained in general use for many years.

Nellie had become engaged to a handsome, well-built young fellow whose father kept a public house not very far away. His name was George Butler, and he worked as a fitter at Tangye's engineering works. There was a large engagement party held at the nearby school, with lavish entertainment and wide invitations in the district. This engagement met with wholehearted approval from both families, who were compatible in every way.

Neither of the boys liked working in the business or desired to take it over. Ernie's piano teacher tried to persuade his father to apprentice him to organ building as he had such a sensitive ear, but the boy himself longed to be apprenticed as an engineer, and pleaded long and earnestly. However, his father was adamant in his refusal, and for this he was never forgiven. He did, however, allow him to attend night classes at the technical college in Birmingham, where he did well, although this far from satisfied him.

95

Harry gave far more trouble. He ran away from home and school and the business to find adventure and be a soldier in the Boer War, lying about his age to the recruiting office.

In the course of the several years that followed, the Butler family moved to Lancashire, where Nellie's handsome George in no time at all found another sweetheart he liked better and married her. Nellie, a very popular and attractive girl, was soon being courted by another young man, the Edwin Norton who had once been Ernie's much beloved Sunday School teacher. He drifted to Nellie from a Miss Penn, a woman some years older than himself, whom he had been fitfully courting, and who belonged to one of Handsworth's 'genteel' families, very much like his own.

Nellie's second engagement was not nearly so acceptable to her parents as the first had been, for a number of reasons. In the first place, Edwin's family, although very intelligent and exceedingly nice people, had very slender means, and as a matter of necessity praticed frugality and economy to make what they had stretch to the limit of possibility in a way of life completely foreign to the Haynes's. None of the men in the family drank or smoked, and this, far from being considered practical commonsense, was interpreted as meanness. Both Edwin's father and Nellie's were Church Wardens, the former being chosen as 'Vicar's Warden', the latter elected by the congregation as 'People's Warden', and on this account there was considerable jealousy and rivalry, each believing his office to carry more weight and be superior to that of the other. The Nortons were decidedly 'genteel', and as such heartily despised as snobs by most of the forthright Haynes family, although they all liked Edwin's mother as a sweet and lovely woman, and also her daughter Amy, who greatly resembled her. As a last straw, the Nortons, who in their own way were just as interested in politics as were the Haynes's, were dedicated supporters of the rival Liberal Party, with very strong leanings towards Trade Unionism, and policies which, later in the twentieth century, led to the formation of the Labour Party. Among other beliefs outrageous to the Haynes's were starry-eyed enthusiasm for public ownership, and the making of travel on all forms of public transport free to all, and above all, an incomprehensible opposition to the Boer War. This latter was a particularly sensitive issue in a family that had a son in South Africa fighting for Queen and Country, albeit strongly against the wishes of his parents. With closer contact between the two families, argument often became heated and bitter, and they did not always find it in their hearts to forgive one another,

Edwin, although an intelligent and skilful young man, did not find it easy to get or keep employment, and this did not endear him to his future father-in-law who, however, gave him a job as traveller for the firm. This was far from being a success; even Ernie, his staunch admirer, had to confess he was no good at all and could not sell a thing. Unquestionably the selling of rope and twine products was not one of Edwin's natural gifts.

Harry and Hannah were very disappointed in their children. The boys hated the business, from which one had already escaped, and the other, while dutifully doing his best, could not put his heart into it to make a resounding success as his father and uncles had done. The father knew that it was his enthusiasm alone that was carrying on his life's work, which he had so confidently expected his sons to continue with like dedication. In addition to this disappointment, the rope walk was not so prosperous as it had once been; times were changing, machinery was being introduced into the trade, there were new methods of working, and rope walks were being covered over so that men could be employed all the year round, and need not be laid off in the winter. Harry would not change, and so he could not compete with those who did. Ernie tried to persuade his father to introduce machinery, which would have inspired the boy with new interest, but he was stubborn in his refusal, and his word was law.

He was very uneasy too about his daughter's forthcoming marriage to a young man he was not convinced could keep her. So, to consolidate his business and help safeguard his daughter's future, he decided to give up the premises and warehouse in the town, and to give his future son-in-law the option to buy the extensive contents for a nominal hundred pounds, for him to dispose of to his own advantage so that the couple would have the chance of starting their married life on a safe financial footing. Edwin jumped at the opportunity, and his family lent him the money.

Nellie took her approaching marriage very seriously, and began to identify herself completely with her future in-laws, who were quite different from her own folks. She began to adopt their habits and their 'genteel' way of life, their frugal economy and dedicated aversion to alcohol. Not satisfied with this, she tried to change her parents and young brother, and 'improve' them too. Ernie in particular was stubborn. He liked and was happy in the way of life in which he had been born, and both at that time and for the rest of his life refused to be dragged upwards by anybody or anything, even by the hair of his head, into a gentility he had been taught to despise. Her parents too resisted, but they found it incomprehensible and bewildering that their beloved, precious and cherished daughter had become ashamed of her parents and home, and were hurt to the quick by what they felt was humiliation and rejection, and could not think what they had done to deserve it. Nellie completely upset the home, and was able to make more changes than might otherwise have been the case, owing to the deteriorating health of her mother at the time and her father's grief and anxiety on account of this and his declining business.

And now young Harry came back from South Africa after three years in the Boer War, to a troubled home and sister changed almost beyond recognition. She had, so he said, developed a 'hush-hush' respectability, and even her father seemed to have become shy of talking and laughing about his brother Charlie's exploits, and Dick's philanderings with the barmaids in the Potteries, which eventually led to his 'judical separation' from his wife, and incarceration for refusing to pay the alimony awarded to her. This shyness about the skeletons in the family cupboard was something quite new and unexpected.

At first young Harry enjoyed being the centre of attraction as a brave young hero in his smart uniform and pill-box hat, and he wallowed in the awe and admiration he inspired wherever he went. He told thrilling tales of the Zulus with spears, hide shields, goats hair and war paint; of heat, dust, thirst and flies; of treeless veldt with huge rocks and boulders giving cover and camouflage to advancing

Boers; of the camaraderie and adventure of army life. He recounted to a wide-eyed and spellbound audience first-hand experience of the siege of Ladysmith and Boer forces entrenched around the town; of their vain attempts to storm the garrison which was weakened by exhaustion, privation and sickness almost to the last gasp, and the severe loss to the enemy in men and guns from the unsuccessful assaults; of the arrival at last of General Buller and the British and the relief of the town; of the route of the Boers in disarray; and the capture of the railway and the bringing up of supplies; of the advance on the Boer strong-holds in the Transvaal and Orange Free State, and their last ditch resistance; of the flight of Kruger and the taking of the dirty tin-town of Johannesburg on the edge of a barren, almost waterless desert, and the capture of its gold mines. The war, so Harry confidently assured them, was now as good as over; Mafeking had at last been relieved by that fine, light-hearted, good-humoured Baden-Powell, adored by his men; Kitchener, a good chap, had been left in charge of the mopping up; there was land there, miles and miles and miles of it, and opportunities for everyone with a thirst for adventure and a pioneering spirit. The stubbornness and cunning of the Boers had been no match for the toughness and grit of the British Tommy. Long live our Glorious Empire.

Before long the glamour of Harry's return wore off, and as a matter of course he began to work again in the family business. This time he was allowed a wage of a pound a week, of which he had to give back ten shillings for board and lodgings. His brother, now a youth approaching man-hood, was still working for pocket money. Harry took over the book-keeping, and it was not long before he realized how serious was their financial position. He tried to make his father understand they were living much too extrava-gently, that spending and giving money away with both hands was no longer possible and that economy was vitally necessary. His father simply refused to believe him, but his brother and sister did.

Both father and son had violent tempers, and all this led to a fierce quarrel in which young Harry announced his intention of going back to South Africa. His tearful father accused him of breaking his mother's heart, but, so he said, he had become so used to hearing that, it did not upset him.

So off he set, taking from the till ten pounds needed to pay the steerage fare for ex-Boer-War soldiers back to South Africa, leaving behind and soon forgetting the girl to whom he had become engaged, and, as it was then thought, ought to have married. He did not again set foot in England for well over twenty years.

Young Harry's words of wisdom proved to be correct, so that even his father, now a sick man himself, could no longer ignore the situation. The first step towards economy was to dismiss the house servants. Bertha, who had been with them since her early girlhood and loved them with selfless devotion, refused to go, saying she would work for them without wages. And this she did. Hannah became ill, and although Nellie and her future in-laws did their best in caring for her, she died. The crash came. They were declared bankrupt, and everything they had was sold to pay their debts, nothing being saved from the business except the proceeds of the warehouse, which had been sold to Edwin Norton some time before. Harry Haynes's heart was quite broken, and he died not long after his wife.

All this was a great shock to Soho, as Harry had been the guiding influence in the neighbourhood, greatly beloved by many and deeply respected by all. At his funeral the church was packed. His brother Charlie, as one of the chief mourners, had to wear a top hat. Trying it on just before the funeral, he thought it looked a bit shabby and, deciding to smarten it up, gave it a coat of varnish. It was a very hot day, and it dried quickly. On arrival at the church, the hat stuck to his head and simply would not come off. It was some time before the combined efforts of verger and several helpful relatives succeded in removing it. All this had occasioned considerable commotion, and the eyes of everyone in the congregation were focussed upon him. In spite of the solemnity of the occasion and its sadness, the mourners collapsed in mirth, and the service proceeded amidst tears of helpless laughter.

Nellie and Edwin, safely protected by the proceeds from the sale of the goods in the warehouse, as soon as the funeral was over went ahead with preparations for their wedding, which occupied them far too deeply for them to have time to think of or bother about Ernie.

Ernie had lost his home; he had no job and no money. Nellie, absorbed for some considerable time past with plans for her wedding, had left him virtually alone to struggle with the business in its decline and collapse. He felt very angry with his brother, who had realized what was happening and should, he thought, have stayed in England to help him and take a share in the responsibility. He did not even have enough money to pay for lodgings. He tried a night or two at Rowten House, the shelter for homeless men, but found the dormitory accommodation in coffin-like beds crudely revolting, and feeling too proud and ashamed to beg from friends or relations, preferred to stay out on the streets. He knew nothing but the rope trade, and could not get a job at that or at anything else. In order to eat, he played the piano when he could at public house concerts for five shillings a night, and, although still not having enough to rent a room, he managed to persuade an old lady to let him lie down on her sofa every night for half a crown a week. The only one who understood and showed him sympathy and kindness was Edwin's mother. She herself was a widow with the slenderest of means, but she did what she could to help him by washing his shirt and socks and talking to him, and he loved her dearly.

At last, Nellie's wedding took place. Ernie, who gave his sister away, was forced, under protest, to wear a top hat. All went well until the photograph of the wedding group was being taken. Just before the trigger was pressed, Ernie removed his hat and set it on a railing spike at the side. When the picture came out, the anger of his sister was beyond words; by doing such a 'common' thing, he had completely spoiled the atmosphere of her wedding.

Ernie was already grieved and sore that his sister and her husband had set up their home, as indeed they were legally entitled to do, on the proceeds from the warehouse, which was all that could be saved from the business, and should, so he and his brother thought, have been shared equally between them. On top of that, those snobbish and unjust recriminations about a stupid hat were just too much. He waited till they had returned from honeymoon

101

and were installed in their new home, a modest little house next door to Edwin's married sister Amy. He got up one morning in the early hours, and, armed with a bag of brick ends, made his way through the silent deserted streets to his sister's home.

WHAM! WHAM! WHAM!

The peace of the morning was broken by the crashing of broken glass, as every single pane was shattered.

For this Ernie was sued, either by Edwin and Nellie or more likely by their landlord, and he had to appear in court. He refused to pay for the damage, and had to 'go down' and 'do seven days'.

What the rights and wrongs of either side were was always hard to judge, but it is thought-provoking that old Mrs Norton and her two daughters had considerable sympathy with him, and took him under their wing for a while.

10

Life's Path Takes New Directions

Edwin's sisters Abigail and Amy were both married to men who worked at Cadbury's, and they used their influence to get Ernie a job there, and there he stayed till he retired. The quarrel was patched up, no doubt under the influence of the peace-loving Norton family, but it was never forgotten.

In the early years of her marriage, Fate dealt Nellie a very harsh blow. On the birth of her child she had a severe epileptic fit, and continued to have them for the rest of her life. This must have been shattering for both of them, but the response of Edwin and his family was exemplary; they came to terms with it, talked about it freely and did not try to conceal it in any way, as was the practice of the times, and they learned to live a natural, happy and fulfilled life within its limitations. Edwin had by this time obtained a clerical job in a small factory in a little Cotswold town. This proved to be just right for him. In the course of time, he worked his way up to be a partner in the firm and stayed there for the rest of his life. Here in this little town where everyone knew everyone else, Nellie went out shopping, to church and social functions quite freely; everyone knew her circumstances, and rallied round when need be. She was sheltered and spared from any feeling of embarrassment or shame until her husband died many years later.

Both Nellie and Edwin had all their lives been involved in the social activities of the church, and continued to do so right through their marriage. Edwin was full of fun, a teller of jokes and amusing tales, a skilful conjurer, inventor of tricks and puzzles, all of which he combined into shows and entertainments for the YMCA and other church and chapel organizations, and on this account was eagerly sought out by many of the little towns and villages around. He had literary talents too, and could make up little poems and parodies to suit any occasion.

Edwin and Nellie's little daughter and only child, quite understandably, was most deeply loved and cherished. From the day of her birth, Nellie determined to bring her up a 'lady' in a 'genteel' home, and never relaxed one minute in impressing upon her table manners and social etiquette so that it became second nature. No doubt as far as possible to frustrate undesirable knowledge of her own family and relations, she never told her much about her early life, nor did she ever take her to Handsworth to see her old home and former friends and acquaintances, many of whom still lived there, although they were constantly in Birmingham visiting Edwin's relatives. Perhaps Nellie's brothers were too hard on their sister for gravitating to the 'gentility' of her husband's family. After all, their own Grandmother Haynes herself and their Aunt Ellen, through 'good' service, had both had instincts for gentility, and perhaps Nellie had inherited some of these instincts without the opportunity to express them in her childhood home.

Only once, a year or two after Nellie and Edwin went to live in the Cotswolds, was Ernie invited to their home, but he so disgraced himself and let them down he was never asked again. It fell out in this way. The Norton family thought it too 'common' to buy fish and chips from a shop, and always fried their own, and never went near a public house. The incorrigible Ernie went out one night, had a glass of beer in a little pub, and brought back some fish and chips for supper. Horror of horrors! What would people think of the newcomers when they had such 'common' relations at this? Undoubtedly Ernie was prompted by malicious devilry to show contempt for what he considered foolish affectation, but he was a guest in their home, he knew their feelings on these matters, and out of courtesy should have respected them. Of course he was never invited again, although for the rest of her life Nellie made a dutiful visit to see him in his own home when she visited Birmingham, and was given the best hospitality they had. Sometimes Nellie came alone, came sometimes with her husband, whose presence helped to ease the tensions of these visits.

Ernie's early, uncritical admiration for Edwin did not long survive their Sunday School days, and over the years never ripened into friendship. But he never ceased to like his brother-in-law, in spite of the uneasy contact with his sister. Indeed, the two men had much in common; they were both skilful in woodwork; they both enjoyed making gadgets and 'inventing things'; they both, in different ways, were excellent entertainers. Ernie liked listening to Edwin's stories, and in other company often included them in his own. Some of them survived over many years as being too good to be forgotten.

One of the favourite tales was of two friends who died, one of them going to Hell, the other to Heaven. Some time after, they met in the passage between the two places and greeted each other warmly:

'Why Jim, fancy seeing you here. How are you getting on up there?'

'Oh! its blooming awful! What with tuning up and polishing the harps and tittivating the angels' wings, we are worked to death. What's it like down your way?'

'It's top-hole down there, a bit of alright. We only have to stoke up twice a day, and there's thousands of us to do it.'

Another story was of a drunken Irishman, who regularly repented at Confession and was told by the priest whenever he passed the door of the pub to say loudly, 'Get thee behind me, Satan.' The priest was disappointed to hear the same confession the very next time and sadly asked:

'Didn't you do what I told you, Paddy, and tell Satan to get behind you when you went past the public house door?'

'Indeed I did, yer Riverence,' came the reply. 'But when he got behind me, he give me a push and shoved me in.'

A particular favourite was the tale of the parson who preached the same sermon at both the morning and evening services, and nobody ever found out; in the morning he preached with his teeth in, and in the evening he took them out.

Ernie was quite definitely the black sheep of the family, but all the same he was never coarse or rough, and had always been more liked by his relations, friends and work-people than either his brother or sister, who had alway had a ruthless determination to excel, rise and shine among their peers, as indeed had their father. To the end of his life, Ernie was completely indifferent to what others thought of him, completely content with what he had, entirely without ambition, and seems in this respect to have been like his mother, whose favourite child he was.

When Ernie started his new job at Cadbury's, he found lodgings with an elderly widow who lived within walking distance of the factory. She had a daughter who was very interested in their new lodger, but Ernie had never had any time for girls, although he was pleasant and friendly in their company, and most of them liked him. After his pleasant family home with its lavish table and comforts, he found lodgings a sad change, but he did not complain and accepted everything as it came. Once, however, he could not even pretend to eat his dinner; going to work one morning, there was a cat outside the house that had been run over, and that evening, when he sat down to table, he could not help associating it with the rabbit stew put for his dinner. But his landlady was kind to him, and he never moved away.

For a long time, he was very heartsore and lonely. Every evening after his meal, he cycled over to Handsworth to seek out his friends. This went on for months until eventually he made friends with two unmarried brothers who lived near his lodgings.

The Banks boys were very musical, one playing the violin, the other the concertina, both having good singing voices. Their mother often invited Ernie, and they used to enjoy some pleasant musical evenings together. Ernie already had contracts for playing the piano at public house concerts, and he sometimes took his friends along with him. The three were so popular they decided to advertise themselves as an entertainment group, and soon found themselves plenty of engagements for socials, weddings, parties and assemblies. It became quite a profitable sideline, and there were few weeks without at least three or four engagements.

Unfortunately, Ernie's employers got to hear about his public house activities, although they took place right the other side of town. He was called to a stern interview, and was threatened with the sack if he did not keep away from places offering such temptation. He was very angry, but forced himself to swallow his wrath as he did not dare defy them. However, it helped to make his talents known in the factory, and he was often called upon to play for various functions there. The Banks boys did not work at Cadbury's so they were not affected. Gradually his visits to Handsworth became only intermittent, as wider interests and contacts grew.

Arriving at work one day, Ernie was sent to another department to take the place of someone away ill. His fate was sealed. Working in the department was a young girl he thought the prettiest he had ever seen, and instantly, and for the first and last time in his life, fell head over heels in love. He was far too shy to speak to her, but contented himself with the bliss of sitting in her chair when he thought no-one was looking. On enquiry, he found out her name was Gertie Witherford, she was eighteen years old, lived in Selly Oak and went regularly to St Mary's Church on Sunday evenings with her mother and sister.

The following Sunday, Ernie, in his best light grey suit, bowler hat and walking stick, was loitering outside the church as the congregation came out. His heart thumped and gave a leap as he saw her walking along the path, but he did not dare to approach or speak to her. This went on for several weeks, although in the meanwhile a colleague at work had introduced him, and he had exchanged a few words with her. Then one Sunday, he took his courage in both hands. He begged from Mrs Banks a pretty cream rosebud with small, dark, shiny leaves, from a bush growing in her garden. He waited at the church porch until he saw her, then hesitatingly stepped out and offered it to her, asking her to press it in her Bible. Gertie was greatly surprised, as even in those days an approach like that was considered sentimental and old-fashioned. But she liked it. As he wrote many years later; 'My fate was sealed the day I gave you that rose. You have had my love ever since. God bless that day.'

They shyly went for a walk together. Ernie knew what he wanted, and made no secret of it; he wanted her to become engaged that very night, and to put a ring she was wearing over onto her engagement finger until he could save up and buy her another. But Gertie was far too attractive and charming a little fish to be caught on the very first baited hook she met. From then on, their friendship ripened; letters and little notes were exchanged at work every day; sometimes they went out for a walk on weekday evenings, Gertie receiving strict instructions she was to be back home by ten o'clock at the latest. Eventually Ernie was invited to Gertie's home to meet her mother and two sisters. They all liked him greatly, and he soon became a regular welcome visitor.

And so their courtship went on for the next three years before they became engaged, and another year after that before they were married. In all this time, although sometimes they had each had a holiday, they had never gone away together, as there was no-one to chaperone them. Ernie had not yet introduced her to his sister, but he had taken her to Harborne to meet Edwin's two sisters who lived there, and they liked her and gave strong approval. The next day Gail's husband found Ernie out at work to congratulate him on his fiancee, and to tell him that if he were not already married, she might have another suitor to worry her, Ernie's pride and joy knew no bounds.

He must have been a very satisfying sweetheart for a girl from a good, orderly home, strictly brought up. In a letter just before they married, she told him she had loved him first because his eyes were gentle and kind, and later she loved him more and more because never in all their years of courtship was he ever anything but a gentleman in anything he said or did. She said too how happy it made her to see her mother's eyes shine with pleasure when he walked in and sat by the fire to talk to them.

Many years later he wrote of those times; 'I knew when first we met no-one else had ever really mattered before or would again. I was no love-sick boy on the quest for anything, but there comes a time when one woman seems quite different from all the rest, and you are that woman. The first time I saw you I thought, "What a radiant girl". I always seemed to be finding something new about you; you were to be just like an intricate puzzle, the piecing together of which was most enthrallingly interesting. When I thought I had you completely analysed, you made all my careful observations come to nought by a temperamental change which I had not noticed before, and I had the delicious task of reconstructing you all over again. Yet all your moods and passions were quite natural and all the changes were made by quite reasonable causes. And when I found these causes I never failed to understand. You always have been like a delicately strung harp vibrating to a fixed order of things and sometimes to a mere whim or fancy. Yet still you had love and sympathy for me, and all this is mine for all times.'

His future in-laws used laughingly to say they had never seen a man so much in love with a woman as he was.

And so they prepared for their wedding. They saved up in a local Building Society to buy one of the new houses being built out in the country about a mile away, the cost being £250 for a five-roomed house and £350 for a six-roomed, the mortage to be paid off after five years. The house was to be ready for them to move in after the wedding. Several of their friends had saved with this Building Society, were already installed in their new homes and were very happy and satisfied. Unfortunately, just two months before the wedding, the Building Society collapsed, and Gertie and Ernie lost everything they had. They decided nevertheless to go ahead with the wedding, and to live with Gertie's mother and unmarried sister till they could make other plans

Neither Nellie, Edwin nor Edwin's sisters were invited to the wedding, the couple being afraid that, as dedicated teetotallers, they would be shocked at the wine they intended to have at the reception, which was to be given by Gertie's mother in her own home to a few close friends.

The day of the wedding arrived, and Ernie came along early to his bride's home to make sure not a stone had been left unturned to safeguard their future happiness. With sparkling eyes he inquired carefully that she was wearing 'something old, something new, something borrowed and something blue' to ensure good luck, as one and all laughingly believed, and no-one would have dared to tempt fate by defying the tradition. Being reassured on these matters, he turned round all the mirrors in the downstairs rooms to face the wall, so making sure his wife in her wedding clothes did not again tempt fate by seeing her own reflection before the ceremony. He then made his way up to the church to make sure he did not see her either before meeting her there.

At the ceremony, Ernie was not satisfied with the service as written in the Prayer Book. Repeating the phrases after the parson, when he came to the words, '. . . till death do us part', Ernie transposed them to '. . . for ever and ever'.

The parson repeated, '. . . till death do us part.'

Ernie said louder and more clearly, '. . . for ever and ever.' The parson was a stickler for propriety, and took the book over to him and pointed out the line. Ernie looked him straight in the eyes and said firmly; '. . . for ever and ever.'

So the parson gave up and left it at that.

Gail and her husband found their way up to the church to see them married, and were amongst the onlookers who waved them on their way home in a mauve coloured taxi with curtains at the back windows, the first to appear in the village of Selly Oak, and considered the very latest thing in stylish elegance. All this was duly reported later to Ernie's sister, and was approved.

After the reception, Ernie took his young bride on honeymoon to Bringsty, where they stayed with 'Uncle' Manny and 'Aunt' Polly, not telling them it was their wedding day. But the shrewd 'Uncle' Manny soon guessed because, so he said, they were so spoony, – and he played all sorts of tricks on them. That night Gertie knelt down at the side of her bed to say her prayers as she had done every day of her life, and was surprised and hurt when her young husband laughed at her.

Their deep affection was mutual. All her life, Gertie kept every letter or card she had ever received from him, together with any of her own to him that survived. She kept too the little sugar cupid from the top of the wedding cake, as well as the white silk tie her young husband wore on the occasion, rolled up carefully in the same box.

And so into the future, through good times and bad, through good health and sickness, of which there was far more than a fair share to both of them; through sorrows, disappointments, poverty, struggle, exasperation, mis-understandings, quarrels (Oh yes, there were plenty as time passed). In extreme old age, as Gertie, a widow by that time, lay dying, she asked for her engagement ring and wore it to comfort herself. And so the bond that had been forged, remained strong and steadfast throughout the years, right to the very end.

Part 2

IN PARISH
BOUNDS

11

Gertie's Family and Place of Origin

Gertie's family, the Witherfords on her father's side and the Partridges and Lees on her mother's, were just as typical as were the Haynes's of families caught up in the Industrial Revolution, but in an entirely different way. The Haynes family, restless and ambitious, left their rural place of origin to seek the new opportunities industry offered to them. The Witherfords and Partridges had no ambition whatsoever for bettering themselves, or for prosperity or influence; they were completely content with their way of life, making the best of whatever they found at hand. They did not move to find the Industrial Revolution and its opportunities; the Industrial Revolution moved close up to them, and they naturally and instinctively used what arrived on their doorstep.

The family lived in Worcestershire in the parish of Northfield, a few miles south of Birmingham. Their ancestors had lived there for centuries, and although through marriage, seeking for work and the like, they had moved from one part of it to another, virtually the whole of their lives had been spent within or very close to its boundary, and they were part of every social and historic aspect the parish had experienced over the centuries. Like her ancestors before her, Gertie spent the whole of her life in the parish; it was her world, and she could not conceive even the thought of being uprooted from it. Everywhere outside its boundary was foreign land to her, and the possibility of making a home even twenty miles away would have been a greater upheaval for her than emigration to Australia for a modern family.

In collecting material for these records, and pondering

what she had heard and knew of her relatives, it came as a revelation to the author to realize what depths of sorrow, emotion and courage lay silent and unexpressed in a number of members of this quiet, orderly and unassuming family.

From Saxon times till well into the eighteenth century, the parish of Northfield had consisted of little more than the village of the same name, two tiny hamlets of Bartley and Selly, and the castle of Weoley with its parkland and estate. Earlier still it had been traversed by the old Roman Saltway, a part of the ancient Roman road network, through which legions were marched, on which settlements and camps had been built for controlling the country, and along which minerals and products of various kinds had been transported to the coast and thence to the continent, in this case salt from the brine springs at Droitwich, just a few miles to the south.

The word 'heath' in so many local place names is indicative of the nature of much of the area. The prefix or suffix 'green' to a place name indicates usually that it was formerly common land. It would be interesting to know in what the 'common rights' for each consisted: the pasturing of sheep, cattle or pigs, geese or poultry, the digging of peat in boggy places, the gathering of acorns, mast, firewood or the like. The name 'Gallows Brook' is self-explanatory.

In pre-Reformation times in the village of Northfield, there had been a monastic grange (a place to which a few monks were sent to live and work looking after monastic land and property in the neighbourhood). After Henry VIII's dissolution of the monasteries in 1537 and his annexation of their land and wealth, the grange at Northfield was converted to a rectory, paying an annual rental to the crown, and in obedience to Royal Decree, the newly-appointed Protestant clergy, in Northfield as elsewhere, were obliged to start a register of all the baptisms, marriages and burials that took place in the parish. These were the first systematic records ever made which included ordinary poor folk. Gradually, over the years entries became more explicit, to include parentage of infants and marriage partners, status, age at decease, trade and a variety of other information.

116

In many places in the country, there was violent resistance to the new Protestant form of worship, and there was much plundering and desecrating of churches. Everywhere, for more than a century there was confusion and hostility, when Protestant Edward, Catholic Mary, Protestant Elizabeth, High Church Stuarts, Puritan Cromwell, all tried to force their own religious beliefs through their ministers and agents, and martyrs at the stake were burnt on both sides. Northfield was lucky in having members of the White family as Parish Rectors during this century of upheaval. They were a peace-loving lot, and bent with the political wind from whichever direction it happened to be blowing. They too were probably lucky in having simple peasants as parishioners, with no pretentions higher than a few yeomanry (prosperous, independent farmers), unlike the neighbouring parish of Kings Norton, where there were a number of arrogant gentry, mostly Puritan, who were more than ready to make their presence felt, particularly at the time of the Civil War and Oliver Cromwell's Commonwealth that followed it.

Few crimes seemed to occur in Northfield that could not be dealt with by the Parish Constable by means of fines, stocks or the whipping post, as was the order of the day. Only very occasionally did anything of a serious nature occur, involving attendance at the Quarter Sessions at Worcester. Such a scandal occurred in 1609, when Edward Byrche and Thomas Guest were taken before the Quarter Sessions for assault on John Sergeant. Ten years later, George Taylor, the ale-house keeper, found himself in Worcester charged with allowing drinking and gambling in his house almost all night long, jeering on his customers to drink more than they should, and generally being very aggressive and offending his neighbours. The verdict is not recorded, but it is to be hoped he thereafter mended his ways. More seriously, 'Allen's wife' was summoned in 1623 for witchcraft. What could she have done to arouse such suspicion in the village or, if she was young and pretty, to arouse such jealousy?

In the sixteen-thirties a case of sheepstealing was referred to Worcester, and several more of deer stealing from Weoley Castle Park. No parish record was kept of the punishment given, although the gallows at Row Heath were there, ready for such eventualities.

The seventeenth century saw an enormous increase in the prosperity of Northfield. Since Medieval times, the Midland Counties of Worcester, Stafford and Shropshire had had a widespread and flourishing cottage industry making nails, and this prosperity was multiplied many times after 1686, when slitting mills were invented for cutting iron bars into rods, instead of chiselling them into strips as formerly. These slitting mills had been invented near the rivers Tame and Stour, on the banks of which they were situated. Nail merchants, known as factors or iron-mongers, delivered nail rods by pack horse and took back completed nails for sale. There were certain well-used routes for this trade, one of which ran between Alcester and Halesowen, taking Northfield village and its hamlet of Bartley en route, which places flourished as never before, and in the parish register about half the references made to trades between about 1700 to 1840 were for nailmakers, the other half being for husbandry and other essential village crafts.

This nailing industry was the circumstance that helped to cushion the parish from the sorrow and hardship of the interrelated Enclosure Acts and the Industrial and Agricultural Revolutions which in the eighteenth century took place simultaneously in many places. No evidence exists of hardship in Northfield over this period, probably because of the thriving cottage industry of nail making, as yet quite unaffected by the Industrial Revolution which naturally absorbed those being deprived of rights of common land, and also augmented agricultural wages for those working for the prosperous yeomen, among whom the parish land gradually became divided into self-contained farms, each with its own farmhouse.

The eighteenth century was a time of great migration into the parish. The large new farms and farmhouses needed more labour than the prosperous nailing village could supply, and labour was brought in from further afield. Two neighbouring parishes each had hiring fairs, where farmers and workers came to make annual contracts over employment. A great number of new names appeared in the parish

118

register, mostly of people from neighbouring districts. Many probably were dispossessed peasants, victims of local enclosure acts who gravitated to Northfield as a prosperous area of cottage industry, not dependent upon the current vicissitudes of agricultural change. Many apparently did not stay long; maybe they were disappointed in their expectations, packed up and tried again elsewhere; maybe they found among the indigenous villagers hostility to those seeking to share their prosperity, so they gave up the struggle and moved on. As became evident in later years, competition among an expanding population gave opportunity for greedy exploitation among the ironmongers and nail merchants on whom the supply of iron and sale of completed nails depended, and whose ruthless greed caused unnecessary hardship.

The social upheaval and displacement of so many people, their homelessness and hunger, reduced many to become little more than beggars, and the provisions of the old Elizabethan Poor Laws broke down completely under the strain. Many experiments in reform, often sincerely and compassionately made, were tried right through the century with varying degrees of success, and eventually parish workhouses were built about 1783 for the care of the homeless and distribution of relief. These workhouses varied greatly, depending upon the character of its master. Not all of them were harsh institutions, but were orderly and well-run and popular, others were little more than brothels. But certainly they were widely used, and a crippling burden on the economy of the country for many years.

At the end of the eighteenth and beginning of the nineteenth century, undreamed-of changes began to take place throughout the country. In the parish of Northfield a time of unprecedented activity began. First came the making of the turnpike road along the route of the old Roman road which, like most others, had fallen into dereliction since the Middle Ages. This was followed by the cutting of canals known locally as 'cuts', even to living memory. According to records of the time '. . . unruly hordes of Irish navvies descended on the district, and with gunpowder, pick and shovel, cleared a way through the clay

119

... to construct the Birmingham to Worcester canal.' Another description of the time refers to 'the cannibals of Northfield', so there is no doubt of the reputation the migrant workers brought with them, or perhaps inspired in its indigenous population.

These canals were completed by 1815, and from then on, the coal and iron of the Black Country, and in due course the products of the factories that arose on the canal sides could be exported all over England, and through the sea ports to markets all over the world. Men were needed on the spot to attend to both the turnpikes and the locks and tunnels of the canals, some of which were very complicated and needed considerable maintenance. Selly became a centre for maintenance, and in this hamlet, near its old oak tree, cottages were built for the necessary workers, and also for their inspector. All the same, for another fifteen years the local inhabitants of Northfield remained constant to their tradition of nail making and husbandry, with intermittent mention in the parish register of such occupations as 'Wharfinger' or 'Boat Builder' or 'Tollgate Keeper', and an unusual number of blacksmiths, for whom no doubt work was brisk on account of the number of horses towing the canal barges, and the predominantly horse-drawn traffic constantly passing on the turnpike.

It was not till after 1830 that any significant changes began to take place, when a phosphorus factory, known for years as 'the soap hole', probably on account of the effluent it discharged into the canal, was set up on the canal side. It later became used as a metal works, and gradually other manufacturers followed, and people seeking work and higher wages were attracted from outside the parish.

There was no precipitant development till after 1876, when a battery company arrived at what was now known as 'Selly Oak' and established itself on the canal side, first making pots and pans, and later heavy steel goods. Thereafter expansion in Selly Oak became rapid, although changes in the rest of the parish were slow in coming, till early in the twentieth century the Cadbury family extended their model village of Bournville into its virgin countryside at Hay Green. Development at Bartley was even later, and until almost the middle of the century it was little more than a rural hamlet.

A factory for machine-made nails was built at Selly Oak in the middle of the nineteenth century, and the cottage industry gradually declined, Bartley being its last stronghold, where it lingered till the turn of the century when it completely died, Gertie's grandfather being one of its last nail makers. Descendants of the nailers still lived there, working in factories at Selly Oak or in the nearby Black Country, or continued with their agricultural tradition. Gipsies still came for harvesting as they had done from the end of the eighteenth and right through the nineteenth centuries, and Irish labourers who came over annually for the same reason. The latter lived in barns, doing their own cooking and washing, and according to local stories, surpassing most of the villagers in their drinking and fighting, as also their conscientious attendance at church for Mass on Sunday morning.

Of course the rise of factories and consequent influx of labour, sometimes from quite distant places in the country, necessitated the building of houses for workers to live in, and taverns for their leisure and recreation. And so, between about 1825 and 1840 the parish register began to record such occupations as sawyer (clearing away timber prior to development), brickmaker, bricklayer, timber merchant, excavator, builder of new houses, artisan, carpenter, painter, glazier, tilemaker, clerk, bookkeeper, while further up the social scale were Contractor of Public Works, Engineer, Architect, Surveyor, Manufacturer, Attorney-at-Law, Chemist, Merchant of Calcutta to the East India Company, and others of like ilk.

Over the centuries, homes, both rich and poor, had mostly been built of easily available materials found locally. In the Midlands these had usually been of half-timber, wattle and daub, with stone-slabbed or earth-trampled floor, and roofs of thatch. Labourers' homes had often been little more than one-room dwellings, sometimes with a sleeping loft above, approached by a ladder. Often the ground floor living space also sheltered some of the family's livestock, the others being easily accessible in adjacent barns and sheds, as also the nail making workshop, with its little forge and simple tools. Few of these simple hovels survived to modern times, their nearest equivalent perhaps being the primitive cabins in lonely parts of Ireland or the 'black crofts' of remote parts of Scotland, which existed till the latter part of the twentieth century.

Many generations of a family had often lived in the same old cottage, possibly having originally built it themselves on the heath, claiming 'squatters' rights' when the area was 'waste' land, and the deserted cottages fell into dereliction and eventually disappeared or were claimed by opportunists. These new 'squatters' often repaired or rebuilt them in brick, which, from the beginning of the eighteenth century, had been increasingly used to replace the traditional timber, which, after centuries of exploitation, was becoming far less plentiful. This process was going on in Northfield, as elsewhere, right through the eighteenth and nineteenth centuries.

Northfield was fortunate in having a plentiful supply of heavy clay suitable for brickmaking, and this was dug out of many parts of the parish, leaving hollows which later collected water as dells or ponds, a distinctive feature of the area right into the present century. Development in the last century greatly stimulated brickmaking, and brickworks built on the canal side found work for a number of men. In parish records there are considerably more brickmakers than bricklayers, even at the time of intensive local development, most of the bricks made being transported by barge to wider destinations.

In the latter part of the eighteenth and beginning of the nineteenth century, a number of small brick cottages, often built in short terraces, were put up for nail makers. Most of them were around the village of Northfield and the hamlet of Bartley, but a few were scattered in other parts of the parish. Many of these survived well into the twentieth century. These new cottages usually consisted of a living room, with a kitchen and nail-making workshop at the back, and a stairway leading up to a bedroom and a large open landing also used for sleeping. Possibly to compensate tenants for the loss of their traditional 'common rights', there was usually a garden at the back large enough to put up a pig sty and a fowl pen, with allotments nearby, where those who wished could grow vegetables. If a convenient

122

Nailers Cottages at Northfield (by permission of Birmingham Central Library). In their day the last word in up-to-date convenience, built of local brick, with a scullery nail making workshop behind the living room with its modern iron-fire grate for cooking, a garden and pig sty at the back, a privy shared with next door, and a well nearby to serve the row. Above was one bedroom and a sizeable sleeping-landing reached by a wooden stair instead of the ladder common in earlier times.

well did not already exist, one was dug near at hand, usually for the use of several families. Privies too, were often shared.

To house the workers which the new industries attracted into the area, this basic cottage plan, with minor differences, was continued right through the nineteenth century. They were often built in blocks of back-to-back terraces facing a sizeable central space consisting of gardens, a shared well and privies, with washhouses (or brewhouses as they were alternatively called), instead of a nail-making workshop. As need arose, patches of these units were built along the turnpike in Selly Oak, as well as several taverns

123

and a few other amenities. These cottages, impossibly tiny, dark, unhygienic and cramped by twentieth century standards, were considered very desirable little homes by those who first occupied them, and a great improvement on what had gone before. It was not till almost the turn of the century, with still more pressing need for development, that a new design of six-roomed terraced identical houses with gardens at the back were built in long, monotonous streets off the turnpike. These were greatly prized by those who rented them, as a step up from the little four-roomed cottages in older parts of the parish.

The immigrants of higher social standing also built new houses for themselves, or rebuilt in brick those that already existed, usually on or near the turnpike. All were set in spacious gardens, with large shrubberies, conservatories, coach houses and sometimes a pool, all of which needed an army of servants to maintain. They filled them with elegant, new veneered furniture of graceful design, inspired by Sheraton, Chippendale, Hepplewhite and others. They hung them with damask, velvets and brocades, all mass-produced on machines in England's new factories, as also glass, porcelains, silver, ornamentation of every kind, as well as pictures and portraits, original or convincingly reproduced with newly-invented processes.

The homes of the poor had always been very bare, with furniture almost non-existent, other than essentially functional home-made stools, settles, benches for various purposes, and beds of straw. Food was mostly eaten and drunk from vessels of wood, horn, earthenware or pewter, with the use of spoons, knives and forks being little in evidence till comparatively modern times. Most food was cooked in an iron pot standing on three legs in the ashes, suspended over the fire, or roasted on some sort of spit, or baked on the hearth stone. Drinks were equally simple, milk or buttermilk, ale, cider or various home-made beers or wines, fermented from roots, berries, leaves or flowers gathered in season. It was not till the middle of the nineteenth century that tea became cheap enough for the poor to buy, when it was often drunk cold without sugar or milk.

As the nineteenth century advanced, cheap, mass-produced articles from the new factories were eagerly saved for and bought to furnish the new cottages. In time many of them had beds with flock (sheep's wool) or feather overlays on the straw mattress, blankets and sheets, bedsteads of wood, iron or brass, a wooden table and chairs, and even a wall clock. Various knick-knacks, ornaments, covers, cheap picture prints, often bought at the fair, were displayed in number, and later on, family photographs, a Family Bible and even a few books, all an oppressive clutter to modern taste, but an enormous joy to their owners. Glass and crockery came into common use, and so did muslin and chintz curtains, and even ones of Nottingham lace. Round about the middle of the century, the open hearth was replaced by an iron fire grate with hobs on each side, an oven, and a crane above the fire with hooks to suspend the pots. Gradually too a paraffin lamp replaced the rush tapers and candles, hitherto the only lighting available, and very sparingly used on account of the cost.

Of course, through the years some of the cottages degenerated into dirt and squalor, according to the life and possibly drunken habits of some of their occupants, but to a great many they were prized little homes, a source of bursting pride to those who lived in them, who struggled against overwhelming odds to keep them clean, scrubbed and polished. They would have found it unbelievable that their descendants in later generations could hold them in so much shame and contempt.

Incredible to modern eyes is how well people throve in these conditions. Entries in the parish register in the nineteenth century began to give the age of those who were buried, and although infant mortality was very high indeed and child life precarious, those who could reach the age of about twenty had a good chance of living to a ripe old age, even to an advanced old age of more than eighty or ninety years. All this, considering that most of them had practically no medical attention beyond traditional family remedies for the whole of their lives, and epidemics of one sort or another were frequent, and tuberculosis was rife; that they worked physically hard all their lives, often to the day they died, retirement being unknown.

They had existed from their birth on a parsimonious diet

consisting of plenty of bread spread with dripping, or lard flavoured with rosemary or eaten with a chunk of cheese and a raw onion. Potatoes, turnips and porridge filled up the empty spaces, with home-produced vegetables, particularly cabbages, overcooked to the destruction of all its vitamins, according to modern philosophy. Luxuries were rarely more than butter, eggs or jam.

Little fresh meat came their way, its place being taken by fat, home-cured bacon from fat pigs, the fatter the better, kept in a stinking sty in the back yard or garden. It was cooked in a frying pan with plenty of lard, with fried bread later to mop up the fat.

No water supply existed except from a well or stream, or a pump if one was lucky. It was often a distance away, so that it was hard work to get it and consequently was used as economically as possible, particularly in regard to the washing of homes, clothes and bodies. Even soap was an expensive luxury till the middle of the nineteenth century, and scrubbing was done with sand.

Tiny two-, three- or four-roomed cottages for even the largest family were the norm, with overcrowding taken as a matter of course, and often shared with mice, cockroaches and bugs. (Even Buckingham Palace employed a bug-catcher to deal with the royal beds.)

There was almost universal abuse of alcohol, mostly among men, who nevertheless were almost invariably pampered by their wives and given the best of what the home had to offer, often to the detriment of their children and certainly to that of their wives, who instinctively thought the breadwinner must be supported at all costs.

Sanitation was nonexistent beyond a privy in a hovel down the garden, the contents of which were emptied from time to time into a hole in the garden or allotment to fertilize the vegetables.

We must beware of thinking our ancestors regarded their own life in the same light that we do looking back on it. Above all, we must beware of pitying them, for the simple reason they did not pity themselves; most of them accepted the conditions of the age, and adapted themselves instinctively. To understand them, we must try to see with their eyes, think with their thoughts, and divorce ourselves completely from the standards, conceptions and aspirations which, through the whole history of mankind, are unique to the late twentieth century.

One cannot help wondering how many people in our own age would survive exposed to such conditions, and if not, are modern conditions, with their elimination of all trouble, danger, effort and inconveniences, virtually breeding the health and stamina out of the human race, pleasant though the amenities undoubtedly are?

Is the reversal of Nature's policy of 'Survival of the fittest' to include 'Survival of the unfittest' the wisest course for the health and survival of the planet of which Man himself is a part?

Be that as it may, it is certainly true that conditions in the parish of Northfield in the nineteenth century, and its expansion in the early twentieth century to become a suburb of the rapidly encroaching town of Birmingham, was typical of what was taking place in one form or another in countless rural parishes, from one end of Britain to the other.

12

Victorian Values

In the sixteenth and seventeenth centuries, religious zealots of various kinds used their wealth, power and influence to force those who had none of those things to accept religious beliefs and practices they themselves held, and imposed every penalty they could think of on those who resisted. Martyrdom for principles, either Church or Nonconformist, appealed to few, and Christianity could scarcely complain that in the instinct for survival, both its pastors and their flocks learned to blow with the wind and embrace the wisdom of expediency. The ensuing apathy, complacency and indifference to the deep significance of religion which took place in the eighteenth century is an understandable reaction from the intensity of the two preceding centuries. And so, throughout the eighteenth century the Church's moral lead and influence lapsed, and social life reached a depth of depravity in the twin upheavals that followed the Industrial Revolution and Enclosure Acts. By the end of the century the situation could no longer be ignored, and a new spirit of religious zeal arose in the church, inspired by John Wesley and others, who recognized the need for a reforming mission, and a return to a belief in Christian values.

In the parish of Northfield, the making of the turnpike and canals, with subsequent industrial development, brought ever-increasing prosperity, but there was a heavy price to pay. The arrival in a quiet village of gangs of strong, rough, virile young men, billeted on local families or accommodated in barns or some kind of temporary settlement, earning good money, probably having, or at least acknowledging, no family responsibilities, and with nothing to spend their wages on except entertainments that the public house and local girls could provide, inevitably led to drunken brawls, lawlessness and a dramatic increase in illegitimate births. It was understandable that the heads of many young girls were turned by dreams of romance or the temptations of prostitution, each according to her individual temperament. No doubt too, these gangs of rough, loosely-disciplined navvies, like the army, attracted girls who trailed round after them as 'camp followers', finding no accommodation or support, particularly in childbirth, except that provided by the newly-founded workhouses.

Many girls had nowhere to go for the birth of their 'base-born' babies (as they were so described in the parish register) except to the workhouse, where the maternity business boomed. These institutions generally described the work or trade of those who found their way there. Local girls who had their babies there were usually entered as 'nailer' (helping in their home workshop) or 'labourer' (working on the land or in brickmaking), or as 'servant'. Some girls had no description other than 'single woman', so presumably they came from families well enough off to support them without working. The names many gave were not those of village families, and never occurred again in the parish register, so apparently they went away after the birth of their baby, some probably having been sent there in the first place to have it away from home and so avoid local scandal.

Right through the parish registers from the very beginning, a small number of illegitimate children had received two surnames, that of its mother and that of its natural father, often used subsequently in either order, one or other sometimes being dropped altogether in the course of time. Gradually, at the end of the eighteenth and beginning of the nineteenth century, this practice became abbreviated to include the father's surname as a form of second Christian name. There is nothing to indicate why some illegitimate entries carry this Christian-surname and others do not. Maybe the father in question acknowledged responsibility and helped to support the child. Or could it be that its mother, probably made pregnant by the son or master of some house where she worked as a servant, so named her child in revenge? In any case it seems likely this was the origin of the practice first made fashionable in the nine-teenth century, of giving a child two Christian names, one of which might be the maiden name of the mother. Later, the assumption of a double-barrelled surname could be another form it took.

Among this depravity, reforming evangelists began work in Northfield parish. Their first campaign centred round the sacrament of baptism, which normally was administered rtly after birth, the significance of which was being taken far less seriously than had formerly been the case, and many babies, even in good orderly families, were not being done. A public baptism took place in 1795, no doubt as a way of focusing attention on the campaign and setting an example for others to follow.

Whatever the source of inspiration, it was certainly very successful, and from the turn of the century to its first three decades, a great number of older children were baptised. They included illegitimate children, whose birth, under-standably, had not been emphasized, children from pros-perous homes, whose parents presumably were too affluent and successful to recognize any great religious need, children from old village farming or nailing families, where some of the children in the family had been baptised and others had not. Sometimes the baptism of a new-born baby stirred the consciences of its parents, who brought along older children to be done at the same time. Sometimes whole families of children were presented for baptism, or, more likely, rounded up. As a rule, although there were exceptions, parents who had older children baptised seem not to have offended again in this way.

Evangelism went from strength to strength. It strove to spread its message by catching the young generation through the influence of education as a first necessity. There had been a Charity School in Northfield for at least 200 years, where some children were taught free, although most had to pay a copper or two a week. Only the lucky children had gone to school. Most of them, as soon as they were able, helped their parents in their daily tasks, and even those who went to school were not excused their share of domestic duties. Even parents who could afford it often sent only their boys to school, saying it was a waste of time and money for their girls. All the same, the little school at Northfield had done well under the circumstances, and in the eighteenth century, much to its credit, about forty per cent of young people married in the parish could sign their names in the register.

Now, in 1820, the wide-spreading Sunday School Movement augmented the Charity School's work, and Northfield Church hired a room for the purpose. The first Sunday Schools were not only for religious instruction, but also for the teaching of reading to older children and adults who were out at work during the week, and for whom Sunday was their only free day. Later, in 1838, a new Church of England National School replaced both the Charity and Sunday Schools. It was built on glebe land near the church with 100 places for children, including both boys and girls, who paid fees varying from 1d. to 6d. per week, depending on parents' income.

The hamlet of Bartley was not forgotten. A small Charity School had been opened there in 1832, and a Sunday School eight years later. Both were replaced in 1845 by a small day school for about fifty children under one schoolmistress ('governess' as she was known), and a cottage, attached to the school, was built for her to live in. Formerly, the hamlet children who attended school at all had gone the long walk to Northfield.

The hamlet of Selly owed its evangelism to Charles Bridgwater, the inspector of the maintenance workers living there. He founded a Wesleyan chapel in Selly Oak in 1835, with a Sunday School attached, but it was more than twenty years before Selly Oak had a day school of its own. Although the hamlet had grown considerably since the turn of the century, it was still a tiny place, and its new National School of 1861 had only forty-three pupils between the ages of three and eleven years, the leaving age of the time. No doubt the fact that as yet education was neither compulsory nor free, must have influenced the number attending.

The spiritual renewal emanating from the Church also found expression in the renewal of the very fabric of the church building itself, which had fallen into neglect and decay under the influence of eighteenth century religious indifference. Extensive repairs were carried out in 1843

131

when a new roof was put on the chancel, stalls erected instead of pews, and a new pulpit installed. But the wheels of renovation did not stop turning there, and little more than ten years later further repairs and alterations were carried out, so extensive that the church had to be closed for nine months while they were being done.

As an incentive to spirituality, a 'Chapel of Ease' had been built in Bartley Green in 1838, to provide services for those who found the long walk to the parish church more than they could manage, although baptisms and marriages were still carried out there. A daughter church with full religious rites was opened in Selly Oak about the same time that its school was built.

The Industrial Revolution had brought appalling conditions to working people of all kinds, and there were many men and women in the nineteenth century whose hearts had been moved to compassion, and who strove to do all in their power to help those who were powerless to help themselves. But many of these philanthropists and reformers, and certainly Society at that time, felt that among the unfortunates were many who, if inspired to a new attitude to life, could, with determination and perseverance, do a lot for themselves to ease their own burdens.

As a first step to independence and self-respect came the tightening-up of conditions governing workhouse relief. At first workhouses had given shelter and relief almost indiscriminately to all who asked, and over the years many people had come to rely on them. In the Northfield locality, considered a fortunate and prosperous area, by the early years of the nineteenth century no less than one third of the burials in the parish were described as those of paupers (people receiving some sort of workhouse relief). In 1828, in a list of 178 people given relief at Northfield Rectory, twenty-two were described as widows or children of widows; four were old; one blind; one a wife with an insane husband; relief for about ten sick children. All the rest were unspecified, and presumably able-bodied; of these, most were from around Bartley and the village of Northfield, but a number lived outside the parish. Only very few were from Selly Oak, presumably the most prosperous part of the area.

132

Parish relief on this enormous scale could not be maintained, and in 1834 Parliament passed an Act designed to cut it down to manageable proportions, by deterring the able-bodied and giving help only to those really in need. It swept aside the practise of unrestricted relief to the able-bodied and their dependents, except in well-regulated work-houses, under conditions inferior to those of the humblest labourer outside. These drastic measures of deterrence provoked widespread resentment, but they succeeded in reducing the volume and cost of pauperism. As time went on they were widely relaxed, but henceforth workhouse inmates, for the most part, tended to be children, the very old with no-one to care for them, the sick, idiots, imbeciles, lunatics and vagrants.

Another step to self-help for working people was the Friendly Societies, founded about 1820 to make provision for times of sickness. A description of one society includes the following, and gives a clue to the universal pampering of husbands, even bad ones, at whatever cost to their wives and children:

'. . . They (the Friendly Societies) tend to keep the mind at rest, for it is probable every man will enjoy his days of health with superior relish, when impressed with considera-tion that he has treasure laid up for days of sickness. A member of a poor man's family may be sick, the father or husband still remaining to provide the necessaries, but if the father or husband be disordered also, the supply frequently vanishes, which evinces the great utility of such institutions.

'Sick, infirm and superannuated members of some of these societies receive 7/- per week, others 10/6. Benefit also extends beyond life, by terminating with a present to the widow or near relative . . .'

These societies, however, were careful as to whom they received as members, accepting only men between the ages of sixteen and thirty-six, all of whom must have had smallpox, cowpox or measles, i.e. having a built-in immunity common scourges of the age. Orderly behaviour, on pain of fines or expulsion, was expected at their meetings, and families and children were often included in church services they held as well as annual processions and tea parties.

133

The most far-reaching of all self-help movements was that of the Trades Unions. They grew slowly from small, scattered uncertain beginnings, and it was not till well on in the twentieth century that they assumed a power and strength that influenced all national life.

Right through the nineteenth century, not only the Established Church, but every other religious denomination, strove to mould the minds and direct the aspiration of all sections and ages of the working class to what, without exception, was believed to be a wholesome and fulfilling way of life. Various movements were founded, which offered most enjoyable entertainment, combined with emphasis on Christian principles as examples to be followed.

Perhaps the best-known of all these movements were the Temperance Societies, which tried to influence working people to better their lives by using wisely the money they earned for the benefit of their wives and families. Realists in the movement recognized from the start that there was only a slender chance of redemption for those already sodden under the selfish, degrading influence of strong drink. They did their best by improving stories and the like to move them to remorse and shame, but for the most part nobody except the Salvation Army persevered optimistically in this field. The others pinned their faith on the new generation, particularly young children in the Bands of Hope which most churches and chapels organized weekly. Here the children sang rousing temperance choruses, played games, were entertained by magic lanterns, conjurors, outings, socials, anniversary celebrations and every activity that could be devised by the unpaid, dedicated men and women who ran them. One and all, the children 'signed the pledge', received attractive cards of membership that could be hung up in the home, and were given books of improving stories as prizes for attendance. The Band of Hope meetings were universally popular and enthusiastically and regularly attended by working-class children. Undoubtedly they had a profound influence on many of them, and helped them in later life to control their consumption of alcohol, even though they did not turn out a great number of 'total abstainers'.

As the children grew to adolescence and on into young men and women, the good work was continued by all sorts of guilds and societies, the best-known and widest-reaching of which was the Young Men's Christian Association (YMCA), founded in 1844, with its complementary YWCA for women a few years later. Their meetings were a combination of Bible reading, prayer and social activities. In the course of time they ran classes, lectures, holiday homes, cycling and other clubs of many kinds, all of which were immensely well-patronized.

The religious denominations did not limit their efforts to children and young people, but later on in the century turned their attention to women, particularly the wives, for whom the Mothers' Union and similar other Nonconformist societies were founded as a social outlet and helped to managing their homes with Christian ideals. These too usually met weekly, and over a cup of tea did crochet work, sewed, knitted, gossiped over their families, heard talks on the upbringing of children, management of husbands and other aspects of domestic life, as well as on a variety of interesting topics. A number of them published for a copper or two some kind of 'Family Reader', with all sorts of useful, interesting and entertaining articles, often very well-written, with illustrations and stories. The issues were carefully collected, and could be bound into a book at the end of the year. Often these were the only reading material, with the exception of the Bible, that came into working-class homes, which rarely bought newspapers, and when, even at the end of the nineteenth century, a great many people were virtually illiterate.

All these movements were popular and flourishing, and there was something for everyone who wanted to reach out and take it, from the intelligent and 'respectable poor', to those who were neither intelligent nor respectable and who tended to gravitate to the Salvation Army, whose appeal for them had just the right touch.

The dedicated men and women who inspired these movements and a great many other aspects of social reform, had a deep knowledge of human nature, and great skill in the methods they adopted to pursue their aims, which, over the decades, had a great measure of success. A new spirit of the age arose, which in the late twentieth century is known, and often derided as 'Victorian values'.

Be that as it may, it is impossible to understand our Victorian ancestors without a knowledge of the age in which they lived and the spirit of their times, and to realize that in the twentieth century, those born before the end of the Second World War had the roots of their formative years firmly planted in these very same values.

13

Roots in the Past

The ancestors of Gertie's father, Will Witherford, went back into the very earliest parish records, when surnames were first being given to distinguish individuals in an expanding population. It undoubtedly indicated the family living near a ford where withy (willow) trees grew. A list of incumbents in Northfield Church from the thirteenth century gives the name De Witheford among the earliest. As was then the custom, he must have been a local boy of intelligence, considered by some local monastry to be worthy of education and training for the priesthood, possibly also possessing some musical ability and a good voice that would be a credit to the church in the chanting of church services.

The next Witherford record in Northfield was not till 1685, when Elizabeth Witherford was buried there, although there were about this time individual families with records not only in Northfield, but also intermittently in adjacent parishes of Cofton and Kings Norton, the names of John, William and Joseph persisting through the generations from 1705, when John Witherford was married in Northfield, and 1711, when Joseph Witherford of Cofton had a son baptised there. Consistent records increased, indicating that about this time a branch of the family, living on the southern boundary, migrated further into the parish and settled there.

A second Joseph Witherford, the son of the Joseph from Cofton Hacket, headed the Northfield Witherfords right through the middle years of the eighteenth century, and thereafter his descendants, right up to the early years of the twentieth century. This second Joseph, described as a nailer, was a prosperous man whose name appeared in the tithe list of 1754, and after whom a part of the parish was named, and where Gertie's Witherford grandparents were living at the end of the nineteenth century, in the same cottage that to family knowledge had been occupied by Witherfords for several previous generations.

In 1738 Joseph Witherford had married Sarah Rogers, both of them being literate and able to sign the marriage register. Of the great number of children they had, the boys were all nailers like their father and, with the exception of Thomas, were also literate, while on the other hand the girls, who seemed to marry into other nail-making families, were not.

There is no record in the parish register of any of Joseph's numerous family behaving in any but an exemplary way and not being able to make an honest living, although the illiterate Thomas seems to have been the least fortunate. In 1776 he married Sarah Traunter, by whom he begot a large family of at least eight children, for whom he received parish relief from the newly-founded workhouse for at least part of his life. Nothing exceptional is recorded about his sons, who also were nailers, but two of his daughters were a problem; Phebe, at the age of twenty-one, gave birth in 1806 to a 'base-born' son, followed three years later by a 'base-born' daughter; in 1810, another 'base-born' grandchild was born to a younger daughter, Hannah, at the age of nineteen. But events turned out better than might have been expected, considering the profligate times in which they lived, and in due course Phebe and Hannah married two brothers, nailers named James and Job Withers, and presumably settled down into respectable married life. Phebe was widowed very soon after, but had no difficulty in quickly finding a second husband.

Thomas's younger brother James, who lived in the next parish, had similar problems with his granddaughter Dina, who proved herself to be 'more than a bit of a lass'. In 1825, at the age of twenty, she gave birth to a 'base-born' son she named Joseph Harrison, after a nailer of that name, who was living on the borders of the parish. A year or two later she again gave birth to another illegitimate son, calling this one George Harrison. There is nothing to indicate why the father of these two children did not, or could not, marry their mother.

From then on, Dina's story took a different turn. Over the next few years between 1830 and 1839, she gave birth to three more illegitimate children, little daughters she named Hannah, Harriet and Dina, two of whom died in childhood. None of them were given the second name of Harrison nor any other, so apparently neither Harrison nor anyone else was prepared to accept responsibility for them. There is no known record that Dina ever married, so one can only wonder how she maintained herself and her family.

The story was continued into the next generation, when a cousin, Susan Witheford, trod the self-same path as the ill-fated Dina, and between 1838 and 1843 gave birth to three illegitimate children.

This Witheford reputation was a scandal in the parish to the orderly, quiet 'good living' families, and it was held in memory over many years. Even at the end of the century in 1884, when Gertie's mother had married one of the Witherford boys, there had been strong opposition on the grounds that the family was not good enough. One must wonder whether this degeneration had been due to Witherford influence, or an element introduced at marriage somewhere along the line.

Gertie's mother had been Jane Partridge before her marriage to Will Witherford.

The first mention of the Partridge family in the Parish Register was in 1608, when Francis Partrych married Isabell Prychett at Northfield Church. They lived in the hamlet of Bartley bordering on the three neighbouring parishes of Frankley, Halesowen and Harborne, where records of other branches of the family may be found. In such boundary areas, families often took part in the social life of adjacent parishes as well as in that of their own, and frequent inter-marriages took place, weddings and christenings being arranged in either parish as convenience dictated, although there seems to have been a gravitation at death back to their parish of origin, no doubt for burial in family graves.

Throughout the seventeenth century, the Partridges were recorded as nailers in the Parish Register, as were a number of other families in this hamlet of Bartley, which was fortunate in being on the well-used nailing route between Alvechurch and what later became known as the Black Country. The Partridges shared the general prosperity of the nailers, but this, however, did not deter them from earning an honest

139

penny by other means when opportunity presented itself, and in 1676 the Parish Constable employed Will Partridge to mend the Pease-Croft bridge, and paid him 1s. 2d. for so doing. Will's wife Bridget was also an enterprising woman, and took advantage of the 'Burial in Woollen' Act to earn a bit on her own account, no doubt for the benefit of her family.

This Act was passed in 1676 to stimulate the decline in the wool trade, which had been the basis of English prosperity since the Middle Ages. It decreed that everyone who died should be 'buried in woollen', i.e. in a woollen shroud, and at least one, usually two witnesses, almost invariably women, had to declare that this had been done. This law occasioned great resentment, as those who could afford it liked their loved ones to be buried in fine linen and lace. Some tried to fulfil the letter of the law by putting linen and lace on top of the flannel shroud, but this was forbidden. In suspicious circumstances an affidavit had to be produced that the corpse 'had been buried in wool only'. Family members naturally acted as witnesses, but frequently others were called in too, most probably women who acted as midwife or layer-out, and so it was natural for them to perform this duty. A number of the women performing this task were widows, doing it probably as a way of supplementing slender resources in their widowhood. The work also seemed to run in families. In the last decades of the century, Will Partridge's wife Bridget, and later Ann her daughter, received intermittent mention as such witnesses.

During the seventeenth, eighteenth and nineteenth centuries, the Partridges were an unusually quiet, orderly and unassuming family. Whether through poverty or indifference to education, few of them until the nineteenth century could, with one exception, write their names in the marriage register, and all of them married spouses with the same degree of literacy or illiteracy as themselves. None of the Partridge daughters disgraced themselves with 'base-born' children as many did, not even in the time of upheaval when the turnpike and canals were being built, and this says much for their character. The worst that could be said against them was that between 1816 and 1824 the church had to catch up with several of them for late baptism. The only exceptions to this moral rectitude came later in the family of John Partridge, where, among his several daughters, the eighteen-year-old Ann, and twenty-year-old Mary each gave birth to an illegitimate child about 1830. Two other daughters behaved virtuously, keeping their virginity till wedlock, and a third died an old maid at the age of twenty-nine.

John Partridge had forsaken the family tradition of nailing and was an agricultural labourer, where wages were very low, only about 7s. per week. This did not deter him and his wife Obedience from taking in his old father William Partridge after he lost his wife and fell on unhappy times. They found it a struggle, and had to apply for parish relief to help support him. The old man kept going till 1833, when he died at the ripe old age of eighty-eight.

There were a number of Partridge relations in the neighbourhood of Bartley, the names of William, John, Isaac, Joseph and Benjamin persisting in most of them right through from the seventeenth to the twentieth centuries. Among them was one Isaac Partridge, who in 1762 had come from nearby Halesowen to marry Elizabeth Fruin in Northfield Church, and stayed in the parish. This family were poor and sick, and of their six children baptized in Northfield Church, three died while scarcely out of childhood, probably of consumption, the scourge of the times, and were buried as paupers. Their son, also named Isaac, became a Private in the 39th Regiment of Foot during the Napoleonic Wars, and in 1802, at the age of twenty-two, married an older woman of the village, Nancy Lea, a widow. Of the several children born to them over the next eight years, only two survived beyond infancy. Perhaps they too were victims of consumption.

Gertie's maternal grandmother, born in 1810, had been Jane Lees before her marriage in the mid-eighteen-thirties to Benjamin Partridge, a nailer. Her family were among the earliest recorded in the parish, not, however, as nailers but as husbandmen. Their first mentions in Northfield register were between 1584 and 1610 with the baptism of John Lees's children, Thomas, George and Ralph. These were followed by the burial of his wife Hester in 1625. Right through the seventeenth century there were a number of Lees entries, among whom the names William, Thomas and John persisted.

The Lees were a prosperous family in the seventeenth

141

century, and in 1656 William Lees and William Mucklow each built and caused to be erected at their own cost, two seats in the main aisle of the church, 'for the better hearing of ye word', going from the chancel to the bellhouse door, and donated 2s. 6d. each to the church for the privilege, the necessary consent of the parson, church wardens and parishioners having first been obtained. Other seats by other parish families had been built in the church on similar conditions during the previous twenty years.

This is probably an indication of the beginning of the practice of furnishing the church with family pews maintained by an annual rental, which survived into the twentieth century. In earlier times, churches had had no seating. Originally they had been used as a kind of community hall, in which all kinds of parish functions, even markets, had taken place, as well as religious services, the worshippers standing or kneeling in the nave. The only seating provided was a stone bench against the wall, where the aged and sick sat. Hence the saying, 'the weakest to the wall'.

No more mention of seating in Northfield Church is made till 1843, when extensive repairs were carried out in the chancel, including the erection of stalls instead of pews.

Later in the seventeenth century, Elizabeth, the wife of John Lees, like her neighbour Bridget Partridge, was a witness for 'burial in woollen' on at least a dozen occasions between 1680 and her death in 1693. Other members of her family, including her daughter Catherine, carried on the practice later, as well as her relations Mary Lees, and Ann Lees, widow.

One notable seventeenth century entry for this family was in 1692 when William Lees, aged 112 years, was buried on the twelfth day of June, Dorothy, wife of John Warwick, being witness that he too was 'buried in woollen, according to law'. His death merited a special entry in the parish register, no doubt the whole village being proud of its oldest inhabitant, who must have had an impressive list of descendants to his credit.

The longevity of William Lees was not, however, a local record. The adjacent parish of Harborne had done much better; James Sand had been buried there in 1588, aged 140 years, having outlived five leases of twenty-one years, each made after his marriage. His wife lived also to 120 years.

No doubt as a result of their antiquity and continuity of settlement in the area, there were a number of branches of the Lees family in Northfield and adjacent parishes, with varying social grades. One prosperous branch of the family was Edward Lees, a yeoman of Halesowen, who lived on the borders of the parish, his children being baptized in Northfield Church, and he and his wife buried there when they died, in 1718 and 1721 respectively.

From time to time in the eighteenth and nineteenth centuries, the Lees and Partridges were related by marriage. The first one recorded in Northfield was in 1726, when Richard Partridge a nailer, married Sarah Danford, while in 1733, John Lees married her sister Ann.

During the eighteenth and nineteenth centuries, the Lees family extended their original occupation of husbandry to other trades, and tow-dressers (preparing flax), nailers, shoemakers and brewers are found amongst them. Most of them were prosperous enough to send their children to school, and their sons could sign their names in the marriage register, although, as was customary at the time, education was a privilege given only to their sons and not to their daughters. One exception to this rule was John Lees, a farm labourer who, either through lack of opportunity or lack of intelligence, was illiterate. His marriage, from the start, had been beset with difficulties; he had got Hannah Walker 'into trouble', and in 1773 a 'base-born' son was born to her, whom she had called John Lees after him. There was, however, a happy ending to the affair; the erring father was stirred to do his duty and 'make an honest woman' of the unfortunate Hannah, and they were married the following year, to beget further children in honest wedlock.

Intermittently through the eighteenth century, several Lees girls found themselves 'in trouble', but in almost every case the girl's family succeeded in getting her married to the man who had seduced her. They obviously stood no nonsense from anyone who led their daughters astray. They must have been one of the stricter village families, that among so many of their entries in the parish register there were surprisingly few illegitimate births, even at the time of the making of the turnpike and the canals, when so many village girls fell by the wayside.

Several of the Lees family fell on hard times at the end of the eighteenth century, were given parish relief, and in the course of time, were also buried by the parish. Richard Lees was one such unfortunate. He had gone off to be a soldier, returning to his family in 1788, discharged or disabled. He had found them either unwilling or unable to receive him back, and had nowhere to go except to the workhouse. There he died.

Gertie's grandmother, Jane Lees, was born in 1810 into a nail-making family who lived just on the boundary between Bartley and Halesowen. Although the family was a large one, she had been fortunate in being sent to the Charity School in Northfield, held at that time in the vestry room attached to the church, where the Schoolmaster was William Palmer, a man remembered with affection by many and feared by some till his death in 1819.

Gertie was brought up on family stories, some from her grandmother, but mostly from her mother, who had eagerly drunk them in in her own childhood, retained them in memory, to recount in the course of time to her own children and grandchildren, who listened to the oft-repeated tales till they knew them as well as she did. Even late in the twentieth century, Gertie, at the end of a very long life, used to say that to her the eighteenth century never seemed very far away.

Gertie, and then later her own daughter heard many times how Grandmother Partridge as a child, and other Bartley children had walked together to Northfield School, crossing over the turnpike busy with carriages, gigs, flys and vehicles of 'the quality', as well as the humbler traps, pony carts, farm carts and timber waggons piled high with trees cut down to clear the land for the big new houses and workmen's cottages being built in places between the village of Northfield and Selly Oak. Sometimes they were lucky and saw the stagecoach rattling by, and waved to it, and sometimes the passengers on the outside waved back. On days when there was a cattle market at Kings Norton or Bromsgrove, Joe Whitehouse, the butcher and cattle dealer, used to drive his animals to the turnpike tollgate, and it was with great interest that the children watched them counted through.

A cousin of Grandmother Partridge's lived with her husband Jack and their two daughters, Annice and Meg, in one of the new brick-built nailers' cottages at the top of Church Lane, and here she often called. She never tired of describing its merits, of how convenient it was, with a long sloping garden back and front, where Jack grew flowers as well as vegetables for the family; of the nail-making workshop at the back, and the pigsty, and a well nearby for all the cottages, so that no-one had far to go for water. Years later, when she was married, she went to live in a similar cottage, built about the same time in Bartley.

She described how, at that time, along the lane between Bartley and Northfield there had been farms and many half-timbered old cottages, some on the roadside, but most of them scattered back in the fields. In one of them lived her Aunt Polly and Uncle Tom and her cousins, Will, Tom and Emma, who all died of consumption when they were little. They had a field and kept some cows, and one day one of them had gored Aunt Polly in the breast while she was milking it. She and the other children liked to call here on hot days in the summer time on their way home from school, when they were given a drink of buttermilk.

Over the years, said Gertie's mother, even in her time many of these cottages fell into ruin and were never repaired, their site being marked only by a few fruit trees and bushes, growing wild where the garden had been.

Grandma Partridge told how an elder sister, Sarah, was a kitchenmaid at a big new house near the turnpike, and had been 'walking out' with one of the gardeners. Once a month, on her day out, her kind mistress allowed her to make a cake to take home to her mother with some vegetables from the garden and a bunch of flowers. When she and Harry Hadley the gardener were married, they lived in a nice cottage in a lane nearby, and they kept bees in straw skeps. When there was a death in either family, they always told the bees, and put a piece of black cloth on each skep, otherwise the bees would be offended and not work for them any more. And that, said Grandma Partridge, was

145

a fact.

She told too how, in her early years, at one period bread had cost four shillings a loaf (possibly on account of the Corn Laws, whereby after the Napoleonic Wars, when trade routes became free, foreign corn had been highly taxed, to keep up the price to the corn-growing landowners who controlled Parliament). It was, so she said, too expensive to eat, when workers earned only about seven shillings per week, so people had mostly eaten potatoes and turnips, which were cheap to buy and which most people could grow for themselves in gardens or allotments. So some of the men in the district, including an uncle of hers and his wife's brother from Bartley, went on a march to London, carrying a loaf of bread on a pole to tell the Government. What the result was, Gertie's mother could not say, as she had forgotten, even if she ever knew.

Apart from Halesowen, where she had a number of relations, Grandma Partridge had never been far away from Bartley, and the few excursions she had made over a very long life were remembered in every detail. Only once did she go to Birmingham, and that in the carrier's cart when she was growing up, and feeling very smart in a new bonnet with cerise-coloured ribbons. According to the story, she was looking in a shop window, when she heard someone behind her say, 'What a pretty girl,' and the next moment a gentleman turned her round and gave her a kiss. Maybe she thought Birmingham too dangerous a place ever to venture there again.

The most significant of her outings was a trip on a canal boat, when a relation of theirs, Ben Pearton, a boatman who lived in Bartley, got up a trip for young people on his washed-out coal barge. She was only a young girl, and this was the first time she had been out in male company, as boys and girls at that time always played their games and recreations quite separately and showed little interest in each other till they were ready for courting. On this occasion she found young Benjamin Partridge from Bartley Farm very attentive, a boy she had known all her life and taken little notice of. To cut a long story short, from that day he began to 'walk out' with her, and in due course, a few years later, they were married.

Ben's family had lived in Bartley Farm for several generations, but it was not a large one, and could not support all the sons, most of whom had to find other work. Ben became a nailer, while an older brother Tom became a cooper, and was perhaps the most prosperous of the family. In the course of his trade, he often went into the Black Country delivering barrels, and always took in Ben's nails for sale to the iron merchant in Halesowen, and brought back the new supply of iron rods for the next lot. This saved considerable expense, as although there was a 'factor' actually living in Bartley, rightly or wrongly, he was not always trusted. With the money they saved they were able to send every one of their many children to the school recently built in Bartley, instead of walking to Northfield.

Another outing of poignant memory occurred one September day in 1840, when her young husband borrowed a pony and trap and took her and Harry, her first-born son, to Northfield to see the first train pass along the newly-laid railway lines between Birmingham and Gloucester. A lot of people had collected on the sides of the track, and there was great excitement, and immense curiosity as to what this incredible new 'iron horse' that ran on wheels could possibly be like. There was a wonderful story to tell later in Bartley, of its size and noise and smoke and steam, and potential for certain danger, so that many who saw it felt they could never have the courage to venture a ride on it. And as far as Ben Partridge and his wife were concerned, they never did.

14

Life in Bartley

In Gertie's memory from the eighteen-nineties, Bartley Green was a place of idyllic rural charm, consisting of a lane with two rows of tiny cottages, two tiny schools known as the 'old' school and the 'new' school, a parsonage, the Cock Inn and the 'Big House' where Squire Atkins lived. And so it remained till the Second World War.

The two short rows of cottages were known as the 'old buildings' and the 'new buildings', and were absolutely indistinguishable, except that in one row the roofs were of tiles and in the other of slate. One of the cottages, known as 'the shop', had two or three bottles of sweets in the front window, backed by a red curtain to draw across and keep the interior private from outside view. The old lady who kept it always delighted the children by letting them weigh their own sweets. Each cottage had tiny windows with shutters outside and consisted inside of a living room opening straight on to the lane, near the open door of which the old folks sat on sunny days to see what was going on outside and gossip with neighbours passing by. Behind the living room was a small kitchen-pantry with a tiny high window. The upstairs of the cottage consisted of one bedroom and a large landing also used as a bedroom. It was hard to imagine how the usual large families fitted themselves in to sleep at night, except that often the older children had left home and gone away to service or as apprentices before the younger ones were born.

Outside at the back was a 'workshop', in which there was a forge, with bellows and various implements for making different kinds of nails. It had small unglazed windows, closed at night by shutters. There were large beams inside

148

across the roof, and here the fowls roosted when it got dark, reaching them by a kind of ladder, made by nailing pieces of wood across a central support. Between the back door and the workshop was a well with a wooden cover over it.

Further out at the back was the earth closet or privy, the contents of which were regularly emptied by the cottagers themselves, and then used to manure the garden. It was not until almost the end of the century that sewage pipes were widely laid, usually only in built-up urban districts, the rural ones having to wait, sometimes till well after the middle of the twentieth century. Even then there was often strong opposition, as the country people felt they were being robbed of the natural fertilizer for their ground.

Further back still was the pigsty. Every family kept a pig, so potato peelings, vegetable waste, little green or windfall apples and the like were never wasted, and when supplemented by acorns and beech mast gathered by the children, and bran and grain bought from the corn merchant, they helped make a substantial hot mash or 'swill', which the animals throve on – no lean pigs in those days – the fatter the better.

For working men, shaving day only came round once a week, on Sunday morning, when they either did it themselves with a cut-throat razor, or took their turn in the barber's shop, which was busier that day than at any time in the week. They then put on a clean shirt, and went round visiting, not to see their friends – they saw them every day – but their friends' pigs, to scrutinize their size and progress, and mentally to compare them with their own. The pig played a vital role in the family diet. Little fresh meat was eaten, its place being taken by fat home-cured bacon, cut from the 'side' hanging from a hook near the chimney. When it was killed, the blood was carefully drawn off, mixed with groats, lumps of fat and onions, and made into 'pigs' pudding'. The fat was rendered down into lard, mixed sometimes with rosemary leaves to flavour it, and then spread on bread instead of butter. The fry was stewed with onions, or minced and made into faggots, which, with lashings of thick tasty gravy, were eagerly eaten by everybody, who dipped their bread in the gravy to clean their plates round, and smacked their lips with satisfaction

149

and enjoyment. The head, boiled to make brawn, the feet cooked for supper, and the chitterlings either eaten for supper or used as sausage-skins, were all equally appreciated. Indeed, as the old saying went, nothing was wasted of the pig except its squeal. Even pigs that had died in doubtful circumstances were not always wasted. Gertie's grandfather once had a pig that died of erysipelas, and he was burying it in the garden when some gipsies who had come for the seasonal harvesting happened to be passing, and asked if they might have it. He refused them, but next day the carcass had been dug up and had disappeared.

With a pig to supply meat, vegetables grown in the garden or allotment, home-baked bread, home-brewed beer or wine, eggs from their own fowl, tasty meals, served on practical pewter plates and dishes, were not short in most families, which were practically self-supporting and did not nee shops.

Gertie's grandparents lived in a cottage in the middle of the 'new' row. The front door had no lock but a slanting piece of wood to latch it, worked from inside with string. The little home was spotlessly clean and possessed many pretty things, remembered by their grandchildren for a lifetime. In the living room was a shining chest of drawers, on top of which, between a number of ornaments of various kinds, sat two large, brown and white china dogs with chains round their necks. Gertie thought they looked very fierce, and did not like them as a child, but in later years, such ornaments were greatly coveted Victoriana. Hanging on the wall was a square-faced clock with weights, and a number of Biblical text cards suspended on coloured cord between framed family photographs. On a little bamboo table in the corner, with pride of place, was the Family Bible with its brass clasp, and here, from the beginning of their married life, were recorded all the births, marriages, deaths and family records of their children and grandchildren.

The fire grate, black-leaded till it shone like velvet, had a crane at the back, with a set of assorted sized pot hooks made in their own forge. A thick rag rug, home-made on past winter nights, lay on the hearth, near to the slatted, high-backed wooden armchair, devoid of any cushions, where grandmother sat. A small oil lamp was suspended

Great Grandmother Partridge.
One of the last of the nail-making families.
The only photograph she ever had for which, about 1896
at the age of 87 she walked five miles along the canal tow
path to Selly Oak to have it taken.

151

from the middle of the ceiling, but it was not always used; a steel candleholder, with a slit in the stalk of it to move the candle up higher as the tallow was consumed, stood on the corner of the mantel shelf and was often lit instead. The little window was tastefully set off by a row of geraniums between very full, white spotted muslin curtains edged with a deep frill. Upstairs there were blue checked curtains to the windows, and valences to match round the high brass bedstead.

Gertie loved the china in daily use in her grandmother's home. It was very thin and white, with raised blue flowers on it. Many years later, long after her grandparents had died and the home had been broken up, a number of her relations, who had shared the contents, sorted out from amongst themselves what was left of it, and managed to make up a teaset as a wedding present for her. It exists to this day as a treasured family heirloom.

Gertie's grandfather, Benjamin Partridge, was a nailer still working at his trade, although he was among the last in Bartley, the trade dying out since the middle of the nineteenth century, when a factory for machine made nails was opened at Selly Oak. His elder sons had followed their father in their cottage craft, but the rest had found other work, and so had his grandsons. When Gertie remembered him, he was a short, very stout man, who, so she said, was always pleased to see his grandchildren. He used to let her work the bellows in his workshop, after she had had her skirt pinned up behind to keep it clean.

His wife had been Jane Lees before she married. She had been a strikingly handsome woman, and was still stately, tall and dignified even in extreme old age. Her husband loved her dearly, and used proudly to affirm, not one of his daughters was a patch on their mother for looks. Gertie, as the youngest child of the youngest child, only remembered her grandmother as a very old lady in her eighties. She remembered her wearing a sunbonnet in the summer time, from which the tapes could be taken to starch it and iron it flat. For best she wore a lace bonnet, and when she sat at home in her fire-side chair, she wore a square of lace, sometimes black, sometimes white, over the top of her white hair. In her clothes she had a most complicated

152

system of pockets; the pocket in her thick, navy-blue serge dress skirt she used to call 'the world', and it had a placket at the back. Through this placket she could reach a secret pocket, worn inside and fixed to a tape round her waist. When asked for money she did not want to give, as a good Christian, scorning to tell a lie, she could always quite truthfully say that she did not have a penny in 'the world'.

During the week, she usually wore a little black shawl with stripes round it, but for best she had a bautiful one of fine wool paisley, which later, when she died, Gertie's mother Jane made into a cover for her little daughter's bed, the remnant of it still being in use as a scarf, more than a century later by her granddaughter.

Gertie's Grandmother Partridge wore button boots made of black felt with black leather toecaps, and lined with red flannel. She wore white or, more often, red flannel under-skirts on a waistband, and two of these are preserved to this day, with the neatest of featherstitch patches. She wore stiff, serviceable, dark grey, heavily-boned corsets, which didn't show the dirt. They had busks at the front, and were built high at the back, with yards and yards of lacing to pull her in to a good figure.

Grandfather and Grandmother Partridge had a large family of at least ten children, of which Jane, the youngest one, was born in 1861, when several of her eldest brothers and sisters were already married with children of their own. They all lived near, and although Jane could not have had the same intimacy with them as would have been natural in a family nearer in age, they were all held in great affection. She would in later years point them out to her own children when they visited Bartley, and tell stories about them all. There was Sarah, who had twelve children and a husband six foot two inches tall, who insisted on wearing his hand-knitted stockings so high up he could 'garter above the knee'. Another sister, Betsy, married a man who worked at a brickyard. One night he fell asleep in a kiln, which was then bricked up and fired. He was found burnt to death when it was opened. The husband of Mary Ann worked at a chemical factory in the Black Country, and his teeth all came loose with the fumes, and eventually dropped out. One little sister had been blinded when a roast potato jumped out of the fire on Guy Fawkes Night. She died some little time after, and her mother had greatly grieved and would not be comforted, until one night she thought the little one came and stroked her hair while she was in bed, and she was unhappy no longer.

One year the whole family fell ill with smallpox, only Jane escaping the sickness, although she was there with them and nursed them all. They all came through safely, although one brother, Jack, a very handsome boy, was badly marked. He was so shocked and grieved over his appearance, he seemed to turn in on himself. He gave up the girl he was 'walking out with', and never married, later turning to drink and becoming a real rascal. He earned his living as a bargee on a coal boat, going up and down 'the cut' in solitude and isolation, with no companion but his pipe and his little dog.

When she was a girl about twelve years old, Jane, or Jenny or Jinny as she was intermittently called, together with her sister Liza, a year or two older, were the only two still living at home. During this time, their eldest brother Henry, or Harry as he was called, a most handsome man, and a 'natural gentleman', who lived in one of the nearby cottages, lost his wife in childbirth, leaving him to cope with his three sons, Ben, Will and Joe. Jane often recalled how she was sent one wild, stormy winter's night to fetch the doctor from the village five miles away. She ran all the way, and the doctor came at once, but it was too late, and the mother and her new baby both died. Harry, with his three young sons, left their own cottage soon after, and moved in with his parents and two unmarried sisters (the old saying, 'where there is heart room there is home room', was not, in those days, an empty platitude). Jane took on the care of her three young nephews, and became a second mother to them. They loved her dearly for the rest of her life, and wept when she died, more than sixty years later.

All these boys had inherited the outstanding good looks of their father. Will and Joe, the two youngest, were quiet and dreamy, artistic and musical, loving to search the fields and hedgerows for wild flowers and grasses, to watch the birds and listen to their song, and in this respect they were greatly akin to their beloved Aunt Jane. Ben, the eldest, a

154

wild, tough boy, was quite different, but all the same was just as much beloved by his brothers and relations.

All the Partridge family were musical. They loved to sing, and some of them, particularly Harry, were very gifted; no doubt, as was usual at the time, they had received their training as members of the church choir. Between them they played a variety of musical instruments; Harry, the double bass; Will, Joe and several of the others played the organ and the fiddle, while Ben took a different line and played the trombone. Jane told how the parson, one day, had offered to teach her how to play the organ, but she was too shy to accept. No doubt the others had also learned this instrument under his tuition.

Ben, the eldest of the three boys, was lovable but wilful and wild, and the least gentlemanly of them all. He did not follow his father's and grandfather's craft of nail making, but got a job at the newly-opened Battery Company several miles away at Selly Oak, walking there each day along the canal bank. After a while he got into bad company and took to drink. His father, brothers and relatives grieved over him deeply, and did all they could to reform him. Surprisingly enough, they succeeded; a year or two later when his father died, cut off by consumption, the national scourge of the time, his brother Will persuaded him to 'sign the Pledge' on his father's coffin. He kept his word, and never touched alcohol again the rest of his life.

Will's first job on leaving school was gardener's boy to Squire Atkins, who, like everyone else in the village, greatly liked him. The Squire wanted to pay for a higher education for him, hoping he could go to a theological college, and perhaps one day come back to Bartley as its parson. For some reason, possibly financial, or even pride, the family felt unable to accept the offer, and the matter fell through, although he did in after years become a well-loved lay preacher. After a while, Will left Squire Atkins to get a job as an insurance clerk, and in time his young brother Joe joined him in the office. Joe was a very delicate boy, suffering like his father from consumption. He was often away from work, so his wages were very little. Will asked his employers if they would deduct 2s. 6d. (a considerable sum in those days) from his own weekly wage and give it to his brother without telling him. This they did till Joe died at the age of nineteen, and he never knew.

In the course of time, Will 'walked out' with Connie Fields, the schoolmistress, who lived in the schoolhouse with her aunt, Miss Hemmings, a dressmaker. For some reason, the understanding came to nothing. Connie never married, but Will married another local girl, Alice Newman, a farmer's daughter. This was a great disappointment to his relatives, as the Newmans were a shrewd, prosperous family, very anxious to buy land and property, and Will's relatives strongly disapproved of what they considered their materialistic outlook. Alice had been a much-loved governess in a wealthy family, with whom she kept in touch all her life. Maybe the undoubted gentility of Alice's manner attracted Will, but she had a fund of commonsense, firmness and financial shrewdness which balanced Will's easy generosity and lack of ambition. These qualities were the foundation of a very happy marriage and a successful family.

Will and Alice went to live in a very nice house overlooking a golf course, and the very first item of furniture they bought was an organ. They had seven children, including two sets of twins, and they all did well. Through his children, Will's interests and instincts found expression. The boys all gained musical scholarships to choir schools, whence the eldest progressed to theological college, and in due course became a parson. One daughter went to art school, two other children became teachers.

Ben lived with his brother's family for some years before marrying. His wife, Rose, was no longer young, but she made him a good, plain, down-to-earth wife, quite lacking in Alice's refinement. They had no children. Rose's family had lived as caretakers in a nice house just outside Birmingham, owned as a country residence by a wealthy Birmingham landowner. Strangely enough, many years later, Rose told Gertie and her husband how she remembered the owner's daughter and her friend, Miss Haynes (Ernie's Aunt Ellen), coming to stay sometimes at their country home.

Bartley had a dialect all its own, which all the Partridge family spoke, and never lost the whole of their lives. It was a

156

strong country accent, very different from either that of Birmingham or the Black Country, using words scarcely known outside the district. Many years later, Gertie's daughter, when studying Chaucer, and later still when learning German, was amazed to find in these sources many of her grandmother's words and expressions:

She always said 'manny' (for many) a time.
She talked about things looking 'prEtty' (not 'prItty').
A confusion of rubbish was 'mullock'.
A ditch was a 'motte'.
Poor quality meat was 'cag-mag'.
She sat on a 'quishin' (cushion).
Swept up the 'hess' (ash) in the firegrate.
Washed down the 'fode' (bricks on the yard floor).
She 'dowted' (put out) the light.
She could not 'abide' (tolerate) a 'blarting' (crying) child, and told it to stop its 'bellocking' (noisy crying).
On summer nights they chased out the 'bob-owlers' (big furry moths), when they flew round the light.
In springtime they picked 'daffydowndillies' or 'daffy-dillies' (daffodils) in the fields.
They caught 'jack bannocks' (small fish) in the brook.

Wild flowers and grasses all had old traditional names:

Poor Man's Weatherglass (Scarlet Pimpernel).
Bandy Boots or Water Bubbles (Marsh Marigolds or Kingcups).
Billy Buttons (Stitchwort).
Birds' Eyes (Speedwell).
Ladies' Needlework (Wild Parsley).
Bread and Cheese (young sprouting Hawthorn leaves).
Parson (or Jack) in the Pulpit (Wild Arum).
Devils' Eyes (Herb Robert).
John (or Jack)-go-to-bed-at-noon (Goats' Beard).

Many of the old garden flowers were never known by anything but their cottage names, amongst which were Old Man or Lad's Love, Fat Hen, Thrift, Pinks, Joseph's Coat or Bells of Jerusalem, Old Man's Beard, Golden Chain,

Hearts' Ease, Love-lies-bleeding, Monkey Musk, Maidens' Blush, Snapdragon, Moses-in-the-Bulrushes and Snow-on-the-Mountain, just for a start.

An interesting story of Bartley Green was of a child who lived there in Gertie's time, in a cottage only a few doors away from that of her grandmother. The girl grew to be one of the tallest people ever known in England, reaching a height of round about eight feet (so it was said), before she died in her teens. Gertie said she was an ugly child, but not feeble-minded, and well-remembered her in the lane, playing ring-a-roses, hopscotch, bowling a hoop, skipping, whipping a top with the other children of her age, and sitting with them in school. People in Bartley accepted her as she was and took no notice of her abnormality, but the family were approached from time to time by circus folks, who wanted to buy her for their shows. Her parents would not let her go, but when she died they allowed the Medical School of the newly founded Birmingham University to examine the body. She was buried in Bartley Green churchyard.

15

Jane Partridge's Marriage

Liza and Jane, the last two members of the Partridge family to leave home, married at about the same time, and each lived in one of the small cottages at Bartley.

Liza married a local house painter by whom she had a large family, in later years getting so very stout she could scarcely move out of her chair, and consequently she rarely went out. Jane married a local lad a little younger than herself, named Will Witherford.

The two sisters each had their eldest child, in each case a daughter, within a few days of each other, Jane's child being called Lizzie, and Liza's child Jinny. Strangely enough, in temperament and looks little Jinny was the image of her aunt whose namesake she was, and Jane always loved her as much, perhaps even more than she loved her own children, and there was always, throughout their lives, an unusually strong bond between them.

Young Jane Partridge was an acknowledged beauty. She had straight, light brown hair, thoughtful grey eyes, a soft quiet voice, and a tranquil, unhurried manner. Like a number of her family, she was artistic, with instinctive good taste in clothes and the things she chose for her home. Also like a number of her family, she was always very reserved and shy, seeking ever to put herself in the background, and never pretending to be anything other than a simple countrywoman, speaking with her local rural accent to the end of her life. But these qualities acted like a charm in any company in which she found herself, and, without uttering one single word, she instantly focused attention wherever she went.

She was always considered delicate when young, having

ruptured herself lifting a bag of nails in her father's workshop. Nothing could be done about it at that time, and she wore a truss from then on. She also had heart trouble, her lips and fingernails going quite blue at times, and she was warned not to marry for that reason, or at least not to have children, all of which advice she ignored. She did eventually die of heart trouble, but not before the age of seventy-eight.

Before marrying Will Witherford, Jane had been 'walking out' with another young man of the village. According to the story, on hearing he was enjoying the company of another girl after escorting her home at night, in anger she broke off the 'understanding', and almost immediately after married Will. There seems later to have been regrets on both sides. On the day of the wedding, the former sweetheart, according to his sister, wept bitterly, and sent her the gift of a large, white silk handkerchief and a brooch. She kept these all her life, and when she died they were found at the bottom of her box of treasures, still wrapped in the original tissue paper, together with an unsigned Christmas card (her wedding took place at Christmas).

Will Witherford's formal education had been almost non-existent. At the age of nine he found himself a job at Elliot's metal works in Selly Oak, five miles away, walking there and back night and morning along the canal towpath. In former times he would no doubt from his earliest years have helped his father in the family nail shop, but now, with decline in the nailing industry, he, and a great many other boys like him, were forced to find work elsewhere, and often gravitated to branches of the metal industry either in the Black Country or Selly Oak.

Will was a very handsome, dark, gay young man, who could sing, clog dance and keep his company in fits of laughter till the tears rolled down their cheeks. He was exceedingly generous with his family and friends, too generous, his wife sometimes thought. He was a very good and reliable workman, and earned more than most working men of the time, but, like many of his sex, spent more of it down at the public house with his friends than his wife thought reasonable. On one occasion early in his married life, when he came home late the worst for drink, Jane hit him on the head with a poker, and knocked him right out. She was terrified to see him stretched out there on the floor, and in panic ran home to her mother to tell her she had killed her husband. Will recovered in due course – and if that did not make him mend his ways, it ought to have done. However, Will dearly loved his wife, and was always ready to be very jealous of her.

Jane and Will lived in one of the small cottages in Bartley for the first four years of their married life. Jane was a capable and conscientious wife, with a well-ordered and very pretty home, filled with vases, ornaments, pictures and china as the fashion then was, all very natty, as the expression went. Her artistic instincts led her to choose the best of what she saw around her, and in due course her daughters, particularly the two youngest, inherited her good taste. Many of these household treasures have survived to the present day, more than a century later, as they were much too well-beloved by her daughters, and still later her granddaughters, to be thrown away lightly to follow the dictates of changing fashion.

In pride of place in this little home, in isolated splendour over the pantry door, was a picture her mother gave her when she first moved in. It was a large, framed family group of the Prince of Wales, his wife, Princess Alexandra, nursing their youngest baby, Prince George, in a sailor suit, his elder brother standing beside him, and the rest of the little members sitting around on the floor, all gazing benignly into that little room. This Jane considered a great treasure, not only out of patriotic pride, but in tender memory of the giver, the person she perhaps loved best in her whole life, and it moved with her wherever she went till the end of her days.

Little Lizzie went to Bartley Green school on her third birthday. Their spaniel dog, Shot, always accompanied her, sitting at her feet all day because nobody dared to drive him away. At playtime the children were sent out into the road to play because there was nowhere else handy, and Shot went with her.

After Jane's second child Nellie was born, they moved to the brickmaking settlement called California (Cali, as it was locally called) which was further up along the canal side

161

and nearer to Will's work. Here their third child was born. Jane was very ill with this child, and the baby was put out to nurse with an unscrupulous neighbour, who almost starved her to death. Mrs Hinton from the public house took pity on Jane and her baby, and helped them back to health. The child was named Gertie after her. This was a surprising friendship, as earlier in her married life, Jane had 'had words' with Mrs Hinton for not refusing to serve her husband when he had spent his money too generously with her, instead of taking it home to his wife and family. All this was now forgotten in gratitude for Mrs Hinton's kindness, and the friendship lasted.

When Gertie was only a few months old, the family moved again, this time to Chapel Lane, Selly Oak, very close to Will's work. Chapel Lane at that time was a very pretty little country lane, just off the main road to Birmingham. On one side was a high overgrown bank with a hedge on top, beyond which was a field with a brook running through it, over which was an old cart in which the children played. Children scrambled up the steep high bank to gather blackberries and pick foxgloves, bluebells and many other wild flowers that grew there in profusion. At the top of the lane on the other side were a few old traditional cottages, in one of which Will and Jane lived for about five years, and at the bottom were several more old cottages and a little farm that kept cows and supplied families around with milk, which the children fetched in jugs. They also kept a couple of goats, so sometimes goats' milk was bought as a change. Between these old cottages was a new development of small, back-to-back four-roomed cottages, typical of Victorian industrial development.

Will had a pigeon pen in the back garden. The birds were not usually confined to it except at night, but were free to fly around. Will loved his birds and the birds loved him, and would flock to him and, to his great delight, would perch on his head and shoulders when he appeared. The pigeons were his pride and joy, and he lavished his love and care on them, and they took up a great deal of his time and money. For some reason, the landlord one day took exception to them, and demanded they should go. Will would not be parted from his birds, so again the family

162

moved, this time to a cottage in the new development a few doors down the lane. Before long, the landlord repented of his hasty words and asked them to go back, but they had settled into their new home and refused.

This new house faced the lane, and was one of a set of four back-to-back houses known as Oak Place. There were two blocks at the front with an entry between, leading to two blocks at the back. The blocks were separated by plots of quite sizeable gardens, all neatly pathed and divided by railings. Most of the gardens were carefully cultivated, and in them were growing beds of lilies-of-the-valley, borders and patches of many cottage flowers as well as rows of kidney beans, potatoes, lettuce, radishes, onions, and other vegetables in season. In the middle of Oak Place, at the side of the gardens, were four well-built lavatories, two families for each, who all owned a key to protect their own from misuse. At first they were only earth closets, the seats of which were holes cut in a thick board, two holes in each board, a large hole for adult requirements, and a small one for young family members. There were four washhouses similarly shared, and two dustbins in a little covered, open fronted shed with a gate across, known as the 'miskin'.

Oak Place was separated from Beech Place next to it by a brick wall over which hung a large willow tree, on the leaves of which great numbers of very hairy woolly-bear caterpillars fed in autumn, and these the children delighted to collect. One of the cottages at the back was occupied by a pleasant, happy-go-lucky Irish family, the father of which made a prosperous living with a window-cleaning round, for which he needed a horse and cart. Each night on returning home, he would leave the cart in the road, and bring the horse up the entry into his own back garden.

When Jane went to this home, there was only one tap in the middle of Oak Place for all eight houses, but what this amenity lacked in convenience, it compensated for in decoration; this tap was a very handsome lion's head in wrought iron, which poured water out of its mouth when its nose was turned. The lavatories and miskins were emptied at regular intervals by the Night Soil (pronounced Sile) men, whom nobody ever saw except sometimes in the early hours, catching a peep through the window blind of their

163

lanterns, their horse-drawn carts, or hearing the clatter they made. Shortly after the Witherfords moved to Oak Place, water was laid on to each cottage and a sink installed. The wash-houses were modernized too, and the lavatories connected to the sewer. In those early days the calls of nature were unbelievably frequent and interesting, when the result could be instantly washed away simply by pulling a chain.

Jane took on the care of the new garden, both back and front, Will taking no interest in it beyond putting up a new pigeon pen, in company with several fowl pens owned by some of his neighbours, as most families were self-supporting in eggs, and the fowls were useful in consuming kitchen waste. The back garden was carefully cultivated on practical lines, with lettuces, radishes, carrots, turnips, young onions, all set out in neat, square beds with a whole row of Jerusalem artichokes, a thicket of rhubarb, and the rest given over to potatoes.

Jane made this new home and its front garden a picture, the prettiest in the lane, and here she stayed almost to the end of her life. Soon after moving in, she made a windowbox, getting the wood, cutting it herself to fit, and painting it green. In it she grew pink geraniums, with calceolarias at the back, lobelia at the front, and Creeping Jinny to hang over it, and intermingling with climbing nasturtiums planted in the narrow border below to reach up and meet it. The front garden flowerbeds were edged with balsam, and gay with pansies, out of which stretched up orange and black tiger lilies and tall, clustered, spotted pink lilies with curling-back petals, which were known as 'turn again gentlemen'. Overhanging the wall was an old lilac tree with a millstone underneath, on which the children stepped to look over into the lane. Round the door was a variety of Virginia creeper with large leaves on long stalks, a glory in its season, and vying with the roses, japonica and hops, which festooned every other door in the lane. The flowerbeds were neatly bordered with dark grey scalloped edging stones, and there was a wide path in front of the window, made with dark grey ridged bricks and known as the 'fode'.

Until very recent years, it has this century been customary

164

to think of Victorian back-to-back dwellings, as well as the long rows of terraced houses that succeeded them, as sordid, squalid, overcrowded slums, but this was by no means always the case, and certainly not in Chapel Lane at the end of the nineteenth and beginning of the twentieth century. With the housing difficulty of recent years, the sturdy qualities of these dwellings, together with the skill of their architects in designing privacy in high-density development, are sometimes greatly appreciated, and where formerly they were never considered anything but working-class homes, now, with appropriate modernization, they are often eagerly sought by young professional couples for their first home.

16

Life in the Cottages

Rooms in the cottages in Selly Oak were larger, some of them considerably larger than those in the cottages of Bartley, and similar ones in the village of Northfield itself, although most of them only had four rooms. They were lit by oil lamps, the glass 'chimney' of which had to be daily rubbed and polished to get rid of the oily fumes inside, which quickly accumulated, making the glass misty, and it needed a lot of heavy breathing inside the glass to help the duster clear it.

Cooking was done on a big range in the living room, which took up most of the space on one wall, leaving only two to three feet on one side of it for big, built-in cupboards reaching from floor to ceiling, and a similar space on the other for shelves or furniture. In homes where there were small children, the hearth was usually enclosed in a high, firmly fixed fire-guard, over which nightdresses were hung to warm before bedtime, and clean clothes put to air.

The range had a central fire, with a hob on each side to support the saucepans while food was cooking. The saucepans were of iron, thick, heavy and black, with long, round hollow handles that did not get hot. Fixed at the back of the range, so that it could swing forward over the fire when necessary, was a long piece of metal called a crane, on which were suspended iron S–shaped pot hooks of various sizes, which supported the big oval stew pan, the kettle with its long curved spout, and the frying pan with its handle over the top, the smoke from the fire, so it was thought, improving the flavour of the food cooked in it. All these utensils were very heavy, made of iron to last a lifetime, and the outside always covered with soot from the smoke.

The fire between the hobs was contained by thick bars in front of it, with a space beneath at least a foot deep to hold the ashes, which did not need to be cleared out each day, once or twice a week usually being sufficient. In front of this 'ash hole' was a heavy iron screen known as the 'ash preventer', which was often highly ornamental, with patterns of birds, flowers, animals and leaves moulded in it, and matching a similar moulded iron fender on which were laid matching fire irons, consisting of a poker, tongs and a shovel with holes in it for riddling ashes, all with very long handles. Sometimes these fire implements were ornamented with brass knobs or fittings of various kinds, and in homes that boasted a front room or parlour as well as a living room, they were even made entirely of brass, regularly polished to gleaming brightness, although seldom, if ever, used.

A small trivet hinged up and down at the top of the fire bars, and here very small saucepans could stand, and their contents regulated to simmer or warm up quickly as required. It was on this trivet that chestnuts were set to roast on winter evenings. Another removable trivet could be hooked on the bars lower down to support the flat irons used after wash days. These were tested by spitting on them; if the iron was hot enough, the spit ran off quickly, if not, it only sizzled. The hot iron was then rubbed quickly over a bar of soap, to make sure it was smooth and clean from ashes. This same trivet also supported the dutch oven, a flat, oblong tin dish with a curved back which could be swivelled from back to front. It had a bar across the top with a row of hooks to hang bacon, sausages, chops, steak, kippers, bloaters and other small items of food, the back of the dutch oven being swivelled over when one side was done, so that the other side of the food could be cooked without removing it from the hooks.

Under one hob was a small oven. Here milk puddings went on slowly cooking for hours, as well as meat in the stew jar, egg custards, bread and butter puddings, stews, and food warmed up. Generally the oven was not hot enough to bake cakes or pastry or joints of meat successfully, unless the flues round it had been well scraped free of soot and ashes, as well as the 'backing', and other flues leading into the chimney. This intensive cleaning was hard work. It usually took place once a week, often on a Friday morning, in preparation for the weekend cooking, and at the same time the whole grate, together with the fender, fire irons and cooking utensils, were black-leaded and brushed with incredible vigour, using special black-leading brushes with a handle over the top to give a firmer hold and increased pressure, till everything shone like velvet. Black lead was used only once a week, but the brushing was repeated every day to maintain the shine.

Sometimes there was a small tank inside the other hob for the heating of water, which was poured in from a lidded hole at the top and drawn out by a tap at the bottom.

Large pieces of meat for Sunday dinner, or the occasional fowl, which was a great luxury, were roasted by suspending them on skeins of wool or string from a meat jack put up in front of the fire place or fixed to the crane drawn out into position. The big, iron door key was twisted into the string or wool, and this kept the joint turning from side to side, ensuring even roasting, the fat and juices dripping down into a large meat tin standing on a trivet underneath it. At a time when many a grandfather or grandmother lived with the family, it was their job, or that of the children, to sit by the fire to watch the joint on Sunday mornings and to baste it when necessary. At the end of the time the children were often rewarded with a thick piece of bread dipped in the juices, known as 'a dip in the pan'. And most delicious it was, too.

Above the fireplace was a high, wide shelf with a decorated border of hand-made crochet work, threaded through with ribbon, or made of dark green or red plush with matching cord or tassels suspended from it. This was called the 'mantel border'. Above this there was often a light, wooden framework of small shelves to hold little ornaments, knick-knacks and little china seaside souvenirs. It often had a mirror in the middle. This was the 'overmantel'. Just below the mantel shelf was a line or brass rod on which sheets or clothes could be hung to air after washing day, or sometimes with larger families this was supplemented by a line stretching right across the room.

Even in the hottest days of summer, a fire had to be lit for a while each day to do the cooking, or a few sticks lighted to boil a kettle for making tea. Every morning to start the day, the soft ashes left in the grate were riddled through into the ash hole, and the residue rough cinders put on one side to help start the new fire. Very often, the night before, chopped firewood and small pieces of coal had been put in the oven to warm up a bit overnight, and so, together with crumpled newspapers and the riddled cinder, ensure a quick start to the fire. Even so, sometimes it was reluctant to get going, when a few splashes of lamp oil (paraffin) or a teaspoonful or two of sugar, helped things along. This, together with a 'draw plate' (a specially-shaped piece of tin with a handle on the front), put over the fire to create a draught, rarely failed. A scuttle or bucket of coal was put in the hearth to replensih the fire during the day. Bundles of neatly chopped-up firewood tied round with wire could be bought very cheaply from many little shops for those who did not want the trouble of chopping up old boxes or scrap wood.

Bread was never burned, in respect to it as God's gift to man as 'the staff of life', and anyone who did was quite solemnly believed to be inviting his wrath for destroying and treating lightly His greatest gift for human sustenance.

Coal was brought round weekly by several coal mer-chants in their wide flat carts pulled by large, slow heavy shire horses, their necks jangling with horse brasses, and housewives came out to respond to their cry of, 'C-o-al, Co-al,' as they went along. The coalman carried the coarse, jute, hundredweight sacks on his back, which was protected by a thick, tough, leather support. The coal was either tipped into a semi-open shed in the garden, and carefully locked against dishonest neighbours, or stacked under the stairs in the coal house there, where about half a ton could be stored. Very poor people often sent their children along to the coal wharf on the canal side, with little hand trucks made of soap-boxes on wheels, where they could buy even a quarter of a hundredweight of coal at a much lower price. Bags of very small pieces of coal, called slack, could also be bought very cheaply. This was packed at the back of the fire grate, and gave out a great heat, lasting for hours, It was sometimes wetted down with water or tea-leaves, to make it

169

burn even more slowly.

Chimneys had to be swept at least once a year, otherwise the clustering soot in the chimney obstructed the smoke and sent it back into the room. Worse still, the soot sometimes caught fire and poured down into the hearth, when the anxious householder would shovel the burning soot into galvanised buckets as quickly as possible, and rush to dump it outside, hoping there was no policeman near enough to spot the effusion of dense clouds of smoke and flames and sparks from the chimneypot. The event was always of great interest to children, who ran towards it from all directions, shouting excitedly, 'Chimney a-fire,' as they converged on it. A chimney on fire was an indictable offence, punished by a fine of five shillings, a lot of money when a weekly wage was only ten or fifteen shillings. After a chimney had been on fire, all trace of soot was cleared out, and the fire burned bright and clear for quite a long time afterwards. Some people took a chance on discovery and deliberately fired their chimney by pushing lighted newspapers up it, with a draw-plate in position to create a good draught. They usually chose a very foggy day to do this, when the dense smoke would be disguised from a distance. Other people bought packets of sulphur which could be lighted in a closed-up chimney, and was said to clear the soot. It did seem to stop the chimney from smoking back into the room for some time, but sooner or later it had to be swept. A sweep was then called in, either by special arrangement, or more often, spontaneously as he walked along the street with his brushes, canes and sacks on his shoulders, or in a little hand-cart, calling, 'Sw-ee-eep, Sw-ee-eep', as he went, to announce his presence.

Chimney sweeping was a great ordeal. When the sweep arrived, the room was cleared out as much as possible, and everything else covered over as, quite unavoidably, dust from dislodged soot penetrated everything, and the room had to be well-scrubbed out afterwards. The sweep was carefully watched to see that the brush went right through beyond the chimneypot, and that he scraped the sides of the chimney afterwards to finish the job well. Some sweeps gave the excuse that scraping was unnecessary, and only damaged the brickwork, but that was never regarded as anything but laziness, and they were never called in again. He was also carefully watched to see he did not put any of the soot in his own sacks to take away with him.

The bedroom too had fireplaces similar to the one in the living room, with hobs at the side, but very much smaller, and without an oven. It was a lot of trouble to take coal upstairs to the bedroom fireplace and even more trouble taking hot ashes downstairs, so they were rarely used except in cases of sickness or confinements. At such times the hobs came in handy for heating milk or gruel for the nursing mother, who, according to the custom of the day, stayed in bed with her baby for a while after the birth. As the upstairs fireplace was so seldom used, it was rarely if ever necessary to sweep the chimney, and consequently birds often nested in it, enjoying its shelter and adjacent warmth. It was quite common to find on the hearth little fledglings which had been pushed out of the nest, and occasionally whole nests tumbled down too.

In most of these cottage bedrooms, it is hard to imagine how anyone could have got round in the room to sweep the chimney. With large families, bedrooms were full to overflowing, and there was little space even for walking, and none for convenient storage. Bulky items such as bed-clothes were usually packed into tin trunks, and pushed under the iron or brass bedsteads, which were made high to allow for this. Frilled valences were usually put around this space underneath, to keep the trunks and other things out of sight.

Open fires had many disadvantages. Apart from the enormous amount of work they needed, they created a lot of dirt, and a thick coat of dust collected in the room, which could never be left uncleaned, even for a single day. The grates, too, held a great deal of coal. Poor people who could not afford much fuel, often put specially-made, very hard 'fire bricks' at the side or bottom, which held the heat and took up a good part of the fire space. But open fires also had a great many advantages. Although the fire was usually allowed to go out at night, the warm ashes left till morning, still gave out heat, and the family never got up to a really cold room. The soot was of great value, mixed with lime to put round tender plants such as lettuces and kidney beans

171

as an excellent protection against slugs. Cinders and ashes made up garden paths or helped to lighten heavy soil. Beds were warmed in winter by the oven plate, or bricks heated in the oven in the evening and wrapped in flannel to preserve the heat. Above all, they were the focal point for cosy evenings and family chat, when mother sat on one side in her high wooden armchair, sewing, mending or knitting, and the children seated either on home-made wooden stools, or on the hearthrug, made by cutting up old woollen clothes into strips four or five inches long, and knotting them in patterns on hessian sacks. Here they contentedly watched the sparks of soot dying out at the back of the grate, waited for chestnuts or potatoes to roast, or looked for pictures between the burning lumps of coal, and made up stories about them. In lucky families, father completed the picture, smoking his pipe and reading the paper, although in many homes, alas, he was missing, drinking with his pals down at the public house.

Washing was done by lighting a fire under a copper built into a bricked-in corner of an outhouse called a wash-us (washhouse), or brew-us (brewhouse) as the same outhouse was used for both purposes. Here the necessary water was boiled, and the clothes pummelled hard in a large wooden tub called a 'maiding tub', which stood on the floor. After vigorous beating with a long, two-handled wooden 'maid' or 'dolly', as it was called, the clothes were boiled up in the copper, after which they went through various processes of rinsing, blueing and starching, before being put through a large mangle with wooden rollers, which took up consider-able room in the 'wash-us'. Then they were dried, with luck out of doors, but if the weather was bad, on a clothes horse in front of the living room fire, the children, when they came home from school, having to sit inside it on stools or on the hearthrug.

The warm soapy water was too precious to be thrown away, so washday ended with all the floors being scrubbed, down on hands and knees to make a good job of it, special attention being given to the front doorstep, which later was whitened with bath brick to dazzling competition with those of the neighbours. Then, with any water that was left over, the children were also scrubbed in a tin or zinc bath in front of the fire.

When the washing was at last dried, it had to be damped down and folded ready for ironing, after which it was finally aired on the brass rod under the mantel shelf, on a clothes horse, or on a line across the living room.

Whenever possible, washing was done on Monday so that sheets and clothes, which were usually changed on Sunday, would not be left lying about longer than was necessary, and also that the remains of the Sunday roast joint and leftover vegetables, could be heated up again for a quick Monday dinner, when most wives were too busy to do much cooking. So cold meat and bubble and squeak were usual for washday dinner. Later in the day the children sat in front of the fire with long-handled wire or brass toasting forks, and made toast for tea, spreading it with dripping from the family joint, the jelly from the bottom of the dripping jar being spread on top for added flavour, which the children especially appreciated, and licked their lips and fingers.

No family was without its cat, not only as a pet, but for its use as a mouser, as often the cleanest family found itself obliged to share its home to a greater or less extent with mice. Tabby cats were the most common, followed by all black, ginger and tortoiseshell. No great originality was usually found in the names they were given, Meg, Tibby, Tiddles, Tommy, Fluffy, Smut, Blackie, Nigger and Ginger being very common. 'Doctoring' of pets was almost unknown, and the numerous unwanted litters of kittens were drowned at birth without ceremony in a bucket of water. Most of the cats had fleas as a matter of course.

Almost every family had its dog too, and an owner had great pride if he could boast it was a good ratter. Dogs kept for guard were usually chained up to a kennel outside, but most of them were allowed to run about freely wherever they wanted. Dog fights were a common sight, and a source of great excitement and entertainment, men particularly gathering to watch, and now and then laying a mild bet on the result. Children, and others too, gathered round and shouted to each other to separate the combatants. For the most part, dogs fought for their own entertainment and enjoyed themselves thoroughly, with no more serious

173

intention than asserting supremacy, but if the battle seemed to be getting seriously vicious and out of hand, a nearby householder would rush out with a bucket of water to throw over them, which usually allowed their separation while the astonished animals got their breath.

17

The Witherford Family

Jane deeply loved her relations at Bartley Green, particularly her parents, her sister Liza, and the three motherless little boys she helped to bring up. She seemed to open herself to them more than to her own husband and children, although she gave the greatest thought in every way to their welfare. With the possible exception of the little Lizzie, she gave them no demonstration of affection, and was never known to kiss any of her children, nor in later years her two grandchildren, although they both loved her dearly. Nevertheless Jane had a delightful way with small children, playing with them for hours. She knew innumerable ditties, starting with play for fingers and toes:

'This little piggy went to market,
This little piggy stayed at home,
This little piggy had roast beef,
This little piggy had none,
This little piggy cried "Wee, wee, wee,
I can't find my way home."'

which ended with a tickle on the sole of the foot and helpless laughter.

Then there was the great mystery of the fingernails:

'Two little dicky birds sitting on a wall,
One named Peter, one named Paul,
Fly away Peter, fly away Paul,
Come back Peter, come back Paul.'

and to infant wonder, the two bits of paper 'birds' on the

fingernails really did fly away and come back.

To their great delight, she called on the Finger Family Twins:

'Toby Thumb, Toby Thumb, where are you?'
'Here I am, Here I am. How do you do?'

followed by Peter Pointer, Tommy Tall, Ruby Ring and Baby Finger, and finally all the family. And then she went on through countless nursery rhymes which they soon knew as well as she did.

As the children got bigger, they were introduced in her soft musical voice to:

'The frog who would a wooing go,
Whether his mother would let him or no,'

and also to:

'The man who had a dog,
Whose name was Bobby Bingo,'

as well as to:

'Old John with his apple tree healthy and green
That bore the best codlins that ever were seen.'

not to forget:

'The carrion crow who lived in an oak
Watching a tailor making a coat.'

and favourite of all, the jolly miller who lived on the River Dee:

'Who worked and sang from morn to night,
No lark so blithe as he
And this the burden of his song
For ever used to be,
"I care for nobody, no not I,
If nobody cares for me".'

They soon knew all the verses and the stories they told, and were ready to join in the choruses of 'Roly, Poly, Gammon and Spinach' from *Anthony Roly*, as well as the 'Hey Derry Down Derry Di Do's' and the rest, all with enormous delight.

She spent hours making rag dolls and clothes for them, or fetching clay from the brook, moulding it into the shape of dishes, tea sets and all sorts of things, and baking them hard in the oven.

When the children were ill, she wrapped them in a big plaid shawl, and sat them in an armchair by the fire to feel sorry for themselves – and how they loved it!

Lizzie, the eldest child, was not so pretty as her two sisters, but she was her mother's favourite child, and all her young life 'got away with' much Jane would never have dreamed of allowing in her two younger daughters. She was a blue-eyed, fair-haired plump little girl, a gay irrepressible child with a turn for comic remark, very outgoing, companionable, warm and loving to everyone, forgiving and forgetting everything undesirable. Later, as she got older, she 'borrowed', without any thought of their consent, her sisters' best clothes and finery – even sometimes exchanging or selling them without their knowledge and quite unrepentent when found out. It was she alone who, when she was growing up, dared to go off to dances and come home very late, knowing her mother would hide her misdemeanours, and excuse them with her father.

Nellie was dark, like her father, but with her mother's innate quietness and gentility ('the best of the bunch', said her sisters). She was clever too, and possibly in a later age, when such opportunities would have been open to her, would have become a conscientious schoolteacher, or a nun if she had been born into a Catholic family. She had a few friends of quiet disposition like her own. Her integrity and truthfulness were absolute, and nothing would deter her from doing what she thought was right. The gaiety of her two lively sisters was quite foreign to her. She simply went her own quiet way, saying nothing to anybody, and gravitating towards the church and its various activities and organisations. At the age of thirty-two she died of consumption, greatly missed. Her mother was told at the time that no-one would ever know what good work she had done and generosity she had shown, quietly and unobtrusively, among poor families in Selly Oak.

Gertie, the youngest child, never felt her mother loved her as much as she loved her two elder sisters, but she was her father's favourite child. He encouraged her with pennies and kisses to sing for him, act and recite poems. She has been described as a lovely child, a ravishing young woman, and beautiful even in extreme old age. She too was dark like her father, with stiff, black, wavy hair, a slim agile figure, artistic and temperamental, with an impulsive, wild, wilful nature and a passionate temper she never learned to control. Throughout her life she liked bright colours and pretty things, reminiscent of a gipsy, and indeed it would not be hard to believe there could be gipsy blood in the family, coming out in Gertie.

With the exception of her Aunt Liza's children, her grandparents and the three motherless little boys, Gertie did not know her relatives very well, although she remembered her mother pointing them out or introducing them when they visited Bartley. Lizzie, six years older, could remember her early years in Bartley, and knew them better. The Partridge and Witherford families did not like each other very well, even after they became in-laws, and had little contact. Of her father's people, Gertie only remembered as a tiny child seeing a very pretty woman looking over a gate, and being told it was her father's sister. On another occasion, her father's brother Enoch was pointed out to her, standing on a canal barge on which he worked. Lizzie, as a little child in Bartley, had known some of them, and had been a favourite with her father's mother.

One other loved relative, an unmarried cousin of Jane's was in service with two bachelor professors at the University. She sometimes visited the family, bringing with her cake or other dainties she had cooked at her place of employment. She too had the quiet gentility of her family, and was greatly liked by her employers, who sent for their own doctor and cared for her as one of their own family when she became ill with consumption, and eventually died.

Jane took great pride in her daughters' appearance and

clothes, as well as that of herself and her husband. Early in her married life she had bought a treadle sewing machine, the only thing she ever bought on hire purchase. It cost £7, which was a great deal of money in those days. On it she made her children's clothes when they were small, little dresses and coats, nightgowns of grey flannelette with white stripes, petticoats, two of which were always worn, one of white cotton and one of white flannel, both of which were embroidered, trimmed with lace, frilled at the bottom, and worn on top of a hand-knitted woollen vest and home-made flannel 'bodice', the forerunner, no doubt, of the later, ready-made 'Liberty bodice'. She made too their white cotton drawers, consisting of two separate legs fastened on to a front and back waistband, and held up by a large linen button at each side, the back band over the front, so that it could be let down as required. The frilled legs were just long enough to show beneath the dress, and were much admired. Times changed and it became fashionable for the legs to be made shorter, so that the frills no longer showed, a fact much resented by the little Witherfords, who were proud of their display. After visiting at Bartley Green, little Gertie pointed out that her cousins there wore drawers that showed frills below their dresses. She was comforted by the words they were country children, and consequently a bit behind the times.

Pinafores were worn almost constantly, with little frills over the armholes, fastening at the back of the neck. Like all the other little girls, the Witherford children went to school in them, in their case dark blue with tiny white spots, or something similarly practical, that did not show the dirt. On Sundays, however, white silk ones came out, which required quite as much care as the best dresses they covered. This was no great problem on a day when much time was taken up with walking backwards and forwards to church or Sunday school, and active games with balls, hoops, skipping ropes or playing at hopscotch were strongly forbidden.

The children and their mother all wore black, woollen hand-knitted stockings, kept up in the absence of elastic by hand-knitted garters (the origin, no doubt, of the so-called 'garter stitch'), or a piece of corking made by four nails hammered into a cotton reel. The children substituted the black woollen stockings for white cotton ones on really hot Sundays in the summertime, but these were strictly for best. They were worn with boots, buttoned or laced. Oh! on school days, what a trial it was for the children, sitting on the floor, to lace them up, especially when the tags wore off, and it took an eternity of sucking to make them go through the eyelets. Their mother always left them to struggle alone till the very last minute before helping them, and there was a danger of their being late for school.

Jane also made shirts for her husband and three nephews. She knew nothing about paper patterns, and had had no instruction other than that passed down from her mother, but she made a very good job of all she attempted. As there was no shop in Bartley Green in Jane's early married life, the materials had to be ordered from the packman, who came round periodically with samples and patterns to choose from. Later, in Selly Oak, a much larger and quickly growing village, there was a big draper's shop owned by Mr Walton, who kept a pattern book permanently, and allowed would-be customers to take it home and study it.

Even Gertie, the youngest child, never had 'passed down' clothes. When new clothes were necessary, all the children had them at the same time, last year's 'best' now being taken for everyday wear, while the new clothes, made with large hems that could be let down to 'allow for growing', and wide seams to be let out as required, became the new 'best'. When they got older, the dresses and coats were always made by a dressmaker, of whom there were plenty about to choose from. Within reason, their mother always let them choose the style and material they wanted. Gertie's first dressmaker-made coat was of light brown teddy bear material with two pleats at the back that swung out when she walked. And what delight it gave her!

Selly Oak also had a boot shop, and here again the children were generally allowed to choose for themselves. On one occasion, however, Lizzie's own choice being considered unsuitable, she was bought instead a light tan pair of 'Kidleyvant' (Kid Levant). How she hated them! The fuss she made! declaring quite untruthfully that they hurt her, as that, she knew, was the only argument likely to move her mother, and with luck they might be changed for others she liked better. Her mother took the hated boots back to the shop, and exchanged them for another pair exactly the same, but a size larger, which took far longer to grow out of.

Will Witherford for one reason or another was not a handyman, and his wife did many things a husband would normally do. This included mending her own and her children's boots, using a foot iron for the purpose. She would draw round the sole on a piece of paper, cut it out, and send one of the children to the bootmender's shop for leather of a suitable size. The leather was soaked in water overnight, then hammered out hard to make it thin and tough, before being cut to shape and hammered in place with brass nails which would not rust.

Although the children did not have 'passed down' clothes, Gertie at least had 'passed down' toys, kept under the living room sofa in a box. She remembered a big, ugly, battered wooden doll with a ghostly wax face from which most of the colours and features had long since been washed away. This she used to push around in an old 'go-cart', the forerunner of the perambulator. Her cousin Ben once bought her a large new one in a box, but the nicest and best-remembered of all was one her sister Nellie won as a school prize; it was dressed as a prince in a white silk blouse, with a white silk front, black satin knee-length trousers with a lace frill at the bottom, white stockings, black patent shoes, a blue satin cape, and a black velvet hat with a drooping white feather. When they were small they also had an old pram with its wheels off, which rested in a corner of the kitchen, and this they played in as a rocking boat. Of course they had tops and whips of various kinds, and played hopscotch by the hour in the street, or trundled wooden hoops called 'bowels' (to rhyme with 'towels'), hitting them along with a little stick. Balls were never allowed. They never questioned why, although possibly it was for fear of damage to windows or gardens. Gertie said she longed for a skipping rope with painted wooden handles, but her mother saw no necessity for such extravagance, and she had to be contented with a piece of clothesline bought by the yard from the ironmonger's shop.

The children were all sent early to bed in the wintertime

181

with a candle which cast long, moving shadows up the stairs. This was left alight in the room till the children had settled, when their mother fetched it down, calling, 'Good night, good night, good night,' one for each as she left.

The cottage had only two bedrooms, and all the children slept in the same room, Lizzie and Gertie in a big bed and Nellie in a single one. On the big bed was a patchwork quilt, and the children amused themselves by choosing patches they would like for dresses. Lizzie, who was six years older than Gertie, would tell her little sister stories, poems, riddles and rhymes till they went to sleep, Nellie listening with interest. When they had new dresses, they were hung up by the door so that they could enjoy and admire them when they first opened their eyes in the morning, and refresh themselves with the sight of them before closing their eyes in sleep.

The children were always packed off to bed especially early if friends of their parents, or visitors called. Sometimes the company downstairs sounded very lively, and the three little girls would creep out of bed in the dark and tiptoe to the foot of the stairs, where they sat as still as mice, listening with all their ears, and scampering back up again at any movement in their direction.

When visitors came, Jane's home-made wine came out. She herself, not even once in her life, went into a public house, but in true country tradition, made wine of various kinds, rhubarb, cowslip, dandelion, elderberry, beetroot, parsnip, potato (which the family swore was indistinguishable from whisky, a beverage well beyond their means) and also stout. Not much of this was for family consumption. On brewing days, one of the children was sent with a jug to the public house for balm, Gertie saying that when she fetched it, she always came home with clean fingers, it tasted so nice. These home brews were strictly not for children. For them a large jug of lemon water was kept in the pantry, and from this they could help themselves freely. It was not till many years later they realised that its bitter taste was due to a tablespoon of Epsom Salts stirred in to keep them 'regular'. However, Espom Salts or no, they enjoyed it, and were not subject to any more drastic potions, except once a year in the springtime, when a large

182

basin of brimstone and treacle was made 'to clear the blood' and a spoonful administered each day, while it lasted.

Opposite the Witherford home was a tiny shop, con- verted from a four-room cottage, and kept by Mrs Coldrick. It had a high window, covered at night by wooden shutters, stored in the daytime on brackets underneath. Here were displayed, higgledy-piggledy, striped rings of peppermint rock (Gertie's favourite), bright fishes in boiled sugar, white, pink and brown coconut chip, kali suckers, stripy humbugs, dolly mixtures, licorice allsorts, gobstoppers, pineapple lollipops, licorice bootlaces, monkey nuts, trays of home-made treacle toffee, locust beans as well as troach drops and aniseed balls. These were overlooked by a row of sweet jars on a shelf at the back, containing such delights as acid squares, raspberry and lemon drops, sugar 'rosebuds', pink on one side and white on the other. There were also jars of heart-shaped, flat, brittle sweets called 'Mottoes' or 'Love Hearts' or 'Cupid's Favours', on which were written all kinds of appropriate sentiments. They were all sold at 4 oz. a penny, and served with 'bumping weight'.

Inside the shop, stacked up at the back, was a selection of vegetables in round wicker hampers, bottles of pop with a glass marble in the neck, bundles of neatly-chopped firewood, a cask of vinegar, bundles of candles and a tank of lamp oil, complete with a large, sharp-spouted tin jug to serve it.

At the back of the counter was a board with a joint of bacon, a primitive bacon cutter with a wheel turned by hand, a barrel-shaped piece of very sharp cheese with thick, cloth-covered rind, as well as big stone jars of jam, treacle, pickled onions and pickled cabbage, all sold 'loose', customers bringing their own basins to put them in. The counter had a slot in it, where the children's pennies dropped through to a drawer beneath.

Gertie was a favourite with Mrs Coldrick and used to dress up in old lace curtains and her mother's and big sisters' clothes and perform antics for her entertainment. All the children were not so popular, some of whom would deliberately taunt the worthy soul, when she would rush out with a cane and shake it at them, as they disappeared into safety over the wall. She did a brisk trade in canes, always

183

popular with conscientious parents.

Jane and Mrs Coldrick were not on very friendly terms, as Jane did not patronise her shop for general groceries, preferring the better-class shops in the High Street. Mrs Coldrick, however, did a considerable amount of business around, mostly because she allowed her customers to make purchases 'on the strap', or 'on tick', as it was called. She had, however, learned to be very shrewd in the choice she made of these customers after one unfortunate circumstance, when one customer had run up a considerable bill and was taken to court. A court order was made against the customer of two pence per week, which even in those days was derisory. So from that time, if payment from a customer seemed uncertain, Mrs Coldrick cut her losses and refused to supply any more.

18

School and School Days

All Jane's little girls were confident enough in their own home but very shy elsewhere, and not one of them, throughout life, ever tried to assert herself above the company in which she found herself. At school, they were never fearless enough to be really naughty. All of them were quite bright, and could hold their own with their fellow pupils, and the tables and lists of spellings they took home for 'homework' were conscientiously heard by their mother, as also the collect they had to learn for Sunday School.

Lizzie left school at the age of eleven, as she was good enough to pass the 'Labour Exam', which was in force in those days and indicated she had reached the required standard of achievement, and need not stay till she reached the statutory leaving age of thirteen. She got a part-time job in a nearby bedstead works till she was old enough to apply to Cadbury's chocolate factory, opened a few years before at the new, model village of Bournville, just over a mile away, where jobs were greatly coveted by the local girls. In due course she was accepted, and here she stayed till she married. Nellie also went to work there when she left school.

Gertie did not like school much, but her mother stood no nonsense, and made sure she did not miss a single day. The only absence she remembered was when she had chickenpox. How pleased she was, and proud of the scabs, and how she enjoyed sitting by the fire in the big shawl, and how sorry she was when the spots disappeared, and the plaid shawl was washed and put away for the next invalid.

All three children were amazingly observant throughout life, and had phenomenal memories for the most minute

185

detail, and so indeed had their mother. Gertie well remembered her first day at school on her fourth birthday, when her mother, wearing a fawn woollen shawl, patterned all over with brown half moons, and which later with true Victorian thrift was made into an ironing blanket, took her by the hand into a cake shop on the way up, and bought her some ABC biscuits, as they were called, made in the shape of letters of the alphabet, and covered with pink and white icing. At school she was handed over to her teacher, who remarked, 'So this is the last of the little Witherfords.'

She remembered sitting in school, and watching through the open door the leaves falling from the big trees outside, and then at playtime sitting at the school door in a round iron boot scraper that just fitted her bottom, nursing in her lap a little boy she knew; she remembered taking a rag to school to wipe her slate clean when the teacher came round from time to time with a wet sponge on the end of a stick to give each slate a dab; she remembered taking her slate pencil out at playtime to get a fine point on it by scraping it on the granite stones with which the school was built. She remembered too, about that time, the parson visiting the house, and lifting her up in front of framed pictures of the Lord's Prayer and the Ten Commandments and asking her if she could read them, but she was too young and could not.

Soon after starting school, she begged to go in her new straw bonnet, and this she was allowed to do on condition she took great care of it. Little Gertie did her best, she was afraid to leave it on the cloakroom peg, so she took it with her into the classroom and sat on it.

All the children at that time took some food wrapped up in paper for their playtime lunch. Gertie was never very interested in food and did not want it, but her mother insisted, so she used to take a tiny, thin piece of bread and butter, which was put on a side table with all the other lunches. One day she was last out to fetch hers and found that her own had gone, and the only one left was a thick chunk of bread and lard wrapped in newspaper, which she refused to eat, saying it was not hers. The teacher did not believe her, and in mistaken zeal of family support, told her she must stand in front of the class until she did. She stayed there the rest of the morning, but did not eat the bread and lard.

Once Gertie even played truant. Her teacher was leaving to get married (women teachers who married had to give up their job at that time, and so did girls in most other types of employment), and the children were asked to contribute towards a present. She was given a penny to take along, and no doubt thinking her contribution would not be missed among so many, little Gertie, so she believed, put it to better use; going back to school after dinner, she spent it on sweets, which she ate sitting by a coal cellar grating under the shop window. By the time they were eaten it was getting late, so instead of going to school, she made her way up to the newly-opened park, where a row of swings had been put up.

After school there was a lot of competition for these swings, and the timid little Witherfords never got a chance among the rougher, more boisterous children. Gertie thought this was her opportunity, she sat and swung quietly to herself all afternoon. Unfortunately she misjudged the time, and was so late getting home, her family were becoming anxious and were already making enquiries. So she did not have long to wait for retribution.

The teacher's present was duly bought, a very pretty tea service, packed and nicely displayed in a clothes basket, and Gertie remembered walking round it with the other children to admire it, with no pangs of conscience.

How Gertie hated Arithmetic, particularly 'problems', saying her mind was always more interested in, and insisted in thinking about the apples, oranges, eggs etc. in the associated narrative, than in the numbers. However, in spite of this early aversion to Arithmetic, she never forgot her multiplication tables, nor how to use them, and never throughout life was she at a loss to cope quickly and easily with everyday household calculations.

In English, Gertie came into her own. Grammar, analysing and parsing, spelling and composition (free writing), had no terrors for her, and her handwriting was beautiful. Her greatest love was poetry, which she learned by the yard, amazing poems for teachers, instructed by their visiting inspectors, to put in front of a small girl. Her favourite was

'An Ode on the Death of the Duke of Wellington' by Alfred Lord Tennyson, whose full title was quoted on every occasion of recitation. 'Barbara Fritche' was another of her favourites, and many poems by Wordsworth, even some of the longest. She never forgot a line, and many years later, at the age of eighty-eight, was still word-perfect. For a long time after leaving school, she eagerly sought out poems she liked, and wrote them in an album she kept all her life. With no-one to guide her, it was amazing how this simply-educated girl instinctively sought out poems of outstanding literary merit.

School also fortified her with a sound knowledge of the mountains, rivers, bays and capes of Britain, as well as the principal events, dates and personalities of British History, which she knew by heart and never forgot.

Needlework was practiced on specimen pieces of unbleached calico, with red cotton to show the stitches. She learned tacking, running, hemming, oversewing, run-and-fell and french seams, as well as blanket stitch, chain stitch and daisy stitch, leading on to feather stitch, herringbone and hem stitch, as well as a variety of embroidery stitches, all of great practical use in the domestic requirements of the time. She remembered learning to knit a long red scarf and a pink vest, knit two, purl two, as well as a pair of stockings, none of which her mother would buy, although the finished articles were for sale. When this happened, the children were expected to take the articles round to friends and relations to see if they would fancy them and buy them, and so, in one way or another, there were few left over.

The children and their Teachers went back to school every Sunday morning for religious instruction, extra to that taught first thing each weekday morning. Later they went up to church two by two for the service there, although the small children were let out early before the sermon. There was much the same procedure in the afternoon. According to Gertie, as far as children were concerned, the only significant difference between Sunday School and Day School was that the former started at ten o'clock instead of nine, and everyone wore their best clothes.

More than once, from the penny her mother gave her for the collection, Gertie was tempted to spend a halfpenny on 'rosebuds' at the sweetshop en route, which was always open on Sunday mornings, and no doubt other children too were sometimes tempted to fall by the wayside.

Once a year there was a flower service at the church, when the children handed over cottage posies for the local almshouses and the workhouse. Jane made sure all her children had flowers, and they loved the occasion.

The Headmaster, who at that time lived in the School House next door to the school, was a greatly respected man. He had been appointed straight from college to the headship more than thirty years before, when there were less than fifty pupils all told, from the starting age of three to the leaving age of eleven. With the making of education free and compulsory in 1870, the development of industry in Selly Oak and consequent increase in population, the school had grown around him. His teachers were mostly the daughters of local shopkeepers, who had attended the school as children, and they stayed on, first as monitors, then as pupil teachers, attending the newly opened Pupil Teachers' Centre in Birmingham. In Gertie's time, there were Carry and Aggie, the coal merchant's daughters, Edie from the pork shop, as well as the Headmaster's own daughter.

Every year in the summer, the dedication of the church and school was celebrated by a school treat. The children assembled at the school in the morning, forming a procession and singing on their way up to the church for a service. In the early afternoon, the children re-assembled at the school, where the shopkeepers had provided cleaned-out and decorated carts to give them a ride to a local field, in later years the park, where the treat was to take place. And so, the village band preceding, off the procession went, all the children having a cup tied round the neck on a piece of string, and waving a little flag. Proud and excited parents walked alongside, some of them, particularly a local comic named Mrs Banner, dressing up, beating dustbin lids, bowls, buckets or the like, in accompaniment to the band, and performing entertaining antics on the way, to amuse a gay and very appreciative crowd and add to the sense of occasion.

At the field, to the increasing accompaniment of the

189

band, races were run, jam jars full of wild flowers were judged 'for arrangement' and prizes given. Then came the highlight of the afternoon, the distribution of bread and butter, slab cake and buns, out of cloth-lined washing baskets, carried round by willing grown-up helpers, and the pouring out of an inexhaustible supply of hot sweet tea out of enormous brown enamel tea pots.

In a similar setting the other side of Birmingham, such an occasion gave rise to the story Grandfather Haynes loved to tell about a little boy he found crying on one of the school treats he had organised. On asking the reason for his tears, the little fellow answered he could not eat his cake. 'Never mind' said the kindly Mr Haynes, 'put it in your pocket, then.'

'I can't,' came the reply, 'they are full up.' No doubt at Selly Oak too, many children arrived home with pockets full of unaccustomed tit-bits for smaller brothers and sisters, or because they could not find room to consume them on the spot.

Tea over, there was a Punch and Judy show, after which the whole assembly made its way to the church for a short thanksgiving service to end the day.

Also in the summer was a Sunday School party on the Vicarage lawn. But that, according to Gertie, was not in the same street.

The children had their weekly pleasures, which included one evening down at the Band of Hope, where they sang temperance songs, said recitations and were entertained periodically by a magic lantern show, most of the pictures shown giving edifying warning of the dangers of strong drink, the deepest and most widespread cause of poverty and misery at that time, which nowadays is no longer suffered in the same way. The children all 'signed the pledge', a formal renunciation of alcohol. Few families took this very seriously, although one little boy the Witherford children knew liked to tell, in later years, how his mother had sewed a blue ribbon (the teetotaller symbol) on his shirt when he left home, to remind him. Later, as the children got a bit older, interest for most of them was transferred to the Boys' Brigade or the Girls' Brigade, where Gertie and Nellie learned some simple dressmaking

190

and, among other useful accomplishments, how to crochet mantel borders and lace for their chemises.

There was no Christmas treat at school, as became customary in later years, but nevertheless Christmas was a time of great delight for the Witherford children; and not only for them, but for their mother, too. Mrs Coldrick adorned her shop window with wire hoops on which were hung fragile glass balls and decorations of various kinds – angels with spun glass wings, birds with wings and tails also of spun glass, paper birds in tiny cardboard cages, as well as various shaped objects, such as watches, clocks, hearts, boots and so on, all made of rough, coloured sugar, and having a hole in them so that they could be hung on the Christmas tree. Spread out below were white and pink sugar mice and sugar pigs, all with tails of string, and all very tempting for the spending of the 'Saturday Penny'.

Jane watched with interest as her little daughters chose each week from November onwards some decoration from Mrs Coldrick's shop, putting them in a shoebox under the sofa. Nearer to the time, she bought coloured tissue paper and got busy with scissors and paste, showing and helping her three little girls to make paper chains and decorations to festoon the living room. Then there was the making of the puddings, a ritual that lasted at least a week, stoning raisins, preparing peel and breadcrumbs, cutting up suet (butcher's plums as it was called), mixing it with home-made stout, the children each having a stir and a wish, and taking it in turn to lick the spoon. They were finally boiled in a big, oval, black, iron pot, kept between whiles on a large hook, in a corner of the coal house under the stairs.

Three or four weeks before Christmas, all the children went out after tea carol singing, long before anyone wanted them, but nearer to Christmas they were welcomed, or at least tolerated, and suitably rewarded. Gertie, one year – but only one year – collected ninepence, and this was a great help to the Saturday pennies and the shoebox under the sofa.

On Christmas Eve the tree was brought in, usually a holly or some other evergreen cut out of the hedgerow. Out came the shoebox, and the decorating began. Finally any bare places in the greenery were filled by tiny, sour Christmas oranges, into which later a lump of sugar would be stuck, before they were squeezed and sucked, and also bright rosy apples suspended on string. Then the candles were lit. One year the tree caught fire, and was put out through the door with difficulty, but this did not deter Jane; the tree found a place in the living room corner right till Gertie was married, and then it was time to start all over again with her grandchildren.

Lizzie, Gertie and Nellie hung up their stockings on Christmas Eve, clean ones in honour of the occasion, on the rail at the foot of the brass bedstead, of which the elaborate ornamentation of leaves and flowers had all been unscrewed, polished and screwed back again to make them worthy of this annual honour. The stocking always contained an apple, an orange, some nuts, sweets and new pennies, all counted out fairly, and with them a pair of new stockings.

In the days before Christmas, the Waits went round playing carols at street corners, making a final visit on Christmas morning, when they knocked each door to wish the family the compliments of the season and receive their reward. On Boxing Day, public houses always put out plates of cold beef for customers to eat with their beer, and indeed they gave away bread and cheese every Sunday morning throughout the year. This custom was not popular with wives, who said it spoilt their husband's dinner, the most ambitious meal of the week, over which they had been slaving all morning.

Jane often went to Bartley to see her dearly-loved parents and numerous relations, taking some 'family biscuits' as a gift for her mother, and saved-up copies of the *Family Reader* she bought weekly – the family never had a newspaper. In the summertime she would get up very early before it was light, and walk the five miles to Bartley along the canal towpath, getting back in time to give her family their breakfast and bringing a bunch of wild flowers and grasses for the mantel shelf.

During the three weeks of the long summer holiday from school, and also at Christmas and Easter, the family 'went on their holiday', a whole day with the children's grandparents at Bartley Green. They went all dressed up in their

192

best clothes, Jane taking some of the food to help out. The children stayed with their grandparents while their mother visited her nearby relations, and her husband visited his, and also his pals and cronies at the Cock Inn.

It was always dark when they started back for home, and little Gertie, feeling very tired, was carried on her father's shoulders most of the way, pleading to be taken 'to the next star'. In some places the towpath had worn away and become very slippery and dangerous. On one occasion Will had just put his daughter down when he disappeared from sight into the water. Poor Jane was terrified, not knowing how to help her husband and look after her children at the same time. It was pitch dark, and there was no-one to turn to in that lonely place, so she came on home. To her great surprise, there was her husband, arrived home before her. He had not bothered to get out of the canal, saying it had happened to him so many times before, that he knew his way in the water as well as on the path. It was only lucky he had put his daughter down in time.

Occasionally Jane's mother visited her, walking along the canal side till she was well over eighty, when she got a lift in the carrier's cart. On these occasions, when she left, she always slipped a gold sovereign into the matchbox on the mantel shelf for her daughter to find later. The last time she came was to have her photograph taken, the only one she ever had, as far as is known. Soon after, she had a stroke and lingered for several years. With sturdy Victorian independence, the family took it in their stride, and between them contributed eleven shillings weekly to pay a daughter-in-law who lived near to come in daily and care for her.

There were very few photographs of any of the family. Jane herself, throughout her life, was most unwilling to be photographed, and there is no known photograph of her husband, nor of her children before they went to work and bought them for themselves. School groups were taken from time to time, but Jane never bought them. It seems strange and unnatural for her not to have wanted a record of three very attractive little girls, in whose appearance she obviously took much care and pride.

19

In the Streets

Lizzie and Gertie, at least, were very glad the family had moved from quiet little Bartley Green to Selly Oak, where there was always something of interest going on.

During the daytime the lanes and roads were busy with horse-drawn traffic of every description, from the little ponies and traps the better class folk used to get about, to the flat lumbering coal carts, brewers' drays, transport wagons coming to and from the metal works, drawn by heavy, powerful shire horses. Between these were carts of every size and shape, for every imaginable purpose, drawn by every type of horse you could think of, and all trundling or rattling on the dark blue brick cobbles with which the streets were paved. With all these horses street cleaners were kept busy, although the horse droppings were never wasted; no sooner was a dollop observed on the road than somebody, usually a child, appeared down an entry or out of a doorway with a bucket and shovel, and got busy on behalf of the rhubarb, the kidney beans, a favourite rose bush or the vegetable patch.

The street was the children's playground, most gardens being regarded with the serious purpose of cultivation. Its pavement was covered with small blue ridged bricks, which did not get slippery when wet, as after rain the water soon drained off, leaving it dry and clean and an ideal surface on which to play.

When the children got home from school, from then on till their bedtime, even in winter when it got dark early, the streets were alive with their noisy play. After a brief rush indoors, many emerged with 'a piece' (a slice of bread and jam, or dripping or lard), just 'to keep the grubs from biting', as the saying went, till teatime. Babies were put in prams for big sisters – and not such big sisters – to take out and mind, and very serious and competent they were too, without making any great burden of it, being quite ready to push the pram to some handy spot and keep an eye on it, while they joined in the skipping, hopscotch and singing games, or spun and whipped their tops. Other children in the meantime, down on their hands and knees, played marbles along the gutter, or sat on a step or kerbstone to play five stones. Naughty boys swung on the backs of passing carts till the driver, when he noticed them, turned round and slaked at them with the whip, to make them drop off.

In due course they were called in for tea, but were out again immediately after, this time without the babies, who had by now been put to bed. Between teatime and their bedtime about eight o'clock, the fun really warmed up. Boisterous children, particularly the boys, kicked cans, screamed up and down entries, hiding, seeking and chasing. They climbed up lampposts, or swung on them with skipping ropes they had tied on the arm at the top. And then, as if by magic, the noise would cease, and every child would melt into thin air; the policeman was walking round on his beat. But he had soon gone by, and in no time at all they were out again. From time to time when the noise got unendurable, a door would open, and an irate householder would shout, 'Get off! Go and play by your own house up your own entry,' but it made little difference. In any case it was not long before they were all called in to bed, and silence took over.

The weekdays always had plenty to offer. The German Band came round regularly, and many children liked to dance to it, making up their steps as they went along.

A couple of dirty fellows used to come along with a performing bear called Joey on a chain. He danced to the fiddle one of them played, or caught a pole thrown to him by the other. A neighbour of the Witherfords, a very old lady, was so sorry for the animal, she one day went up to it and stroked it, with the words 'Poor thing' on her lips, to the anger and fear of the owners, who threatened and warned her off with the pole and the most colourful of expletives.

Every week the Italian organ grinder came down the street with his hurdy-gurdy and its dirty little monkey on top, dressed in a red coat and a pillbox hat, which it held out to the audience for pence after it had performed its tricks. What a job sometimes it was for the children to get their mothers to part with half pence to put in it! Jane was never easy in this respect, and Gertie remembered how she had sometimes grizzled all day long for a half penny, to no avail.

The rag and bone man with his barrow was also a regular visitor, and the children found it easier to coax a jam jar, some old stockings or rags out of their mother than the precious half pence. In exchange they received a little flag on a stick, a clay bubble pipe, or a paper windmill, or, if they were very lucky, a balloon from some he had blown up and tied in a bundle to the handle of his barrow. For a really handsome donation, even a gold fish in a small round bowl was sometimes forthcoming; although they rarely survived longer than a day or two at most.

Sometimes small street roundabouts came to give the toddlers a ride, when their mother handed them over the low wicket put in front of the open door to keep them from straying while she was busy, and watched with pride and joy to see them slowly turning as they sat in the small attached chair they were placed in for the ride.

In the evening, there was the lamplighter with a taper on the end of a pole to watch for.

Knife grinders pushed their barrows along at infrequent intervals. They pedalled away at their grindstones for customers and did a brisk trade, particularly in sharpening scissors, as most people could keep their hand-forged steel knives at their peak of sharpness by constantly whetting them on suitable garden stones till they were very thin, narrow and worn down almost to the hilt, and were quite outlived by the forks, which had two or three, long, almost needle-sharp prongs and bone or horn handles.

Travelling tinkers arrived from time to time, set up a little brazier on the doorstep, and mended pots and pans on the spot or put rivets in broken china without any fuss or trouble.

Clock menders came round from door to door. They took

broken clocks to bits on a sheet of paper on the kitchen table, and were seldom unsuccessful in putting them right, making a charge well within the modest means of their customers.

Umbrella menders made spasmodic rounds, putting in ribs and ferrels from spares they carried, or exchanged for a small cost old umbrellas for ones they had reconditioned, or buying old ones for a copper or two.

The sandwich-board man sauntered up and down the gutters, walking slowly so as to give passers-by time to read the message written in bold letters back and front, of goods advertised for sale, interesting news or local announcements, warnings on Sin, or instructions for Salvation from earnest Christian missions.

Occasionally a beggar came along, wearing dirty, ragged clothes, broken, worn-out boots, and singing aloud with an unbelievably tuneless voice as he (or less often, she) shuffled up the gutter. He was only trying to earn an honest penny, he explained to the 'copper' who came down to move him on.

About once a year the gipsy women came, very dark and handsome, with black, greasy hair, coal-black eyes, large brass earrings and bright vivid clothes. They usually sold clothes pegs or artificial flowers they had made, which they carried in wide flat baskets. The men who accompanied them sold baskets they had woven themselves or twig besom brooms for garden use. They begged old clothes and boots, and were strongly suspected of taking eggs from fowl pens, washing off the line, or anything else left around, so they were carefully watched. Gertie one day, passing two in the lane, heard one say to the other, 'Look! There's a pretty wench.' Remembering family tales of children stolen by gipsies, she fled home in terror.

Most intriguing and best of all were the quarrels and fights which took place at turning-out time at the public houses on Saturday night. These were always awaited and watched with absorbing interest.

If there was nothing else going on, the children, and grown-ups too, sauntered along to the blacksmith's shop to watch him from the doorway, peer into the dim smoky interior, and enjoy the smell of burnt hoof. The sight of the

197

patient horses, standing in the midst of the noise and sparks from the anvil, afforded endless fascination. The schoolmaster sometimes visited the blacksmith with a more purposeful intent; he begged pieces of pared hoof, which he carried round with him in his pocket. When he saw a child in school biting his nails, he used to put a piece on the desk in front of him, telling him to have a nibble at that instead of his own fingers when he felt hungry, as it was just the same. In this way he often shamed, or perhaps ridiculed nail biters out of their unpleasant habit.

As Selly Oak was at the confluence of two important canal systems, there were always many barges and horses about, and blacksmiths were in constant demand. There were two in the village itself, and another only a quarter of a mile away, and they were always busy, mostly with an audience at the door. Near the canal was a very steep hill, and Gertie was always so sorry to see the horses dragging loads much too heavy for them, being cursed and beaten by their drivers. Once, to her haunting distress, she saw one fall down dead under the onslaught. A happier memory was of May Day, when the drivers vied with each other in grooming their animals and decorating their manes and tails with braids of every colour, and polishing their jangling brasses to gleaming splendour.

Sunday was always an exciting day, in spite of forbidden toys and games, best clothes and Sunday School. The adventures started in the late morning with a parade of the local band, known as 'The Bum-a-Toots', which was always followed by a number of children trying to keep in step and mime the instrument players, grown-ups looking on over the garden wall. Just before dinnertime, a blind man used to come singing up the lane, when even the poorest families used to send out one of their members with a copper. Later in the day, the Salvation Army Band clashed the tambourines, beat the big drum, sang hymns and saved souls in number on the green by the Oak public house, while in the evening, outside the chapel a Tolley Alexander or Moody and Sankey mission continued the good work.

The Industrial Revolution had infiltrated well into the parish by the middle of the nineteenth century. There was now plenty of work in a variety of local industries, and the tradition for the girls of 'going out to service' was for the most part discontinued, and with it was lost the knowledge of skilful cooking, learned in the kitchens of the 'big houses' where they worked. Hence the mothers, doing their best on the by now almost universal black-leaded fire grate with its flanking hobs and tiny side oven, were not as a rule, such skilful cooks as earlier generations had been. They did not, however, find it necessary to think too much about culinary skills, as there were plenty of tasty cooked dainties to buy for teas and suppers. As well as the by now universally popular fish and chips, there were faggots and peas, chitterlings, tripe and onions, cow heels, pigs feet, pigs pudding, and a great variety of cooked meats and sausages, not to mention whelks, cockles, mussels, winkles, bloaters, oysters or kippers, all very plentiful and cheap, and within the reach of most.

A number of these delectables were sometimes brought round by street vendors, generally on Sunday morning, when wages were comparatively intact, and most folks liked to get something special for Sunday tea. Little Benny was one of these traders. He pushed a small handcart with a box of kippers and bloaters on it or a barrel of herrings, sold by the handful rather than weight, straight onto the dish or plate brought out to receive them, without the formality of wrapping. Another old fellow used to come round with a clothes basket filled with watercress on his head, which also was sold by the handful straight into the dish.

In the winter, the roast potato seller came round regularly, pushing his wheeled stove, his wares being first pressed with his dirty fingers to make sure they were done, and then served to his customers with a large pinch of salt from a box at the side. In the autumn, chestnuts were sometimes substituted for potatoes, and these were equally popular.

Gertie had a little friend whose parents kept a shop. They made and sold pikelets on Sundays, and Gertie loved to see them cooked on a stove out in the washhouse, and watched with interest the bubbles rise in the dough and then break to form the holes that would soon be filled with melting butter after they had been toasted on a long, wire toasting fork in front of somebody's fire. She used to help her friend

199

carry them round in a clothes basket covered with a white cloth against the dust of the road. It never occurred to her to expect payment for her help, nor did she ever receive any, the pleasure of the task being sufficient reward.

This family also made ice-cream in the weekend, and again Gertie liked to help her friend fetch the ice from Birmingham, four miles away, walking there and back along the main road, and sometimes, as a great privilege, she was allowed to turn the handle of the freezer – and how good the ice-cream tasted, made only from milk, ice and eggs. Mrs Coldrick also made ice-cream, and sometimes on Sundays in the summer used to take it up to the park in a little hand barrow from which she sold it, cornets and pies for a halfpenny each while wafers were a penny.

About this time an Italian ice-cream shop opened in the High Street, and it was considered very special indeed to sit inside at one of their small round tables, and eat hokey-pokey, as it was called, out of a little glass dish, with a tin spoon. But this was a sophisticated refinement, not meant for young children. Young people at work formed the majority of their customers, especially youths taking out their girls and wanting to cut a dash with them that was not beyond their slender financial means.

Gertie's pikelet friends also sold milk from their shop, making two deliveries a day, most families having half a pint in the morning and half a pint in the late afternoon. Gertie sometimes went with her friend after school to do the afternoon delivery, serving the milk from the can in a ladle-type measure straight into a jug. When they had finished, her friend always gave her a drink of milk out of the lid.

Occasionally the travelling theatre, known as the 'Blood Tub' on account of the harrowing nature of the plays they performed, was erected on some waste ground at the end of the village. The most expensive seats cost fourpence, but a considerable number of their patrons – but not the little Witherfords, who were much too scared – got in for nothing by crawling under the canvas at the back. Jane's children never went till they could pay for themselves, with the exception of Lizzie who, one day, being sent on an errand to fetch half a pound of lard from the grocer, spent the money instead on a seat in the Blood Tub, risking what awaited her when she got back home.

The circus came too from time to time, but this cost real money, at least sixpence, and a great many children, including the Witherfords, had no hope of seeing it till they were earning. However, all was not lost, and they were quite content and happy to crowd into the street to watch it arrive, with the elephants leading the way, lions and performing tigers wheeled along in their big cages of strong iron bars, prancing horses, riders and clowns performing in the procession, and to watch the Big Top being erected.

Periodically the fair came and stayed three days on the same waste ground off the High Street. The fun began in early evening, when its hurdy-gurdy blasted out unceasingly l a very late hour, and its tow and naphtha flares lit it up to the sky, the smell they made and the shadows they cast on the thronging crowds all adding to the thrill, mystery and romance. One evening, when big sister Lizzie was allowed, albeit reluctantly, to take her little sister Gertie to see what was going on, the excitement took an unusual turn; the large, veiled, flowered and feathered hat of a young woman standing near caught fire in one of the flares. No harm was done; a young man standing not far away, nattily dressed in his best suit, rushed up, dragged it off her head and stamped on it, putting out the flames. This fortuitous occurrence served as an introduction, and the two went off together to enjoy the fair's safer delights, the young lady no doubt feeling that the hat, in an unforeseen manner, had fulfilled its intended purpose.

Gertie loved the horses with their barley-sugar-twist brass poles for the rear riders to hang on to, and the horses' ears for those at the front, but she was terrified of the more adventurous turns, particularly the swing boats. For most of the things, she found more pleasure in watching than in participating.

The fair was the cheapest and most popular of all the visiting entertainments, and when it came there were few children for whom a few pennies were not found from somewhere.

20

Social Life

Selly Oak Village, as it was now called, could in one way or another supply all the interest and social life most of the working-class families wanted. First and foremost, of course, came the public houses, of which there must have been at least a dozen in the High Street and in two or three of the side lanes, all with their sawdust-strewn floors and spittoons, very necessary in a society where all men spat without inhibitions, and where it had not as yet been found an unacceptable practice.

Each public house was favoured by its own bunch of cronies, who gathered every evening after tea, enticed by its warm fire and congenial company, very different in many cases from their own homes, crowded with children, washing drying or airing round the fire, and a wife still busy, overworked, tired and possibly very irritable and untidy as a consequence. Many husbands took all this as a matter of course, and gave no thought that perhaps their home might be happier and more comfortable if their wages, which they were convinced were completely their own to do with just as they liked, had been spent on family obligations instead of at the pub, treating each other to pints of beer, which they paid for on the spot if they had money, and if not, running up an account with the publican, who 'put it on the slate' or 'chalked it up' over the bar, as the expression went, to be paid for with future wages they had not yet earned. Often on pay night men went straight to the pub to pay their debts before going home to their wives, who sometimes, knowing their husband's habits, were waiting for them at the pub door, and then quarrels broke out between wives and public house landlords they felt should not have allowed their husbands to run up such debts, which forced wives often to find the rent and food for their children by cleaning, sewing, or taking in washing for people more fortunate than themselves. Even when men stayed at home in the evening, they did not deprive themselves, but often sent their children to the outdoor of the pub with a jug to fetch their supper beer.

Sometimes men belonged to a Friendly Society and, worthy as their concept and intention undoubtedly was, they were almost invariably attached to some public house, so their meetings were not without strong temptation.

Saturday night at the pub was often a most pleasant occasion, and provided the only entertainment of the week for most of the men, when 'Smoking Concerts' were organized for them. Local entertainers were engaged at a modest fee to play the piano or concertina, sing Music Hall popular numbers of the day, clog dance or tell jokes. Some of these amateur entertainers were very good indeed and much in demand.

Women as a rule did not frequent public houses, although there were a few, ususaly ones of dubious reputation, who joined their men there, or even went there alone, particularly at weekends when money was plentiful. Children from such homes, feeling lonely and bored, hung around the public house, catching reassuring glimpses of their parents from time to time through an opening door. When 'closing time' came, these women, often as drunk as the men, joined in the brawls and arguments which occurred outside, before husbands and wives with their trailing children directed their steps towards home, or, if they were incapable of walking, or their disturbance had assumed more than acceptable level, being escorted to the 'lock-up' up the road by the 'copper' on his beat.

Abuse of alcohol at this time was the source of the deepest social misery and poverty. Many individuals and organizations were straining every nerve to combat it, and particularly to win the children; the Band of Home movement, the Temperance Societies, the Quakers, the Rechabites, the Salvation Army, the Boys' and Girls' Brigades, the founders of model villages such as Cadbury's of Bournville, were foremost among many others. They all believed that once the Demon Drink had been conquered, civilized Britain was set for Utopian happiness. Gradually over the next fifty to sixty years, alcohol abuse was greatly diminished or its consequences alleviated, and unprecedented measures were taken for social improvement, such as had hitherto never been dreamed of in any land or age. Alas! one evil was replaced by others equally devastating, proving perhaps to the philanthropists and those who succeeded them in later generations that the root of the evil lay more in the heart of man himself, than in his social conditions.

But beer was not the only way working men had of spending money wastefully as of God-given right. Tobacco was another. Almost all of them smoked, not cigarettes, but pipe tobacco, particularly the strong, compressed, crude kind called 'twist', bought loose in a plug, from which pieces were cut according to requirements. This they often smoked in small clay pipes, or even chewed it, a habit that gave rise to a lot of spitting, so much so that with the increased use of public transport, trams and trains displayed notices, 'No Spitting Allowed' or 'Spitting Prohibited', or 'Spitting will be Prosecuted', posted up in prominent places, and this continued well on into the twentieth century, when the habit seemed to die a natural death, probably due to increased popularity of refined pipe tobacco instead of twist, and the by now widespread use of cigarettes by the working men, particularly the cheap, paper packets of 'Woodbines'.

The innocent-looking barber's shop with its red and white striped pole outside, could also be an unsuspected cause of family misery. All men went there, not only for a haircut, but often for their weekend shave, when the barber, helped by his lather boy, who was working his way up in the trade, often earned more than by cutting hair. The customers sat on a bench in the shop awaiting their turn and exchanging village gossip. It was often at this time that bets were placed for horse racing, the gambler's fancy being written on slips of paper and handed surreptitiously with the money to the bookmaker's tout who stood around, recognized only by the initiated, as street betting was strictly illegal and betting shops for the working man did not exist. The tout probably went on from there to the pub, where he found more customers and paid out anyone who had won, expecting a drink in return. Even the poorest men often found money enough for a daily 'flutter'. Many considered it their unquestionable 'right' to daily beer, baccy and a 'flutter on the gee-gees' as of first priority, the needs of their home and family being met with what might be left over, or left to their wife's ingenuity.

Down the village, on a corner of one of the side roads, three golden balls proclaimed the pawnbroker, or 'Uncle' as he was familiarly called. The window looking into the side street was full of small pieces of jewellery for sale, earrings, brooches, lockets and chains, wedding and engagement rings, as well as household items which their owners had at some time pawned, and had not redeemed within the allotted time, after which 'Uncle' was free to sell them on his own behalf. The pawnshop window looking into the High Street was mostly devoted to new clothes, especially working men's clothes, jackets, corduroy and moleskin trousers, caps, mufflers, neckties, large red handkerchiefs with white spots, used universally by working men, all hanging outside temptingly displayed and flapping in the wind. Long strings of hobnailed boots hung in the door frames. There was a brisk trade for these ready-made clothes.

Where men drank or betted heavily, their families were often in deep distress, and their wives needing money to buy food, or fearing the 'bums' (bum-bailiffs), or eviction from their home if rent was not forthcoming on Monday morning, often pawned anything they had in the house to tide them over. Usually they wisely asked for a shilling or two, or as little as 'Uncle' would give them, so that the pledges would be easier to redeem when funds allowed. A very high rate of interest was charged for the money lent and the pawnbroker, keeping this in mind, and realizing no doubt, that the more he lent on the article the less likely the customer was of repaying it, liked to lend as much as the customer could reasonably be offered. Visits to 'Uncle' were sometimes part of weekly family routine, and no occasion for shame. 'Uncle' accepted not only obvious pledges such as jewellery, but almost anything at all, including Sunday clothes, bedlinen, flatirons, kitchen utensils being amongst the most common. Sometimes women who took in washing for other people, pawned that too when times were bad, trusting to luck they would be able to redeem it in time to return it to its owner on the appointed day.

If unpaid rent mounted up really seriously, and a visit from the 'bums' seemed inevitable, the family packed up all their possessions in a little handcart, and in the dead of night made a 'moonlight flit' to find another home, where the cycle started all over again. It was not difficult to get another home, as there were 'Houses to Let' notices everywhere, and landlords did not ask many questions, but took a chance with new tenants.

About this time, the Mothers' Union was founded by the church, and regular weekly meetings held, when interesting and knowledgeable speakers were invited and talks were given on hygiene, the upbringing of children, household management, home nursing, among a great many other less serious but equally informative subjects. The women sat around and gossiped over their homes and children, and brought along their sewing and knitting so as not to waste time. These meetings were very popular with mothers who belonged to the 'respectable poor', who were willing and eager to be 'improved', but less so with those whose families fell far short of respectability. These latter, if they were interested at all, gravitated to similar groups run by the Salvation Army and Nonconformist chapels. All these societies worked very hard, each in its own way, and membership flourished. Jane, however, attended none of them. Being of a very quiet and reserved disposition, she kept aloof from her neighbours and felt quite alien from the atmosphere of gossip in which these meetings inevitably took place, and which was a source of the greatest pleasure to most of their members. She used her spare time in visits to her relations in Bartley Green, and this afforded her unceasing joy and satisfaction, and fulfilled completely her social desires.

Opposite to the Oak public house was the police station. The police were held in great respect, even awe, by everybody, children and grown-ups alike, and although efforts were of course made to avoid detection in nefarious activities, nobody felt hard done by, resentful, or that it was out of place or unjust to be caught doing wrong. Mischievous boys, disturbing a street by playing noisily round a lamppost, scrumping apples or teasing old folks by knocking doors and running away or such-like tricks were chased by the police and, if caught, given a clout and warned not to do it again. And there the matter rested. By latter-day standards, the chargeable offences were very mild, being drunk and disorderly perhaps the most frequent offence, followed by having a chimney on fire, or riding a bicycle on the wrong side of the road, or without a light after lighting-up time. Dishonesty and theft were, by standards a century later, very insignificant; nobody was afraid of intruders, or took much care about fastening doors and windows at night. In some homes, children were dirty or physically neglected, but callous indifference to suffering, or deliberate sadistic cruelty were practically unknown. Mutual struggle and hardship often brought out the best in people's contact with each other, in a way that affluence in the years ahead could not match.

21

The Daily Food

In the eighteen-nineties there were enough shops and services to supply all the daily needs of Selly Oak. Intermittent shops had been opened in the main 'horse road' by householders enlarging their cottage window, and using their front room as a shop, paving the front garden with blue bricks, and using the back garden for stores or workplaces. In the side roads also, a number of cottages had been converted into little general shops, similar to that of Mrs Coldrick in Chapel Lane.

Until Jane came to live in Selly Oak, she had never tasted any but home-made bread, as there was no baker in Bartley Green. In Selly Oak there were two, both making their own bread. They also made buns, cakes, and pastries of various kinds and degrees of richness, but these were usually bought only for special occasions. One baker produced concoctions that were tiny, dainty and melting, set out in a most artistic manner on glass shelves suspended in the window. The other specialized in size rather than quality, but even his products could compare very favourably with the large, solid, stodgy 'cream' or 'fancy' cakes produced at the end of the next century. Even the cheap, simple, homely buns had a lightness that got lost over the years.

Jane always bought 'cottage' loaves, and these, according to the laws of the times, had to be weighed for each customer, and, if they fell short of the statutory weight, had to be supplemented by an added slice. Occasionally the baker would add 'make-weight', not of bread but of stale cake – and what a treat that was! Any cakes or buns left over on Saturday night would be sold off cheaply just before the shop shut. Another service the baker supplied was to heat up his oven on Sunday morning, and also on Christmas Day, when customers could take along their joint in a tin with their name on it, and have it roasted for a copper or two. This was a great help in homes that had only a small side oven or a dutch oven, and anything sizeable had to be turned on a spit in front of the fire.

Apart from the little general shops in the side lanes, there was only one grocer's shop in the High Street, and that was kept by Mr Pember. It was a very old-fashioned shop, and had a number of large canisters of tea on shelves behind the counter, which the grocer weighed out and mixed according to customers' requirements. Sugar was sold in bags of thick, absorbent deep blue paper, which colour is known to this day as 'sugar bag blue'. Dried fruit, including prunes, figs, apples, raisins, currants, sultanas, pears and others, including candied peel of half-oranges and lemons filled with pools of candied sugar, were supplied in the same kind of bags, only red. It also had various kinds of butter, turned out of their barrels onto a marble slab at the back, as well as several cheeses of varying degrees of maturity, a customer being offered a taste of either cheese or butter on the end of a knife before deciding on a purchase. When the butter had been decided upon and weighed out, it was manoeuvred with butter pats into a neat block before being wrapped in greaseproof paper for the customer.

Inside the shop was a very low stand to hold a number of square biscuit tins, all open to display their contents, and these were weighed out and mixed to the customers' wishes. Gertie remembered one day when the Vicar's sister was in the shop, her poodle, helping himself from one of the tins, got the tin stuck fast on his head. He rushed blindly up the road, followed by his mistress, the grocer, the customers in the shop, and joined on the way by an increasing trail of excited children, all rushing up the street after him in a near riot.

Mr Pember delivered the family grocery every Saturday, and how eagerly the little Witherfords awaited it, as Mr Pember always put in, free of charge, a bag of fondant sweets. The children settled round the table while their mother shared them out with due consideration for each as to number, size and colour.

There were three general butchers' shops. One sold meat he had produced himself on his farm two or three miles away out in the country. Another of the shops had its own slaughterhouse at the back, approached by a wide entrance, and a high gate at the side through which the animals were driven. The drovers did not find it easy to manipulate their charges through scurrying pedestrians, bicycles, horse and cart traffic and excited barking dogs of the village street. Often the animals would get into a panic, or maybe they had an instinct as to the fate that awaited them. At any rate, slaughter day was a very noisy one on the part of both animals and passers-by, each in their own way, for their own reasons, trying to escape, with the drover brandishing his stick and waving his arms, and shopkeepers appearing at doorways with brooms and clothes props to poke any intruding animals and head them off in the right direction if they showed signs of trying to escape into shop premises, as they occasionally did.

The third of the butchers' shops was that of a 'foreign' butcher. He sold chilled, foreign meat, which was considerably cheaper than its English counterpart. Only the very poorest bought from him, and even they would send their children rather than go themselves with the possibility of being seen by their neighbours, who, they knew, very much looked down upon these 'foreign' customers. Even among the very poor, there was an infinity of subtle nuances of class distinction.

The cheapest meat sold was beef, followed by mutton and lamb (not to be confused with each other), while pork was the dearest of all. The general butchers sold only beef and 'sheep meat', while pork was sold only by the pork butchers who, as a sideline, sold home-cured bacon, boiled ham, chaul, brawn, sausages, chitterlings, à-la-mode beef, pigs' pudding, tripe, pork pies, faggots and peas, all of which they had prepared and cooked themselves in the little dark kitchen behind the shop.

Of the two pork butchers in the High Street, one of them was almost next door to a general butcher, who to everyone's amazement, one day offered pork for sale in his window. Then loud voices rose, and the sparks flew, ending in fisticuffs between them. Presumably they settled the matter out to a satisfactory conclusion, as there was never any recurrence of this trade encroachment.

There were several greengrocers' shops, all well-patronised and flourishing, the greatest part of their trade being vegetables, roughly packed in wicker hampers. A great many root vegetables were eaten, including turnips and Jerusalem artichokes, and none of them were ever washed before they were sold, so consequently they did not need to be eaten immediately, as the dry earth on them preserved their freshness. In the summertime, radishes, young onions, the small, drum-headed Tom Thumb or Cos lettuces were there in plenty, to be eaten with bread and butter for tea, and later in the year came freshly-dug celery after frost had been on it to make it crisp, the red variety, known as 'Manchester Red', being particularly popular. All this produce was home-produced and strictly seasonal. Even broad beans, peas and kidney beans, over-flowing into the shops in summer, except in years of bad harvest, were very cheap.

Although greengrocery was so cheap and plentiful, many people liked to produce at least a few carrots and salads in their own garden, and were proud if they could grow some of the less usual varieties, such as the soft, brown-tinged, curly-leaved lettuce, and very long 'French' radishes, which rarely, if ever, appeared in the shops. A row of outdoor mustard and cress, which could be constantly cut at, came in handy for tasty sandwiches, and so did marigold petals and nasturtium leaves, the seeds of the latter being carefully saved and pickled.

In days before chemical insecticides, gardens in summer were full of white butterflies that laid masses of eggs on the cabbages. These quickly hatched into green caterpillars, which, if left alone, made short work of their cabbage home, reducing it to a veined skeleton. Gardeners went round daily and sprayed their cabbages with salt water to wash out the eggs and kill the caterpillars, but a few were always left. Hence summer cabbages were carefully washed in salt water with a dash of vinegar to bring out any that still lurked, and even then were inspected several times before being cooked. In spite of all this, it was by no means seldom that an odd caterpillar escaped and found itself cooked on a plate.

Imported fruit was mostly limited to the winter months and consisted of oranges and lemons, together with oblong blocks of compressed dates, from which pounds or half pounds were cut or hacked. Their place was taken in summer by local English fruits. The first to come were cherries, black ones and light-coloured ones known as 'white hearts', each of which had its own distinctive flavour. These were followed by gooseberries, strawberries and black- and redcurrants, all of which came in large chip baskets holding a number of pounds in each. In August the shops were flooded with plums of all kinds, the most popular being the Victoria and golden Pershore egg plums. The latter, although not so attractive to look at as many of the others, had every other advantage; they were delicious to eat raw; better than any other for preserving; by far the cheapest, costing only a copper a pound. Following close behind came damsons, pears and apples in unbelievable variety, codlings, pippins, russets, all full of distinctive flavour. Just occasionally a few quinces put in an appearance, and even medlars, which were eagerly bought in spite of their likeness in taste (so it was said) to rotten apples. All these fruits were packed in large hampers just as they were picked, without any great care or attempt to make them look attractive, the growers' interest being concentrated not on their appearance but on their flavour. Indeed, all varieties of fruits and vegetables were grown first and foremost for flavour, and it would never have entered anyone's head to reject or destroy a fine-tasting variety in favour of a poor-tasting one simply because it could be made to look more attractive in the shops.

Selly Oak, being on the main road from Worcestershire and its market gardens and orchards, was very handy for farm carts coming into Birmingham in the early hours to drop off supplies at the shop doors, before going on to the wholesale markets in the town. As well as that, a number of families in the village had, in not such distant times, come up from the country round Worcestershire, and still had connections there, who were pleased to supply their shop-keeping relations with many things out of their cottage gardens to sell in their shops. They sent up not only fruit and vegetables, but bundles of rhubarb, and little bunches

212

of mint or parsley or watercress, which were put outside the shop in bowls of water to keep fresh. They sent little bunches of herbs, sage, thyme, rosemary, marjoram, and many others to hang up and dry.

The greengrocer was rarely without flowers for sale, standing around in bowls or buckets of water. There were always cottage flowers sent in by relations in the country or brought in by neighbours around. The earliest in the year were the snowdrops in February, then primroses, violets and wild daffodils about Eastertime. Before Whitsuntide, bunches of gilly flowers and posies of polyanthus and forget-me-nots made an appearance, and then later in the summer came lavender, pinks, sweet williams, sweet sultan, sweet peas and little red and white double daisies. Early autumn brought dahlias, and late autumn a profusion of small cottage pom-pom and spray chrysanthemums of many colours.

For a week or two in autumn, and at no other time in the year, there were mushrooms about, fresh, field mushrooms with strong, rich flavour. While they had been growing they had sometimes become the home of tiny grubs which could not be seen in the gills, but as the mushrooms were frying in the pan, the heat drove them out. They were carefully removed as far as possible, but within reasonable limits, not taken too seriously; after all, they had lived on mushroom all their life, hence they must be mushroom, so what was the difference? In years of plenty, the glut was made into ketchup to flavour the breakfast bacon.

Just before Christmas, farmers and cottagers sent in nuts, chestnuts, cob nuts, and most delicious of all, walnuts, wet from the grass under the trees where they had fallen, the water penetrating inside the shell to the moist, sweet kernel. They cut too, berried holly and mistletoe from their fruit trees, and most people bought some to put behind the pictures in their living room.

A great many of these vegetables, including red cabbage, kidney beans, cauliflower, onions, marrows, beetroot, carrots, were not only eaten fresh, but preserved for winter use in vinegar or salt, and stored in thick brown and cream-coloured glazed earthenware jars, which were also used for the many kinds of jam all good housewives prided themselves on making. Vegetables and fruits of all kinds, wild and cultivated, were preserved as home-made wine. Jane also used to preserve eggs when they were plentiful in the springtime by smearing them over with lard to close their pores, although it is doubtful if modern eggs, with their comparatively soft fragile shells, would be successful with this treatment.

As yet, tomatoes were generally unknown. Gertie remembered her father one day bringing one home for her and telling her it was a plum. She spat it out vigorously at the first bite, and indeed, it was quite a long time before people got used to the flavour and learned to like them.

One of the greengrocers also sold fresh fish, which was laid out on a marble slab just outside the shop and was constantly washed down with buckets of cold water to keep it fresh. Herring, mackerel and cod fish were the most popular as they were very cheap, costing only a copper or two a pound, but hake, plaice and sole were not prohibitive in price.

Rabbits were a cheap and plentiful alternative to butcher's meat. They were hung by their back legs outside the green-grocer's shop, unskinned until they were bought when the shopkeeper skinned and gutted them for the customer, keeping the skin for himself as payment. These were bought later by dealers, who came round collecting them, and who, in their turn, sold them to furriers, who cured the pelts and used them in clothing. The rabbit's white tail was always left on, as this was cut off at home and tied to a long string, and with it the children teased the cat, who found it irresistible. The rabbits had all come from the Worcester-shire countryside, where they hopped about wild in fields, orchards, lanes, commons, everywhere, and farmers and others sent them to market by the thousand.

Poultry was only sold at the greengrocer's, or at one or two high-class poultry shops in the town, and it was hung outside like the rabbits. Except at Christmastime, little was bought by working-class families, as it was very expensive, a real treat for special occasions. The birds were always freshly killed and needed feathering and drawing. For a small charge this could be done for the customer, but most people took it home and prepared it themselves.

214

There were two select little sweetshops in the High Street, and these also sold cigarettes and refined, sometimes scented, pipe tobacco, as distinct from the twist sold at the barber's shop and other rough and ready places. The sweets they sold were expensive quality sweets, served in dainty white tissue bags, square bags for quarters, poke bags for lesser quantities. All this was a strong contrast to Mrs Coldrick's type of shop, where newspaper was the only wrapping provided, but the quantity available for the price made this a negligible factor. The profit these two sweetshops made must have been very modest. One of them, the neatest, most polished and shining and quietest little place imaginable, was kept by two prim little elderly maiden sisters, who were too 'genteel' to go out to work and get employment in a factory, and would have felt equally degraded at going out to service. They fell into the class known as 'shabby-genteel', which nevertheless inspired considerable respect among their unpretentious neighbours.

One of the cottages in the High Street had been equipped as a fried fish and chip shop, the window of the living room having two large metal containers, one for fish and one for chips, and there was a little table in the corner and a bench; knives, forks and plates were provided and here customers could sit down and eat their supper if they so desired, at no extra charge, and wash it all down with a bottle of pop or cup of tea. In the tiny scullery behind, all the preparation and frying was done, the cooked fish and chips, when done, being carried through in large wire baskets. Pieces of beautifully succulent, crisp-battered fish, ranged in price from a halfpenny to about threepence each, according to size, cut and variety, cod being the cheapest, followed by hake, while plaice and sole were the most expensive. A good packet of chips cost a halfpenny, and a large family packet no more than twopence, all served in newspaper without any hygienic white paper lining. Batter bits were strained out of the fat in which the fish had been fried, and a generous scoopful given to anyone who requested, any still left being used next day to help light the boiler ready for a new lot of cooking. Whelks, cockles, mussels and pickled onions were prepared and stood on the counter for anyone

215

who wanted to spend an extra penny. The shop only opened about six o'clock in the evening, but a long queue had formed outside the door long before that time every night, and there was brisk custom from then on till very late, often after midnight at the weekend when money was plentiful.

Corn shops were of great importance in the newly developing suburbs, and there were two in Selly Oak. In each, a number of large hessian sacks stood on the floor containing various kinds of 'corn', which included rye, wheat, oats, maize, and barley sold by the gallon or peck, and not by weight. Many people in their gardens kept fowls in pens, with a large run attached where the birds could run freely and scratch for worms or grubs or grit. They consumed all the kitchen waste, but this had to be supplemented by corn.

Most of the shopkeepers had horses for their business purposes, and so did a great many other people as well. There were plenty of pigs in sties at the bottom of back gardens, and pet rabbits kept in hutches, and bran mash and various kinds of corn were fed to them regularly. All the livestock needed hay or straw for bedding down, and this the corn shop kept in bundles round the back. They also kept various accessories such as drinking fountains for birds, bird cages and crock eggs to put in the hens' nesting boxes to encourage them and give them the right idea. Millet hung up on hooks for the cage birds kept as family pets, the most popular of which was the canary, but finches of various kinds, blackbirds, linnets, thrushes, larks and others were kept too. These wild birds had mostly been caught in nearby country villages, and sold to livestock shops, where they fetched a good price.

The corn shop also acted as a seed merchant's, and at the appropriate time stocked sacks of seed potatoes, sold by the peck, many varieties of peas, broad and kidney beans, measured out by the pint, as well as lettuce, vegetable and flower seeds, weighed out in ounces. Strong white raffia for tying plants, hung in great bunches round the shop, rough handfuls being pulled out for customers. Bundles of pea and bean sticks were stacked up in the corner. Lime in half-hundredweight sacks was stored round the back. A warm, pleasant, sweet, dusty smell pervaded all.

One of the corn shops had a white cockatoo with a yellow crest chained to a perch in the shop. He would screech out 'Good morning' and a few other expressions, and was a great attraction to customers, particularly children sent on errands by their dads.

22

Clothes and Things for the Home

Although ready-made working clothes were available for men, as yet there were no ready-made clothes for women, who either had to try to make them for themselves or get them made by a dressmaker, of whom there were a great number about, varying greatly in skill and prices they charged.

As a rule the dressmaker used only one basic pattern for every garment she made, adjusting it to fit each customer's figure and requirements, individuality being achieved by the materials and the ornamentation required. Brush braid was often put round the bottom of the skirt of 'best' dresses as a protection from the mud, and for the same reason a cord and clip were fastened to it to keep up the front of the skirt without continually holding it. Frills, tucks and ribbons, or tiny black, gold or silver beads or sequins were features of most 'best' dresses, as well as rows of innumerable very small buttons, either covered in the same material or made of metal stamped with a design, which were put on the sleeves and bodice. These latter all had buttonholes, which needed many hours of work, as they had to be done by hand. All dresses, even simple cotton dresses for the summer, were carefully lined to ensure a smooth, crease-free, perfect fit, and so too were blouses. It usually took several weeks and two or three fittings before a garment was ready.

Overcoats and suits for men, and coats and costumes for women who aspired to elegance, were made by a bespoke tailor for those who could afford them. The tailor in Selly Oak had the reputation of being a very skilful cutter. His shop window in the High Street was quite unpretentious, with no attempt whatsoever of making it attractive to passers-by beyond a shelf at the side with rolls of cloth stacked upon it, one or two samples draped over stands in the centre, and a coloured picture or two pinned at the back, of someone wearing the kind of clothes he could provide. Inside, the little dark shop, still and quiet, with its polished mahogany counter, was equally unassuming. The tailor, measuring tape round his neck, worked alone without any assistant. He gave at least three fittings to his customers, and several weeks elapsed before the clothes were ready, but they were worth waiting for. They all had a dark lining, usually striped, of hard, tough, incredibly closely-woven glazed cotton, and were very severe and unadorned, their beauty being in their line and cut. He handed his garments over with the assurance they would last for the next twenty years. That was no idle boast, as indeed they did, and often considerably longer, as the closely-woven material was almost indestructable, and the small, hand stitches tight and firm beyond belief. They were never washed, and dry cleaning was unknown, but they were regularly sponged and pressed, and carefully put away when not in use. If, after years of use, the cloth grew dull and looked shiny, navy blue serge being particularly prone to this, the tailor was requested to 'turn' the garment, that is, to undo it and make it up again on the other side. And so it looked smart till the very end. The description 'tailor-made' was an indication of simple, faultless elegance.

Jane had a black, pinstripe costume made by this bespoke tailor in her middle years, and it lasted her the rest of her life. She wore it with a high-necked black silk blouse, a black silk lace scarf, a severe black toque hat made with swathes of thin black silk and net, with an occasional black sequin in the folds. She looked 'a lady' and knew it, and walked out with pride. All her daughters had bespoke clothes when they were old enough to buy them for themselves. Gertie had a dark, bottle-green costume, and this, together with a heavy brown winter coat made by the same tailor lasted well over the early years of her married life.

Sewing machines, both hand and treadle, were becoming a coverted item in many homes, although they were very expensive, and were often bought on the 'so-much-a-week' or 'never-never', as hire purchase was at that time called. Weldon's weekly pattern books were launched about that time, and many women, following the instructions, began to try their hand at making clothes for themselves and their families, with varying degrees of success. It was nearly twenty years later when a friend of Lizzie's who had emigrated to America sent back wonderful stories of shops that sold ready-made coats, suits and dresses in different sizes to fit many figures, a most enviable state of affairs.

In the High Street was a large draper's shop, well-stocked with materials, selections of which were stacked up for display in the wide low window, and there were plenty more inside, ranged on shelves behind the counter. On other shelves were rolls of white bedlinen (coloured was unknown) in several widths and qualities, and sold by the yard for housewives to make up themselves into sheets, pillow and bolster cases. White striped towelling was also sold by the yard to be made up at home, as well as white damask table cloth material, and Nottingham lace curtaining in many patterns and widths. Most people covered their windows at night by roller blinds, and a selection of these in several lengths and widths stood upright in a container at the side, the better quality being made of cream-coloured linen, guaranteed to last almost a lifetime; the popular poorer quality were of paper, but these too were very durable, and would last for years with reasonable care.

Another department further into the shop supplied corsets, known as 'stays', always made in very tough, tightly-woven cotton material for hard wear. They were sometimes pink, but more often dark grey or black which did not show the dirt as they were seldom if ever washed, being scrubbed over with hot soapy water from time to time. Their busks and bones were tightly stitched in to withstand the strain when the laces were pulled in to make the corset fit as close to the body as possible to give shape to the figure and an elegant line to clothes worn over it. This department also sold stockings of fine black cashmere for those who did not want to knit their own. Black woollen stocking were universally worn, except by young women and girls in the summertime, when they were occasionally changed for some of white cotton.

220

This shop also carried a good stock of gloves, without which no woman with any pretentions to good manners would dream of going out. Woollen gloves were knitted at home for children and workaday wear, but other occasions demanded something better, usually of kid, always in grey, black or brown as being practical and serviceable colours needing little attention or cleaning, and all having press-stud buttons to fasten them firmly round the wrist. On very hot summer days, washable white cotton or wash-leather were worn. The draper stocked all these in many fittings and small graduations of size. A few were lined with cloth or fur, but most of them were not. For elegance, the unlined gloves had to fit skin-tight, and considerable care and skill were needed to get them on, glove stretchers often being used to open up the fingers, and chalk powder blown inside to make the hand slide down more smoothly. At times when it was inconvenient to wear gloves, it was allowable to carry them, but it was essential for them to be in evidence. Umbrellas too, with long handles and long pointed ferrules always accompanied formal occasions, neatly rolled if there seemed little likelihood of rain. Better-class women exchanged these for light-coloured, lace-trimmed parasols in the summer time. At that time, trouble was taken *not* to catch the sun and get tanned, but to avoid it and keep the skin white. The draper had a selection of both umbrellas and parasols.

There were two shops that sold haberdashery. One was a very modest little establishment that dealt only in materials for sewing, knitting and crochet-work, which was a very popular hobby at the time. The stock included coloured sewing cottons of various degrees of fineness, an infinite assortment of gold-eyed sewing needles, buttons of pearl, linen, bone and metal, tapes, fasteners, yards of lace and braid for trimming, cords, beads and sequins, ribbons of silk, satin and velvet in many widths, embroidery silks and wools and iron-on transfers of scalloped edgings, with floral and other designs for use with them. There were steel knitting pins in sets of four for making socks and gloves, and pairs of larger ones of bone or wood for scarves or vests, the necessary wool being sold in hanks, which needed to be wound into balls at home before use. There were little linen mats already transferred with scalloped edgings and various patterns and designs for children to embroider, and labelled 'Bread' or 'Cheese' or 'Butter' or 'Cake' or 'Biscuits', as purpose for their use. This was known as 'fancy work', and was very popular with little girls, their little brothers being equally enthusiastic for cotton-reel corking, their small balls of mixed coloured 'rainbow' wool being also stocked by the haberdasher. Most of these items were neatly stored in innumerable well-polished little shallow mahogany drawers with gleaming brass knobs and handles. They were placed at the back of or beneath the counter, and could be removed entire and placed in front of the customer, so that at a glance she might have the benefit of the sight of the full range on offer. Across the window, temptingly displayed on rows of string, was a selection of lace collars and matching cuffs, as well as 'modesty vests', consisting of lace or attractively embroidered cloth, intended to be put in the neckline of dresses, if an embarrassed wearer considered it too deeply cut.

The second haberdashery shop supplied all this and much more as well. It had a window on each side of the door, one of which not only had the usual collars and cuffs and modesty vests, but also baby clothes, bonnets and shawls enticingly displayed. In a society where babies were in plentiful supply, these were much admired, even by mothers who could not afford them.

The second window was devoted to millinery, and was full of stands or pegs supporting hats, all in the latest models and made from straws of various kinds, of felt, of velvet or velour, many of them resplendent with artificial fruit and flowers, feathers and ribbons, as the fashion and season might be. Inside the shop, behind the counter were rows of deep, wide drawers, all neatly labelled, where other hats, in a variety of fittings and sizes, were carefully stored. As well as ready-made hats, the drawers held basic hat shapes made from a kind of very light, thin, stiff white gauze or buckram. These could be bought very cheaply for covering and trimming at home. Small black or dark-coloured high bonnets tied under the chin with satin or velvet ribbons were very fashionable, particularly with elderly ladies, who, once they had taken to such a bonnet,

222

never changed the style again to the end of their lives. It was a symbol of advancing years. From time to time they achieved variety by getting the milliner to retrim it with another selection of artificial flowers or fruit, feathers, beads, ribbons and the like.

In both the drapers' and haberdashers' shops customers were provided with high, round-seated, spindly-legged chairs at the side of the counter, so that they could consult the shop assistant in comfort, and not get too tired in the leisurely, time-consuming process of making a wise choice. Mr Pember the grocer also gave similar consideration in his shop.

At the very bottom of the village was a boot shop. Cheap felt slippers hung in strings on one side of the door, heavy workingmen's boots on the other, while in the window, artistically displayed on stands, were selections of better-class footwear. Very few low shoes were worn by men, women or children, boots being the order of the day, although they varied from ankle-to-knee-length. Some women's boots were made of dark felt lined with red flannel, but most of them were of soft thin kid or calfskin for the thicker, stronger ones. All were lined right through with very fine, matching leather. The soles of either the very light or heavier ones, were invariably of hide. Boots were either laced up the front, or buttoned up the side with small round buttons, fastened tightly over by means of a button hook. A strong braid tag was stitched to the centre of the back to pull them on. In men's and children's boots the toes were invariably rounded, but in women's there was consider-able variation, pointed toes and 'waisted' heels being very fashionable, and this, combined with the universal admira-tion for small feet, often, in time, brought painful conse-quences to beauty-aspiring wearers. All footwear, even the cheapest, was always sold neatly packed in tissue paper in a cardboard box.

The shop also sold children's gaiters of soft, thin, black or brown leather, cosily lined with felt, and fastened firmly up the side with boot buttons. Hide leggings for men were also stocked. It was many years before rubber Wellingtons came into use, but in the winter, boots were waterproofed by rubbing them over with dubbin, particularly between the uppers and soles.

Keeping children well-shod was a very worrying task in many homes, but although bare-footed children were no longer common, many wore boots that had holes right through the soles, or with soles and uppers gaping apart, and they might just as well have been without them. The two boot-mending shops had plenty of work. They understood their customers and their needs, and patched the tops, stitched soles to uppers, pulled off the old soles and stitched and rivetted on the new, put in new inner soles or stiffening round the back, and never seemed to find a pair beyond redemption. The shops smelled strongly of dirty boots and sweaty feet, and also of the hides that hung around the shop, not only for the cobbler's own use, but also to supply handy fathers who bought leather and repaired boots at home, not only for their own family, but often for their neighbours too, using a shaped foot iron that could be bought from the ironmongers.

Like their working fathers, boys often had big-headed hob nails put in boot soles to make them last longer. They were very noisy and looked clumsy, but their wearers were greatly envied on account of the added speed and fun they gave on the slides youngsters made on roads and pavements on frosty days, in spite of the danger to horses and pedestrians.

Another shop, where the smell of leather pervaded in a pleasanter way, was the saddlers. Harness, horse straps and trappings hung outside on hooks, while he worked within. His business prospered in a community where horses were the chief means of transport, and there was a busy canal with a constant flow of horse-drawn barges.

Further down the village was a large ironmonger's and crock shop, with a floor-length wide window, and a blue-bricked pavement in front of it. Standing on the pavement outside the window were benches, on which were stacks of glazed earthenware, which included pudding dishes, oval or round, stew jars, wide-topped brown or fawn-coloured jars for storing pickles or jam, and wide, very large vessels called 'joels' to stand on the pantry floor to keep bread in, or to contain home-made pop or wine before it was bottled, and while it was still 'working'. On the floor below the benches were round-bellied, black iron cooking utensils, including pots with long hollow handles, kettles with long flowing spouts and gracefully curved handles, and frying pans with handles over the top. On other benches at the side, dutch ovens were on display together with flatirons and their stands, toasting forks and toast trivets, assorted-sized pothooks, meat jacks and tins, not to forget the large, brown enamel, family-size teapots, which were virtually unbreakable, and could stand on the hob at the side of the fire, keeping the contents hot for hours if need be, black, stewed tea, bitter with tannin, not being considered with any disapproval in many families. Ornamental iron fenders and fire irons were out there on the front of the pavement, as well as some in brass for people fortunate enough to have a parlour, where they would be rarely used, but regularly polished and tastefully displayed to create admiration and to give a good impression. The overflow of odd cups, saucers, plates and teapot lids were also placed out on this pavement in a row of clothes baskets, while bringing up the flanks were the largest items, wire fire guards, maiding tubs with maids (or dollies), mops and brooms, standing in them for convenient display. Clothes baskets and galvanized buckets and bathtubs hung out on hooks, festooning the windows.

Inside the shop, on rows of shelves stretching right across the window, were the quality goods; twenty-one or forty piece tea sets (a dozen each of cups, saucers, plates, a milk jug, sugar basin and two large bread and butter plates), for wedding presents, all neatly packed into straw-lined clothes baskets for display and safe transport, and to be used only on very special occasions; prettily-painted trinket sets and matching candlesticks for the bedroom dressing table, sets of matching jugs in half-pint, pint and quart sizes; ornamental vases ('ornaments' or 'vorses' as they were called) in every imaginable colour, size, shape and decorative design; most elegant and spectacular of all, and holding pride of place in the centre of the window, were the water jug and washbasin sets for the bedroom washstand, flanked by two matching chamber pots, the whole often being referred to as 'the upstairs tea service', all magnificently painted, large pink or red cabbage roses decorated

225

with gilt being popular favourites.

The ironmonger did a brisk trade in mouse and beetle traps, as these creatures were practically universal even in really nice homes. Wire mousetraps, to be baited with cheese, bits of bacon, bloater or kipper, were standard household equipment, as not all cats were good mousers. Beetles, cockroaches and crickets often lived behind fireplaces where it was always warm. They particularly liked to eat the paste behind the wallpaper, which sooner or later fell away from the wall. These were baited in traps containing beer, but if they got really out of hand, doors and windows in a room, or even the whole house, were carefully closed, and some sulphur burned on a shovel, the fumes from which, it was hoped, would kill them or drive them away.

In the early twentieth century came two small toyshops, enchanting to children. One of them had a very low broad counter, divided up into numerous compartments to accommodate an immense variety of small toys costing only a copper or two. Among many others were dolls' feeding bottles, tin scales, tops, whips, balls, skipping ropes, bomb-droppers with boxes of caps, pea-shooters, minute cups, saucers and cooking pots, pencils, chalks, slates, paint-boxes, painting books, Japanese paper water flowers, whistles, mouth organs, clappers, toy guns, Indian head-dresses, marbles, strings of beads, toy watches and jewellery, and a great many other absorbing delights.

More expensive items were displayed on shelves at the back. These included dolls large and small, made in china, rag, wood, or with straw or sawdust-filled bodies and limbs, covered with thin leather. Many were jointed and had eyes that opened and shut and real hair, while others had eyes and hair painted on. Some were dressed, others were not, but clothes could be bought for them. They were all beautifully packed in individual boxes trimmed with paper lace, and there was an assortment of beds and cradles to fit them all.

There were needlework baskets and wooden boxes lined with chintz or satin. There were boxes of dolls' furniture for the dolls' houses fortunate children owned, often home-made by handy fathers out of orange boxes and covered with brick-designed paper sold specially for such purpose.

There were cardboard cut-outs of every description and subject, from dolls and their wardrobes to whole farmyards and zoos of animals, and theatres with background scenery.

There were boxes of tin or lead soldiers, boxes of every type of building block covered with pictures, boxes of miniature tea sets and boxes with puzzles.

There were packs of picture card games, from miniature size only an inch or two long to full size, as well as dominoes, snakes and ladders, tiddlywinks, and ludo, even chess, all of which were just as popular then as for later generations.

Monkeys and acrobats on sticks were there too, and clockwork toys of every description, engines, mice and jumping frogs being particular favourites.

On the other side of the High Street, almost opposite, was a similar shop appropriately called 'The Bijou', (pronounced 'By Joe', as no-one had the least idea what it meant, and had no curiosity to find out).

These toyshops also sold fireworks, most of which were of the ornamental variety, bangers being much more expensive and mostly limited to rockets. The Witherford children were never allowed any fireworks, although sometimes they managed to watch other peoples. Their mother did not encourage such wasteful expense – or perhaps she remembered the early tragedy in her own family.

Selly Oak had its pretentions to culture too. At the bottom of the village was a shop that framed pictures, specializing in very large ones in wide gilt frames, popular at the time and giving the owners the warm feeling of having a home of distinction. An example of the framer's work stood on an easel in the centre of the window, with specimen strips of framing on a board nearby. Jane's two best gilt-framed, living room pictures, which hung on each side of her daily-polished mahogany chest-of-drawers, had started life in this shop, early in her married life.

A photographer came later, and had a studio at the top of Chapel Lane in a large old house, behind which was a quiet secluded garden with a tall, old pear tree in it. Gertie became very friendly with the family as she was growing up, and they often photographed her for nothing, putting her picture in their window as example of their skill. As she was so pretty, no doubt it was a good advertisement for them.

23

In Times of Trouble

In the High Street was a large, square, redbrick, comfortable house, where the doctor, a bachelor, lived with his unmarried sister. It had a large, well-kept garden at the back, as well as stables and a coach house, which were approached by a drive leading off a narrow side lane. The doctor was a stocky, red-faced, pleasant man, still handsome although getting on in years when Jane came to live in Selly Oak, and he did his daily visits in a horse and trap. He was a Scotsman and, true to his native tradition, liked his whiskey just as much as some of his humbler patients liked their beer. That, as well as various other peccadilloes he reputedly shared with them, far from detracting from his popularity, endeared him to many as a fellow human being, whose weaknesses he understood first-hand.

The population in the village expanded greatly in his time, but he never took on an assistant. The ever-increasing number of patients was served by a second doctor, who, round about the turn of the century, opened another practice at the opposite end of the High Street. The new doctor was young, and had worked in a children's hospital before starting up on his own. He could not afford a horse and trap in those early days, but went on his rounds on a bicycle. Both doctors as a matter of course did their own dispensing, and also a lot of the treatment which in later years would have been done by a district nurse. The new doctor was very modern, up-to-date in his methods, conscientious and meticulously scrupulous in his attention to cleanliness and hygiene, and was outspoken if conditions in his patient's home did not satisfy him. It was he who first introduced a trained midwife into the village, babies being brought into the world before that time with the help of local women who had gained practical knowledge, usually from their mothers before them. Childbirth was considered a natural event, and doctors were only called in for the occasional complications. These untrained midwives were also called in to to do any 'laying out' of corpses if the family preferred not to do it themselves.

Soon after coming to Selly Oak, Jane had occasion to call in the old doctor to her husband. A bottle of medicine was duly prescribed, and set on the bedside table with a spoon nearby. When the first dose was due, on reaching out to the bottle, it tipped over, and the contents spilled on the floor. Jane gasped in horror as she saw the surface of the lino peeling off as though burned. Her confidence in the old doctor melted away for ever, and she never returned to him. She could not help wondering if perhaps in his cups, his hand had shaken, or he had mistaken the ingredients. From that time on she went to the new, young doctor, who attended her and her family till he retired many years later, well over the age of ninety.

A few doors up from the old doctor's house was a chemist's shop, distinguished as usual by a large glass bottle of coloured water placed high up in the tall, narrow window. Like the doctor, the chemist also was a bachelor and lived on the premises with his unmarried sister. As well as dispensing cough mixtures made up from his own prescriptions, or the personal ones his customers brought in, he sold cod liver oil, sulphur flowers, syrup of figs, syrup of prunes, gripe water, 'cooling medicine', senna pods, and other time-honoured remedies, as well as various herbal preparations and liniments and the late-Victorian standbys, such as Doans and Beechams pills, Fennings Fever Curer, to mention but a few. For most family ailments, the advice of the chemist was sought by many people rather than that of the doctor, and he was held in much respect.

The chemist also acted as the local dentist, pulling out teeth as required, and for this purpose the patient was invited into the private sitting room behind the shop, and sat in a chair by the fire while the operation took place. Children were seldom taken for dental treatment, even to the chemist's shop, it being reasoned that first teeth would inevitably come out naturally, and consequently supplementary help was unnecessary. A neighbour of Jane's did not even go to the chemist for extractions when his teeth became decayed and loose in his middle years. Over a period, one at a time, he pulled them all out himself with a pair of pliers.

About a half a mile out of the village was the workhouse, where young and old who had no-one to care for them were taken to be looked after, and food, clothing and a bed were provided. Although at this time the inmates were certainly not cruelly treated, it was a place dreaded by all, particularly old folks, who were the most likely to find themselves within its walls. Families sacrificed themselves in endless ways to spare their old folks the feeling of shame and rejection universally associated with this institution, and often in their small houses, overflowing with many children, lovingly found room for an aged parent or maiden aunt, but it must often have been a difficult and very uncomfortable situation, demanding patience and understanding on both sides, and harmony could not always have prevailed.

At a time when old age pensions were unknown, the poor who had no children or relatives to take them in had no choice but to end their days in the workhouse. A couple going in together, who perhaps had hardly been out of sight of each other for the best part of their lives, were obliged to separate at the door, the wife going one way to the women's quarters and dormitory, and the husband to the men's. Periodically they were allowed out to visit friends and relations if they wished. If they were capable, they were expected to do some work in the institution. The Selly Oak workhouse had a large garden which skirted the road, and here men could always be seen cultivating vegetables needed for the inmates. Passers-by often handed the men tobacco through the railings.

The workhouse also had a casualty dormitory, where tramps and beggars were given a bed for the night and a meal, in return for some appointed task. From about four o'clock in the afternoon till about six, when the gates were closed, down-and-outs, dirty and unkempt, with ragged clothes and old boots tied on with rags or string, could be seen sauntering along in its direction. One of the conditions of entry was a bath, and on this very account quite a number of tramps avoided this institution, preferring to sleep under a hedge in their comfortable dirt.

Early the next morning, breakfast eaten and their task done, they were on the road again, begging food and money as they went. Householders were surprisingly sympathetic, and a gift of food, old clothes, even beer money, were never hard to come by.

Those in need were not always taken into the workhouse, but supported outside by 'Parish Relief', dispersed by officers known as 'Guardians of the Poor'. For families, this relief usually took the form of food, but for others, for example, widows left penniless and without any means of support, but quite capable of looking after themselves, it often consisted of a small weekly sum to pay the rent and provide a frugal sustenance. The Robbs, a family that at that time came to live near Jane, needed such help.

Towards the end of Gertie's school days, she became very friendly with Elsie Robb, and this friendship, stemming from those early years, lasted till Elsie's death many years later in late middle age, and occasioned constant exchange of visits, much fun and many happy memories and reminiscences. Elsie, two years older than Gertie, had already left school and started to work at Cadbury's. She was the eldest of a very large family that had recently come up from Somerset where they had formerly lived, although they were of Scottish descent. The family was a very poor one, as their father was a heavy drinker. His brother, a prosperous baker, offered to adopt Emmy, the youngest child, to relieve them, and very reluctantly Mrs Robb consented, and so the broken-hearted child went off to live with her uncle and aunt, who immediately dressed her in beautiful new clothes to suit her altered condition.

Very shortly after, to the intense relief of his wife, Mr Robb died suddenly, and although the family were so poor that Mrs Robb had to go up to the workhouse for 'public assistance', whereby she was given bread twice a week for her children, she was unashamedly thankful she would have no more babies to struggle with. Gertie pleaded with her mother to help her friend in those sad days, and any coppers she could earn by running errands for neighbours

231

she handed over to Jane, who had little enough herself, to help buy them a piece of meat for Sunday dinner or some special occasion. They were both dearly beloved for their thoughtfulness and kindness.

Then overnight the Robb family fortunes changed dramatically; a remote cousin in Somerset died, leaving Mrs Robb a modest fortune of several thousand pounds.

First Emmy was called back home, to the intense fury of her aunt and uncle, who took away the clothes they had given her, and sent her back in the old worn ones she had come in. Then the whole family went on a holiday journey to Somerset to claim the inheritance, inviting Gertie to go with them. How thrilled and excited she was, never having been away from home before, and what a lovely time they had. For years after, Gertie and Elsie, who had slept together, loved to relate how frightened they had been the first night, when, looking out of the window over the dark orchard, they thought they saw a ghost, and lay trembling and breathless with fear till morning and daylight came, when plucking up enough courage again to look out of the window, found the ghost was still there – a big white shirt flapping about on the line.

Mrs Robb spent her newly-found wealth wisely. She first spent a sizeable portion of it on a very nice new house near Elsie's workplace, and from this moment the family never looked back. With new-found opportunities, Elsie proved to be a very clever and versatile girl. Like her mother, she learned to do beautiful sewing, knitting and crochet work, and helped her make the kilts, jackets, sporrans and bonnets her younger brothers and sisters wore in honour of their Scottish ancestory. Mrs Robb bought a piano, and Elsie taught herself to play it really well. Elsie also bought herself a camera, taught herself not only to take pictures, but also to develop the plates and make prints, passing on the knowledge she gained to her younger sisters and brothers, who became as skilful as she was. And what a lot of fun she and Gertie made for the family, with musical evenings and amateur dramatics, standing on the front room table for a stage.

Soon after Mr Robb had died, Gertie's father had died too of consumption at the age of forty-six, brought on, it was thought, by a chill caught one day when he got drenched, and, having no opportunity to dry his clothes – or possibly no others to change into – kept them on for many hours. In true Victorian convention, Gertie had been invited to view Mr Robb's corpse, and had not wanted to do so, and in return Elsie had been invited to view her friend's father and had not wanted to either, but it would have been very discourteous and offending to refuse what was considered an honour on one side and a sign of respect on the other. Indeed, Gertie recounted how, as a small child, she had accompanied a neighbour whose sister had died on a journey into the Black Country to go to the funeral, walking every step of the way, at least eight or nine miles. She remembered being taken upstairs to see the corpse, and processing round the bed with the family mourners, and sleeping in the room next to the one where the body lay.

Bodies were never taken out of the house before the funeral. It was usual for a member of the family, or a neighbour, often the self-appointed midwife, to wash it, wrap it in a clean sheet or clean night clothes, tie up the jaw with a large handkerchief, put pennies on the eyelids to keep them closed, and to sprinkle it with salt to ensure that the spirit of the deceased would rest in peace, as ghosts of even the most dearly-loved ones were not as a rule welcomed back. When it was prepared, it was laid in its coffin by the undertaker, who had already been to the house to take the necessary measurements. Often the coffin with the body was put on the kitchen table to save room in the tiny cramped cottages until the day of the funeral, when the undertaker brought the hearse, drawn by sleek, beautifully-groomed black horses with their resplendent black plumes, and it stopped outside in readiness to escort the procession up to the churchyard. The return journey always came back home by a different route, to make sure, so it was said, that the new spirit rested content in its grave, and became confused if it tried to follow back home.

Of course people grieved for the loss of their loved ones, but for the most part death was accepted as a natural event for oneself and for others, and was talked about in a natural way. This is shown by the story told of the old woman who did Jane's washing. Lying in bed with her family round her, she opened her dying eyes and enquired if the neighbours had yet started to collect money for flowers for her funeral. Her last words were, 'If they don't, don't you ever give again for anybody else in the street.'

As the youngest member of the large Partridge family, a number of deaths occurred during Gertie's early years, all duly observed and mourned by her mother, but making little impression on the children beyond the fact that whenever they had a new dress or coat, before very long it had to be dyed black in mourning for one or other of their numerous unknown relations. For adults, after the required year of 'deep mourning' had passed, when everything worn had to be sombre black, a further period of 'half mourning' was required, when mauve or grey could be worn, relieved by touches of white, in preparation for return to normal, everyday clothes.

A very widely-observed superstition, which persisted even till almost the present day, was fear of wearing anything green, which, so it was thought, was always followed by the necessity to wear black. Alone of Jane's family, Gertie defied the superstition, and when it was pointed out to her how often she had had to wear mourning after green, she had wisely retorted that maybe she had, but her sisters had gone in mourning after the same relations, even though they had not been wearing green.

Another superstition Gertie did not regard so lightly. It was believed that sometimes a 'ticking spider' could be heard about the house where a death was imminent; and to the end of her life, with solemn, steadfast conviction, she told how one had been heard in the pantry the night before her father died, and her story was confirmed with equal conviction by her mother and two sisters.

24

The Girls Grow Up

The time passed by, and one day Lizzie found herself accepted for work at Cadbury's chocolate factory. At first she had to give all her wages to her mother for her keep, receiving back a shilling or two for pocket money. After a few years she was allowed to 'keep herself', which meant giving her mother a fixed sum for her board, and keeping the rest for herself. Now she really had money of her own, and how she enjoyed it!

About that time moving pictures had been invented, and a very small picture house was opened in Selly Oak. Nobody enjoyed the cinema more than Lizzie, and she became a lifelong devotee. As well as the cinema, dancing was, to her, another delight. There was no dance hall in Selly Oak at that time, so she had to go into town, where dance halls gave instruction classes during the week, and a social on Saturday night. Getting ready for her evening out, she was quite prepared to borrow clothes or finery from either of her sisters if they were not looking, and gave herself most painful bunions by insisting on wearing shoes too small for her. And oh! what trouble she got into at home when she arrived back later than the ten o'clock allowed and found her parents waiting up for her, or sometimes only her mother, who had pretended to her husband that their erring daughter had returned, and so persuaded him to go up unsuspectingly to bed. But the happy, laughing, amusing, dancing Lizzie was prepared to risk her parents' anger, and gave them many anxious moments.

Lizzie made friends very easily, and the dancing classes brought her into contact with many other young people with similar disposition to her own, a number of whom kept contact with her throughout life. Among her partners was a good-looking, well-dressed young gunsmith named Bert, who fell head over heels in love with her. Although he was already engaged, he was quite prepared to throw over his first love, Minnie, in favour of the enchanting Lizzie, and Lizzie was just as willing. So they decided to get engaged, in spite of the profound disapproval of both families, who each excused their own child and blamed the other. Bert's mother came to see Jane, and there were strong words on both sides. Lizzie and Bert were both of age, so there was little they could do about it except to refuse to attend the wedding, with the consequence the young couple fell further from grace and scandalised friends, relations and neighbours by refusing to marry in church, and chose instead the Registry Office. On the day, Jane so far came to terms with her scruples as to turn up at the time and watch the ceremony from the back of the hall, no doubt to reassure herself that the ceremony actually took place, but no relations from either side were present at the reception, held later in company of their dance hall friends. And so Lizzie's married life began with a clever, handsome, irresponsible, good-for-nothing with whom she was to have a stormy, far from happy life.

To give the couple a start, Jane lent them forty pounds, a great deal of money at that time, to open a greengrocery business in the town. It was ideally situated and should have done well, as Bert's family owned a prosperous pork butcher's shop, so he must have had an idea how a business was run. However, he spent most of his time in a nearby public house, leaving the shop to his inexperienced happy-go-lucky young wife, convinced that backing horses was a quicker and easier way of making a fortune than thrift, diligence and hard work. The business failed, and the money Jane had lent them was lost for ever. Unknown to his mother-in-law, Bert also bought goods in her name, she being later called upon for payment, without Bert ever expressing one word of shame or remorse, only a light-hearted comment that there was plenty more where that came from.

All through his life, Bert spent more time out of work than in it, and annoyed Jane very much when he found a job by immediately treating himself to a new suit of clothes or other such extravagance to celebrate his good luck, instead of paying his debts. He was a clever, versatile man, if he could have put his talents to better use, and had had less bombast and more stability of character. His own family background was a prosperous one, but his parents considered his marriage to Lizzie beneath him, and cut him and his wife off completely, never lifting one finger to help him out of his escapades. In years to come, the rift was healed to some extent, and Bert's people became very fond of Lizzie when they knew her better. But Bert never endeared himself to his mother-in-law.

At that time Jane's landlord employed her as a kind of local agent, interviewing intending tenants and letting his houses for him. After Bert's shop failed, she used her influence to get him the little cottage next door to her own, so that she could keep an eye on her daughter, and no doubt smoothed over many of their financial crises. From the beginning, Bert was an ardent supporter of the newly founded Labour Party, and a dedicated believer in the sharing of the wealth of the fortunate with their less prosperous neighbours, and without any compunction was always happy to participate with his mother-in-law in such arrangements.

Jane's younger daughters were very different from their sister, and never gave their parents one scrap of trouble. On leaving school, Nellie, like her sister, had gone to work at Cadbury's, but her leisure time was very differently spent. She occupied many hours up at the church taking part in the social activities centred round it; she took on the task of polishing the church brasses on Friday nights, went to all the church services, never missed early communion, and taught in Sunday School.

Gertie left school very happily on her thirteenth birthday, glad to have escaped the raising of the leaving age to fourteen, which took place a short time after. She very much wanted to go to work at Cadbury's like her two sisters, and no doubt the thought of never-ending opportunities for eating chocolate, the supreme luxury in confectionery, had a great part in the enthusiasm. Cadbury's never minded work people eating chocolate, no doubt thinking that an

237

Gertie, 1909 aged 18.
Described as a lovely child, a ravishing young woman,
and beautiful even in extreme old age.

238

individual's capacity for consumption, even of chocolate, was limited, and that very likely after the first gorging or two, interest in eating it would moderate, or even be lost altogether, but they were very severe on those caught stealing it, even sacking them. Most other young girls around wanted to work there too, and competition was keen. Gertie was not taken on at first, but the privilege of working at Cadbury's was worth waiting for, and she went patiently week after week to the factory lodge till at last she was successful, in the meantime going each day to help two elderly ladies with housework, for which she earned two shillings a week. This she handed over immediately to her mother to help with her keep. Many years later she described her early years at the factory, and this is what she wrote:

GERTIE'S STORY

I started work at Cadbury's in 1904 at the age of thirteen. I remember how I and many other girls presented ourselves week after week at the factory lodge, hoping eventually to be chosen.

The successful candidates were 'examined', first in their heads, no doubt in search of wild animals which, in those days, might well have been found in those hairy regions, then hands, 'to see if they were cool enough to work in a food factory', so we thought, never having heard of scabies or impetigo. And so we awaited our turn, with our hands pressed against a wall or something cold, to create the right conditions.

And then our first week's wage!

Mine was eight and fourpence.

I ran all the way home to give it to my mother, who gave me back two shillings as pocket money, saying that was twice as much as my two sisters had had at that age.

By this time Selly Oak and Bournville were linked by the railway, and in common with many other girls, it was not long before part of this precious pocket money was spent on a weekly railway ticket, the train journey being both status symbol and adventure, as it was by no means necessary, the

239

journey on foot being, on the whole, probably quicker.

Most of us stayed to dinner, which we could buy as a complete meal in the dining room, or as individual items. Some girls bought a halfpenny worth of potatoes on a saucer, which they ate with bread and butter brought from home. Others brought a cooked dinner tied in a basin, which could be put in the warming cupboard. Sometimes older children of a family brought dinner for all of them in one big basin, and shared it out at the table on plates they could borrow. And what tasty food some of their mothers could cook with very slender resources!

During the morning, the firm provided, free of charge, refreshments of a cup of cocoa and a slice of bread and butter or two bath biscuits. I always chose the biscuits, which I did not eat, but took home for my mother because she liked them so much.

Earlier on, in my sisters' time, every day at the factory had been preceded by a prayer meeting in the dining room. In my day this had been reduced to one morning a week, when we left our work to attend it. It was not very long, consisting mostly of a simple prayer and hymn.

On our appointment we were given materials to make our first overalls. These were usually made by a dressmaker, and how proud we were of them, and how we tried, within the regulations, to make them just that little bit different and individual. And the thrill of doing 'gym' in a real, beautifully-tailored black gym tunic lent for the occasion! I was so proud of mine, and borrowed it to have my first photograph taken.

Then the wonderful, dark red, woollen bathing costume in which we learned to swim in the girls' baths! We thought we looked so nice in them, they almost, but not quite in my own case, dispelled the innate terror of water so many of us had. I never really enjoyed swimming, but got immense pleasure when I got home at night in showing off to my mother how it was done, lying flat over the fireside stool to do the breast stroke. We could also stay behind after work and have a shower bath, borrowing for a copper a nice warm towel. This was an amenity eagerly accepted, as bathrooms were unknown at that time in working-class homes, though we could keep ourselves spotlessly clean by a wash 'so far up and so far down' or, as it was sometimes expressed, 'up as far as Possible, and down as far as Possible', or soak in a zinc bath in front of the fire in warm water and soapsuds after washing day.

We were encouraged to go to night school in the newly-opened Ruskin Hall in the centre of Bournville village. The fee was two shillings per quarter, but this was refunded at the end, depending upon attendance. Here I learned to draw (the least of my skills), more Arithmetic and also English, the latter providing me with the greatest pleasure, as it was the subject in which I could shine. About this time I started an album in which I wrote down poetry I particularly liked, all in my very best handwriting, and this I still have and treasure.

> What a nice lot of girls we were!
> How proud our parents were of us!
> How proud we were of ourselves!
> And how happy!

Not one of us believed without shadow of doubt, that as 'Cadbury Girls', we were just that little bit special.

One must look back with deepest respect and gratitude to the efforts of the founding members of the Cadbury family, who saw, and were moved by the poverty and deprivation around them, and did everything in their power to lift all who came within their influence to experience and enjoy better things, both materially and culturally. Above all, one must respect their wisdom in not forcing these benefits, or making them too easy or commonplace, but encouraging and expecting those who wished to enjoy them to make a personal effort, and sacrifice time and money within their resources to reach out and take them.

Gertie sparkled with interest in her life in the factory, but she enjoyed her leisure time just as much. Her sisters' interests did not appeal to her in the least. She spent some of her time at the church, as was natural in a church-going family, going to confirmation classes, which she took very seriously, making a written promise to God to say her prayers regularly and try to control her temper, no, not temper, but passion, as she truthfully acknowledged, and taking part in the various services and socials that took place, but she enjoyed them without the dedicated zeal of her sister Nellie. Nor were Lizzie's interests of the cinema and dancing any more to her taste. Her mother once allowed her to accompany Lizzie to a dancing class, but this aroused no enthusiasm. She rarely went to the cinema, although she was friendly with Jinny, the manager's daughter, who was about her age, and used to let her sit in the most expensive seats for the cheapest price. The cinema manager and his family lived near. They had been circus folk before they came to Selly Oak, and Jinny inspired Gertie and her other friends with open-mouthed awe and wonder, as they listened wide-eyed to her description of her earlier life in the circus, where her particular act had been to put her head in the lion's mouth. Such courage and daring was beyond admiration.

When Gertie had money enough, she paid for some singing lessons for herself, and joined one of the music societies Cadbury's ran for their work people, but she was far too shy to attempt to win any prominent role. The time she enjoyed most was that she spent with Elsie Robb. They went off together to the fair, the circus or the Blood Tub. They dressed up for amateur dramatics performed on the front room table in Elsie's home, with all the little Robbs as audience, and their mother producing as if by magic, piles of flour and water pancakes, roast potatoes or onion and potato soup for a hot supper or they sang together round the piano, all the popular songs of the day, and hymns too, for a change, Gertie showing off her newly-acquired singing accomplishments and Elsie her skill in accompaniment.

Elsie had bought herself a bicycle and taught herself to ride, held up by her little brothers and sisters, and Gertie had learned too at the same time. One day, when they considered they were proficient enough, they decided to have a trip out into the country, Elsie on her own bicycle, Gertie on one hired for the day for a few pence. They set off in fine style, and all went well till late in the afternoon, when they met a herd of cows wending their way to the farm for the afternoon milking. The terrified Gertie, forgetting all about the saddle, pedalled so fast the bike ran away with her out of control, and she finished over the handlebars headfirst in the brambles the other side of a hawthorn hedge. The sympathetic Elsie escorted her home in tears, covered in scrapes and scratches and bruises, where she was put to bed, and it took a week to patch her up well enough to go back to work. This was the only absence she ever had in her ten years of working life.

Another venture, not quite so dramatic, was at a roller-skating rink that had recently been opened in Northfield. The first occasion they went also ended in Gertie's tears, when, as was natural enough, she fell over from time to time before she mastered the balance, and her beautiful 'best' white cashmere skirt got daubed with grease off the rink. She was not hurt, only fearful of her mother's reaction and the scolding she would get, if not worse, when she got home, and her fears were well-founded.

Gertie enjoyed skating and she and Elsie often went to the rink in company with young people from Selly Oak. On the way home some of the boys and girls would pair off together, but Gertie and Elsie would not be parted. One of the boys, Herbert by name, was deeply interested in Gertie, even to the extent of confiding in his mother, and persuading her to invite her home and speak favourably on his behalf, and this she did. The unsuspecting Gertie enjoyed the invitations, and liked all the family, but was not tempted to a closer understanding with the forlorn Herbert. And so, when she at last realized the situation, coming home from the rink, she tried to divert him to an interest in Elsie, who would have welcomed his attentions, but in vain, she was not the girl of his choice.

Herbert was not the only boy who had his eye on this very pretty girl. A cousin from Bartley Green, who had previously never shown any particular attention to the family or visited them when he came to Selly Oak, suddenly took to calling on his Aunt Jane, and staying for hours in her home. Mrs Coldrick's son, with full approval of his mother, could also very often be seen sauntering over the road to talk to Gertie over the garden wall. But she had no particular liking for any of them, and gave them no encouragement; passion and sexual obsession and indulgence were not considered normal essentials for young people in her days. She never took one of them as a sweetheart, or considered boys seriously till, at the age of eighteen, she met Ernie Haynes at work.

For a long time the attention was all on his side, but persistence won, and eventually he found the longed-for response. He, too, had never been interested in girls, nobody had ever seen him out with one, and certainly he had never had a sweetheart. He was convinced then, and ever after, that she, and she alone, was his Destiny. In time they became engaged. Gertie began to save for her bottom drawer, to sit alone in the park, and in eager anticipation to make out imaginary grocery bills and menus for meals, plans for routine household management, and to dream dreams for the future. They both began to save in a Building Society to buy their future home.

At this time they never went on holiday together, as there was no member of either of their families or responsible older friend to go with them, a condition considered essential in those days, nor did they see each other more than two or three times a week at most, Ernie keeping up his old companions, and Gertie her friendship with Elsie.

Eventually the day was fixed. Gertie gave in her notice at Cadbury's, as girls when they married were expected to give up their job to stay at home and look after their husband, home and family. She and Ernie, like all other young couples at the factory, were called before old Mr George, who presented them with a guinea, a rose and a Family Bible, as a foundation for their new adventure of married life.

25

The War Years

The marriage of the Prince and Princess in the fairy tales, after the overcoming of apparently unsurpassable difficulties during their courtship, and ending in their living happily ever after, was reversed in the case of Ernie and Gertie. In spite of friendship and love that seemed to fulfil all that heart could desire, and resemble the magic of the fairy tales in so many respects, shadows began to cloud over even before the wedding took place. The Building Society in which they had been saving for their new home collapsed a week or two before their marriage, and, together with many others, they lost every penny they had. Another blow, the significance of which they did not realize at the time, was the outbreak of war while they were on their honeymoon. But nothing that Fate brought could destroy their happiness in each other.

Their first Christmas of married life was one to remember fondly for a whole lifetime. The young couple sat in the living room of Gertie's childhood home, she on one side of the fire basting a joint of meat roasting on a string in front of it, and Ernie sitting on the other side reading aloud Dickens's *Christmas Carol* to his wife and to her mother and sister, who were preparing the vegetables and other indispensible concomitants in the adjoining kitchen, with the door open between so as not to miss one single word.

A year later was born a little daughter, whom Ernie insisted on naming after the only two women that had any meaning in his life, his wife, of course, and his mother, whom the child right through life greatly resembled in looks and temperament. In spite of their delight in the birth of little Hannah, she was the occasion of their first quarrel;

245

Gertie at that time was strongly opposed to her husband even visiting a public house, and had refused to become engaged to him unless he promised never to go in one again. This he had readily done, and kept his word till the day his little daughter was born, when his excitement could not be contained; he went out to find his friends and tell them his news, later arriving back home, not nearly so steady or coherent as his wife thought he ought to have been. But his penitence was genuine, and although in later years both he and his wife occasionally enjoyed a drink when they were out together, he never again disgraced himself with excess.

Soon after Hannah was born, Ernie was called up into the army, and his skill with a gun, learned many years before scaring birds in his 'Uncle' Manny's cherry orchard, promoted him quickly to the front line in France. Lizzie's husband Bert was called up about the same time, but was draughted out, in his profession as gunsmith, to Egypt and Palestine. Although they had been married more than seven years, they had as yet no child, and Lizzie, now expecting one, was very fearful and disappointed that her baby would be born while her husband was abroad.

After their husbands were gone, neither Gertie nor Lizzie had any money to live on other than the army allowance of just a few shillings weekly, which was not enough for even the most frugal way of life. So they both went back to work, Gertie leaving Hannah, and Lizzie her baby daughter Cissie for their grandmother to look after. Lizzie went to work on munitions at the Austin Works at Longbridge, and Gertie went to Elliotts, the nearby iron and steel works where her father had once worked. Nellie went to First Aid classes and joined the St John's Ambulance Unit.

Almost all the young people they knew were 'doing their bit' in one way or another. Ernie's special friends, the Banks brothers, joined up about the same time that he did, and so did the two eldest sons in the Robb family. A little while later, Elsie, who was not yet married, went into the WAACS, and found herself in France in no time at all. The Vicar's sister also volunteered, and Ernie, some time later wrote home to say he had met her one day, serving in the YMCA canteen in company with Lady Astor. Eligible young men who for one reason or another managed to escape the call-up, were greatly despised, particularly those who worked in munition factories, where pay was good, in strong contrast to the few shillings a week servicemen received. Women often gave vent to their scorn by approaching these men in public places and handing them a white feather, an indication of what they considered their cowardice. They had no resepct for the philosophy that it was better to be a live coward than a dead hero.

In Ernie's early letters from France, he asks eagerly about his baby daughter, and when told she was becoming a lively little tomboy, his reply was guarded. He did not mind that, he said, provided Gertie made sure to teach her good manners so that she would grow up to be a lady like his own mother. He said he well remembered how, even at the end of their lives, his father's eyes would glow with pride and pleasure when he escorted her out, even though others sometimes found her distant and reserved. But he kept his love for his child in due proportion. He wrote, 'I love my little daughter with a father's love, but the lov I have for my own darling wife is far in excess even to that. Ours was an eternal marriage of souls, in life or death we shall never part.'

Gertie kept all Hannah's new baby clothes, together with some her mother had given her, preserved from her own children's infant days. These were all put in Gaggy's tin biscuit box, which Ernie had sentimentally kept, and periodically, till the end of Gertie's life, they were carefully taken out of the box, washed and put back again. After her death many years later, the box was opened, and a note found on the top:

'These are the baby clothes of my little girl, who was my pride and joy.'

But the note continued in a more restrained tone:

'Only she did not grow up to be the little princess we thought she was.'

Maybe Gertie need not have been unduly disappointed;

there must be a great many parents who have felt much the same about their children, even though they have not expressed themselves so openly.

The men had gone off cheerfully and courageously with no doubt whatsoever that Britain would win the war, and they would soon be back after teaching the Jerries a lesson or two. In one of Ernie's early letters, he writes:

'I cannot imagine we have been married so long, but when I look over my desk and see you and the Babs photo, I thank God that there is one little happy family that have never quarrelled in their married life, but was unlucky enough to be parted by a terrible war, which I think has made our love for each other even stronger if it were possible. My own dearest wife, I am so pleased to know I can address you as such, but you know, it is a great risk to get married, but I thank God I took, or shall I say we took that great risk with all its responsibilities, and have never yet had any cause to regret it.

Hoping shortly to be reunited, and the most happy family in existence.
                    Yours ever,
                              Ern xxx'

In another letter shortly after, he writes:

'My Dearest Wife,
I am just writing these few lines, hoping they will reach you on the 25th (their wedding anniversary). I can assure you my thoughts will be with you on that day, and I sincerely trust that next year we shall again be reunited. What a happy time that will be, when we are relieved of the anxiety this war is giving us. But it has given us a few valuable hints and proved to both of us the true value of each other's love and friendship, so at least we have something to be thankful for. My own dearest wife, I can safely say that in the last twelve months, I have been taught more of your

true worth than in any past time of our married life. I have proved for myself your self-sacrificing nature on my behalf, and I am indeed thankful to think I own such a woman, yes, all to myself. I cannot find words to express myself properly, but I am truly happy with the knowledge that I possess the finest little woman in this vast universe, and one I am exceedingly proud to call my wife. You have had a very trying time, my dearest wench, but you have shown them and me you are made from the right kind of stuff, and therefore I need to be proud. I think honestly we are very near the end, and it won't be such a long time before it is all over, and we shall be able to live again as of old in dear old England after the painful lessons this dreadful war has taught us. But come what may, it is so nice to know we are still united, even in absence, with those precious bonds which naught on earth will ever sever.

My own darling wife, I am indeed grateful to you for the splendid way you have taken your part in this terrible ordeal, and though I have roughed it, I am sure I can stand more hardships knowing that there will surely be a brighter dawn, when my own dearest wife welcomes my return to dear old Blighty and home. True women are very hard to find, and I am certain there are not many left, in fact, I know of only one who is up to my estimation, and I think myself a very lucky fellow.

It seems strange for an old married man to write such lines to his wife, but we are a very extra-ordinary pair, so what matter? I have always thought of you as a good wife, but henceforth I shall think of you as something more, although I cannot think of any word to express it, but you will understand. Your self-sacrificing nature and perseverance under the most trying circumstances has made me more a man than ever I was. I have always tried to be straight and honorable with everyone, and I shall endeavour so to do in the future, my own little wife being the instrument

249

that will enable me to keep up my reputation and
good name through the most difficult circumstances.

God help the man who has a bad wife, but a
good wife is a brighter jewel than any.

xxx Ern xxx'

Ernie was not wrong in his realization of his young wife's
capacity for courageous struggle and devotion during these
difficult years. Her sister Nellie had developed consumption, had had to give up work, and was now permanently at
home, slowly dying. Gertie was a slim, slightly-made girl,
and the work she was forced to do in the metal factory to
keep her mother, her child and her dying sister was far too
heavy for her. Up to that time, she had never had a day's
illness, but now her strength was completely undermined,
and she was robbed of the strength she would need to cope
with the troubles soon to come in the years ahead. She
loved her husband dearly, and tried with selfless dedication, not only to meet her immediate financial needs, but to
save for her future home, and also to send cigarettes and
little treats to him. She spent nothing on herself or her own
needs. But Ernie appreciated it and wrote:

'My dearest, dearest Wife,
    If you can keep on doing as you are, and for
which I admire you greatly, we shall be bound to
come out on top.
    You cannot for one moment imagine my feel-
ings towards you, and what I really think of you
words cannot describe, but you can rest assured
that your darling boy as you term me in your
letter, will be faithful and true to my own darling
and dearest girl, and trustworthy, faithful and
sincere wife. You have had all my love ever since I
gave you that rose. God bless that day. You may
think it very strange, but though I am so far away,
my thoughts are ever with you, and you are
constantly by my side, even when asleep. Love
like mine is not made in one day, it takes years,

250

but then it is true, true to one little woman. Even if you had not married me, I should still have continued to love you in silence, and should finally have died of a broken heart.

Your devoted husband and sincere pal,

Ern.xx'

It was only her husband's love that sustained Gertie, and he poured it on her with all his heart. He wrote:

'. . . My fate was sealed the day I gave you that rose. You remember the parson saying ". . . to love, joined together by God." My own dearest girl, Love is for us, yes, us two, who came together because our beings cried for one another and said "This is my mate". It was not merely a contract with us, was it Darling? If you were married to anyone else, I would still make my vows to you from my soul. . .'

and he continued further:

'. . . if ever a woman was loved by a man, you are that woman, and if ever a man's life, present and to come, lay in a woman's hands, my life is in yours. You are my fate, my other part, with you my destiny is sealed. There is nothing I could not do with you to cheer me, on the other hand no depth to which I could not sink. . .'

In another letter he reminds her:

'. . . The vows we made on that eventful Saturday morning were not for days or years or times. They were for ever, and I firmly believe that nothing can or ever will dissolve them, and that Death itself will be powerless against them. Strange things come into a man's mind out here. Some day I shall tell them all to you. Not that I have ever been quite alone, for I can honestly say that you have

always been at my side since I left you, and there
has been no hour day or night when you have not
been in my thoughts, and I believe that till Death
blots out my senses, no such hour will ever come.
Day by day my love has grown stronger. You
remember my intentions on that first night I went
out with you. You know what I wanted and had
made up my mind to gain, and that was the
beginning of our honourable love. My purpose I
gained, and I gained it honourably, but you could
have led me into temptation, but only you, and
nobody else, then or now.

I am simply dying for that way you used to
rumple my hair that always sent thrills down my
spine in those dear old early days. I guess I look at
the marriage service as it was meant to be.
Perhaps other people don't, but when I took into
my care a young and attractive girl, it became my
business to look after her. It would be very nice to
have all you want, meals well served with shining
silver etc, but it is not to be named in the same
breath with a simple meal, eaten with love as a
sauce and a few kisses from the girl of your heart,
in place of, say, strawberries and cream.'

Unfortunately Gertie's letters to Ernie did not survive.
He told her he did not need to keep them, as he knew every
word by heart, and he did not want them to fall into anyone
else's hands, as undoubtedly they would if he should be
killed, but he eagerly awaited them.

'. . . I do expect letters, letters about anything. I
don't care if they are about Pardoe's cat having
kittens, or anything else, but please write soon,
often and more often. Lloyd George said in his
great speech the other week that all England
wanted was ships, but you can take it from me
that all the English soldier wants out here is
letters from home. If you are getting tired of me,
please say, and I will volunteer at once for the
firing line, when my prayers will be ever with you

252

both, and perhaps we shall all meet again. All I want is news from my only sweetheart, and then everything else can go to Hell. . .'

And so, no doubt she told him, not about Pardoe's cat, but about their dog Sligo, who came home one day with a leg of mutton he had stolen, and what a nice Sunday dinner it made after it had been dusted up a bit, and how she and Hannah had been invited.

She told too of how Pardoe's eldest son Arthur had been chased by his mother, intending to thrash him for stealing sixpence out of her purse, and how he had escaped onto a canal barge moored by the bank and pushed off out of reach into the middle of the water, and what a lot of trouble it had caused to get it back.

She told him of the death of a neighbour's child from consumption, and the sickness of another child in the family who had been taken into a sanatorium, but with little hope.

She told him that the Ring of Bells public house had been closed, and the young doctor had opened a Child Welfare Clinic on the vacant premises, and how she took Hannah along every week, and how she had been universally admired (of course!) as the most beautiful child there (!!!).

She told him about the Chinamen who had come to work at Elliotts, how small they were, the unusually colourful clothes they wore, the difficulty of understanding their pidgin English, the way they never walked anywhere, but moved with tiny running trots everywhere they went, and above all, the strange writing they chalked up on the walls, and the strange language they directed at their foreman, both of which were suspected of being neither complimentary nor kindly in intent.

And so she gossipped on with home news of relations, friends and acquaintances, and the news they received from the front where most of them had loved ones serving. As well as cigarettes, she sent her husband the Lifebuoy carbolic soap he particularly requested, which he said helped to keep down the fleas and lice with which they were infested, and which he used not only to wash with, but to rub into his damp body as an added protection.

253

In one of Ernie's letters he told his wife how he and a mate, a nice young fellow and a lay preacher at home, as he carefully explained, had gone one day into what they had thought was an ordinary café and had been served by a girl without a stitch of clothing on her. This had greatly distressed Gertie, who began to remember all she had heard about the seductive beauty of French women, and men's inability to resist them, and her next letter voiced all her fears.

Ernie's reply was reassuring:

'My dearest of all,
    I can assure you there is no need for you to worry in that respect. You know full well I am a man with extraordinary willpower, and not even the finest woman nor strongest man in heaven or upon earth could turn me to any purpose I set my heart against. You can believe me, I was quite prepared for this state of things long before I came to France, but I am pleased to say it did not affect me in the least.
    The place that we went into was, as we thought, a respectable café, but found out, greatly to our disgust, that it was not so. There are thousands of such places all over France, but then, it takes time to find out which are and which are not.
    You say you may not be as beautiful as some of these women. My dearest, dearest wife, I don't think like some other men, and am not moved by fine clothes and powdered faces, but to me you are the most beautiful woman in the whole universe. I don't really mean in looks, although you can give any of the French girls a start in that, but in disposition. My father used to say it was the little things that count in this world, and I am sure he was perfectly right. I am only sorry you took it to heart so much. But never mind, dearest wife, you have no cause to fear, as you know full well I was never struck on women.
    Look at the time when I kept Charlie Banks a bit straight, and the temptation I had then, but

254

though I say it myself, I never yielded and I was a lot younger then and not married. Don't you think that if I could keep straight then, it is a thousand to one I shall keep straight now that I have a wife that I love dearer than life and a dear little Babs (God bless you both), whom no-one shall ever replace (either of you)?

I am sorry in one way that I told you, but then I am not in another, as I have got a clear conscience to think that my dearest wife knows all about the carryings on in this country, and still there is no secret between us. But think for yourself for a while and put two and two together and weigh things up as they should be. A man who has a very strong willpower, a dear little wife who to him is dearer than life itself, a dear little baby girl whom for which nothing is too good, also has had two Christian parents and brought up in the Christian faith from the earliest childhood and taught to know right from wrong, who has had a very very good mother, the best mother that any lad had, and now has, as I mentioned before, the best wife and bab that any man had, do you think for one moment that this man is going to let himself go at the impulse of a moment to do that for which he has always had the most utter contempt? No, even if I was single, for the sake of my dearest mother, whom I loved as much as you in a different way, I would keep straight. Another thing, my dearest wife, I shall always tell you everything. There have been no secrets between us yet, and there shall not be any on my side. Now I hope you will read this from a reasonable point of view, and banish all the little worries from your mind for ever, because come what may, I shall always keep straight and true for you, as I always have been.

So cheer up and don't think any more about it.

So I will close now, with the very best of love and kisses for you both

Yours, Ern.'

Even so, Gertie could not quite put her fears behind her, and again her husband was reassuring:

'. . . I can only say that in all my wanderings I never saw a really beautiful French woman. The majority are thin-nosed, scraggy-necked, thin-lipped and absolutely ugly, yet merely by reason of their dress, some of the most attractive women in the world. All they live for is dress. But there is no attraction for me. All I want is those two little women at Selly Oak, and I shall be forever satisfied. I loved you as no man has ever loved before. I played for what I earnestly desired. I obtained all I set my heart on. You are my wife and the mother of my child, and all I can say is "God bless you". I satisfied my desires with you. I have had those intimate relations with you that is only, or should be only permissible to man and wife. And I can safely say on my word of honour, I have never been intimate with any other woman. . .

What more could Gertie want?

Soldiers serving abroad seldom got home leave, so when the Armistice came, and men began to trickle back home, the excitement, relief and joy were overflowing.

Ernie's homecoming was one of Hannah's earliest memories of her life; it was of being wakened from sleep one night, and her mother carrying her downstairs wrapped in a blanket to see her soldier Daddy, dressed in uniform, sitting at her grandmother's kitchen table, eating bread and cheese and pickled onions out of a gold-rimmed dish with pink daisies painted round it, then to being taken to the fireplace to see one of the presents he had brought her, a golliwog with a spring in the top of its head, hung up at the side of the mantel shelf.

Ernie had brought many other presents too, which included the prettiest little French apron his wife wore on special occasions when there was company, for many years after. He also brought his little daughter a most beautiful doll's sewing machine that really worked, set out in a box

256

fitted with drawers of silks and cottons and paper patterns, and readymade dolls' clothes arranged around. This was a family treasure for many years, and the tale often told of how he had nailed it down on the boat coming back to England to prevent it being stolen.

Ernie had been lucky and had come safely through it all, and returned with a fund of stories, interesting, amusing and incredible, of life in the trenches, the barracks, the Naafi, of pals he had made, tricks he had played, entertainments he had helped to give, of the strange ways of France, the French and what he thought of them, of contempt for their food and drink, frogs' legs and snails and strange-tasting sauces, as not being a patch on good old English beer and fish and chips. He described the destruction and civilian panic in air raids. He told of the Angel of Mons and the Christmas Day football match with the Jerries – although so he said, like many others at the time, he believed the only good German was a dead one.

His family laughed admiringly to hear how he had been sent one cold, dark winter's night to guard a churchyard in Rouen, and how he had spent the early hours sleeping out of sight in a newly-dug grave. He told how in Rouen Cathedral there were two old fishponds, where an old man had charge of them and bred fish for the hospitals. The smaller pool he used for a nursery. He came down with baskets of food each day, and whistled the fish to come to be fed. He caught them with big nets when they were the right size, and took them to the hospitals. They enjoyed with him in retrospect the night the barman in the canteen was ill, and he had been sent to his job, and how, unnoticed, he had slipped pints of beer outside the door for his pals till they were helpless, and how sorry they were when he was removed, and another chap sent in his place the following night. He told how he had made hammocks for some of the officers to sleep in, and other gadgets to make life comfortable, and how well they had been appreciated.

All these stories and countless others, he told for years afterwards in his own inimitable sparkling way, that could not fail to carry his listeners with him.

Ernie brought back, as a gift from a friend, two watercolour pictures he had painted on army forms in nostalgic memory of his home, and these he framed ready for the time when he had a home of his own. These were to grace the walls long after his death, handed down in affectionate memory of a dearly-loved man and a warm friendship.

Several of Ernie's comrades wrote or visited him for a long time afterwards, always calling him by his army nickname 'Mercy Messoo' (Merci Monsieur). Ernie had known not one word of French, but had done his best with the phrasebook the army had supplied. He hadn't been much good, and his accent was unrecognizable – hence his nickname. One of the friends, whose family had a factory in Dundee, tried to persuade him to go and work for them, but Ernie declined the offer, as his old job was waiting for him.

All the homecomings were not so happy. Ernie's old friends, the two Banks brothers, did not return; they were both killed in France. One of Elsie Robb's brothers returned on crutches with the loss of a leg. Lizzie had not seen her husband for almost five years, as he did not return from Egypt till 1920, and had lost an eye. This handsome, conceited man never came to terms with his affliction, which, together with his general wartime experience, quite destroyed him. He had always liked alcohol, but now this liking had got quite out of control, and under its influence made him very quarrelsome and aggressive. He found it impossible to get a job in his trade as gunsmith, which needed keen eyesight, and he never again had a permanent job of any kind. His army pension, which was a good one, as he had been a staff sergeant, was as much as many men received as a weekly wage, and thereafter this was his family's support. His little daughter Cissie, whom he had not seen till his return could not give him the joy she might have done in normal circumstances. His home was never a happy one, although his wife and daughter too when she was old enough to understand, were completely silent on their troubles and loyal to him. He died of consumption thirteen years later, a totally broken man.

The men had thought to come back to a grateful country, 'fit for heroes to live in', so they believed with starry-eyed trust and conviction. Many, bewildered, found themselves among masses of unemployed, newly-discharged soldiers, with little hope of finding work in the factories now idle after their years of prosperity and activity in munition production. Others had to adjust themselves to maiming and affliction. Many family relationships had become strained and broken. Many young women had to adjust to shattered dreams and widowhood, and the bringing up of their children on their own. The great number of homes that had been freely available for renting were available no longer. The government did its best with the introduction of unemployment benefit and the building of council houses, but the upheaval of national life was in the melting pot for years to come.